Moving Away from the Death Penalty:
Arguments, Trends and Perspectives

MOVING AWAY FROM THE DEATH PENALTY:
ARGUMENTS, TRENDS AND PERSPECTIVES

© 2015 United Nations

Editor: Ivan Šimonović

Design and layout: dammsavage studio

Cover image:
The cover features an adaptation of a photograph of the feet of a man convicted of murder, seen during a hanging. Photo credit: EPA/Raed Qutena. The back cover graphic line represents a declining percentage of United Nations Member States that practice the death penalty (those that have not abolished it in law or practice), from 89% in 1975, ending at 27% in 2015, in 10 year increments.

Electronic version of this publication is available at:
www.ohchr.org/EN/NewYork/Pages/Resources.aspx

Sales no.: E.15.XIV.6
ISBN: 978-92-1-154215-8
eISBN: 978-92-1-057589-8

MOVING AWAY FROM THE
DEATH PENALTY

ARGUMENTS, TRENDS AND PERSPECTIVES

New York, 2015

UNITED NATIONS
HUMAN RIGHTS
OFFICE OF THE HIGH COMMISSIONER

CONTENTS

"The death penalty has no place in the 21st century. Leaders across the globe must boldly step forward in favour of abolition. I recommend this book in particular to those States that have yet to abolish the death penalty. Together, let us end this cruel and inhumane practice."—*Ban Ki-moon*

PREFACE

Today, more than four out of five countries have either abolished the death penalty or do not practice it. Globally, there is a firm trend towards abolition, with progress in all regions of the world. Member States representing a variety of legal systems, traditions, cultures and religious backgrounds have taken a position in favour of abolition of the death penalty. Some States that opposed the abolition of the death penalty in the recent past have moved to abolish it; others have imposed a moratorium on its use. The application of the death penalty appears to be confined to an ever-narrowing minority of countries.

Those remaining States cite a number of reasons for retaining the death penalty, including what they see as its deterrent effect; that it is consistent with public opinion; that it is equally applied against all perpetrators; and that there are sufficient judicial safeguards to ensure defendants are not wrongfully convicted.

Over the past two years, the Office of the High Commissioner for Human Rights has convened a series of important panel discussions on the death penalty, seeking to address these issues. The events drew on the experiences of government officials, academic experts and civil society from various regions which, in recent years, have made progress towards abolition or the imposition of a moratorium. They covered key aspects of the issue, including data on wrongful convictions and the disproportionate targeting of marginalized groups of people. This publication brings together the contributions of the panel members as well as other experts on this subject. Taken as a whole, they make a compelling case for moving away from the death penalty.

The death penalty has no place in the 21st century. Leaders across the globe must boldly step forward in favour of abolition. I recommend this book in particular to those States that have yet to abolish the death penalty. Together, let us end this cruel and inhumane practice.

Ban Ki-moon
Secretary-General, United Nations

"In the 21st century a right to take someone's life is not a part of the social contract between citizens and a state any more...."

— *Ivan Šimonović*

INTRODUCTION:
AN ABOLITIONIST'S PERSPECTIVE

Why yet another book on the death penalty? The answer is simple: As long as the death penalty exists, there is a need for advocacy against it. This book provides arguments and analysis, reviews trends and shares perspectives on moving away from the death penalty.

This book, first published in 2014, has been updated and expanded, providing victims' and United Nations human rights mechanisms' perspective, a new chapter on the role of leadership in moving away from the death penalty. The new High Commissioner for Human Rights, Zeid Ra'ad Al Hussein, appointed in 2014, has provided an afterword.

Abolishing the death penalty is a collective effort which requires commitment, cooperation and time. As a student in 1977 in the Socialist Federal Republic of Yugoslavia, I was allowed to write my high school graduation essay on the abolition of the death penalty. At the time, Yugoslavia practiced the death penalty and had limited freedom of expression. Against this backdrop, I am especially thankful for the courage and support of my teachers.

Much has happened since 1977: Yugoslavia broke up more than 20 years ago, and all its successor states have abolished the death penalty. Globally, most countries have gradually been moving away from the death penalty—by reducing the number of crimes punishable by death, introducing additional legal safeguards, proclaiming a moratorium on executions or abolishing the death penalty altogether.

Amnesty International reports that in the mid-1990s, 40 countries were known to carry out executions every year. Since then, this number has halved. About 160 countries have abolished the death penalty in law or in practice; of those, 100 have abolished it altogether. In 2007, when the death penalty moratorium resolution was first adopted by the United Nations General Assembly, it was supported by 104 states. In the most recent vote, in 2014, it was supported by 117 states.[1] In 2014 there were at least 607 documented executions[2]. While the number of executing states remained the same in 2014 as in 2013, the number of documented executions dropped by 22 per cent.

While this is grounds for optimism, there are also reasons for concern. The number of death sentences imposed in 2014 worldwide was at least 2,446, which represents a 28 per cent increase over 2013.[3] Can the recent steady global trend towards abolition be reversed?

Some human rights achievements dating back to the early 1990s are currently facing renewed challenges.[4] Armed conflicts involving non-state actors, triggering ethnic and religious divisions, are proliferating globally. Many states and regimes face instability. Fear of violent extremism, organized crime and especially drug trafficking make tough punishment for these crimes appealing. It creates an impression of commitment and is much easier and cheaper than increasing the efficiency of the law enforcement and justice systems. It is still to be seen whether these setbacks will stall or reverse the trend of moving away from the death penalty. This book seeks to contribute to efforts to prevent this from happening.

In 2012, 35 years after my graduation essay, now as United Nations Assistant Secretary-General for Human Rights, I was able to contribute to a discussion on the death penalty at the United Nations in New York. The panel discussion on "moving away from the death penalty" that I moderated in 2012 included a distinguished group of member states representatives, experts, civil society activists and a victim of wrongful conviction. The panel identified three main reasons for member states' decisions on the death penalty: the possibility of wrongful convictions, crime deterrence or the

---

1   UN Doc. A/69/PV.73, pp.17-18 (18 December 2014)

2   Amnesty International, *Death Sentences and Executions in 2014* (London, Amnesty International, 2015)

3   The number of death sentences imposed in Egypt—509—significantly contributed to this trend. By the end of 2014 Pakistan lifted a six-year moratorium. The real number of executions is unknown. Some countries—including China, in which most executions take place—do not publicly release data on executions. China appears to be moving cautiously away from the death penalty, initially reducing the number of crimes punishable by death and introducing additional safeguards, which may heavily and positively influence overall trends.

4   A series of world conferences in the early 1990s made significant progress on human rights. But the principles agreed to there are currently being challenged.

lack thereof, and discrimination against marginalised groups in its implementation[5].

Recognizing their importance, the Office of the High Commissioner for Human Rights in New York organized debates on each of these three issues, involving member states, non-governmental organizations and academia. We benefitted from the valuable support of the permanent missions to the United Nations of Chile, Italy and the Philippines as co-organisers for two of these panels[6]. Together with the permanent mission of Italy, we organised an additional panel on national experiences with a moratorium on executions[7]. Finally, in April 2015, at the United Nations Congress on Crime Prevention and Criminal Justice in Doha, Qatar, we also organised a panel discussion on the death penalty, drugs and terrorism[8].

United Nations Secretary-General Ban Ki-moon participated in four of these events as the keynote speaker, and has provided a preface to this book, which presents contributions by panellists at these events and other prominent authorities on issues surrounding the death penalty.

The views expressed in these articles reflect the personal positions of their authors and not necessarily the institutional position of the Office of the High Commissioner for Human Rights or the United Nations. As the editor of the book, I hope that you will find their ideas interesting and challenging, whether you agree with them or not.

The panels on which this book is based, apart from the one held in Doha, took place in New York, thus benefiting from the proximity of a number of top-level death penalty experts, civil society activists as well as two victims of wrongful conviction. Nevertheless, we are fortunate to be able to present an even larger number of articles by African, Asian, Caribbean and European authors.

---

5   See brochure on the panel *Moving away from the death penalty: Lessons from National Experiences* (UN OHCHR, New York 2012, 25 p.)

6   OHCHR Global Panel: "Moving Away from the Death Penalty-Deterrence and Public Opinion", co-sponsored by the permanent missions of the Philippines and Chile, 24 January 2014 UNHQ, New York; OHCHR Global Panel: "Moving away from the Death Penalty - Discrimination against Marginalised Groups", 24 April 2014, UNHQ, New York

7   "Best Practices and Challenges in implementing a Moratorium on the Death Penalty", UNHQ, New York, 2 July 2014.

8   "Panel discussion: Death Penalty, Drugs and Terrorism", 13th United Nations Congress on Crime Prevention and Criminal Justice, Doha, Qatar, 14 April 2015.

The book consists of six chapters. The first three chapters are dedicated to the three issues identified at our initial 2012 panel as decisive for decision-making on moving away from the death penalty and on which we held individual panels in 2013 and 2014: wrongful convictions (chapter 1), the myth of deterrence (chapter 2) and discrimination (chapter 3). They were supplemented with three additional chapters, covering other issues highly relevant to decisions about the death penalty. Values related to the sanctity of life and the limits of state power are discussed in chapter 4. Chapter 5 deals with the role of leadership in moving away from the death penalty. Chapter 6, looking forward, provides data and examines trends.

Chapter 1 addresses wrongful convictions from the personal perspectives of a wrongfully convicted person, an academic, a civil society activist and a former prosecutor. It is not easy for governments and leading representatives of justice systems to acknowledge that, despite heavy investment in the legal process, wrongful convictions occur. It is even more alarming that they occur in death penalty cases, including in the most sophisticated justice systems.

DNA test results have confirmed long-standing warnings by academia and civil society in this regard. In the United States, the first country to use post-conviction genetic testing on a large scale, 140 death row inmates have been exonerated since the 1970s.[9]

Had public pressure to identify and punish perpetrators made wrongful convictions more likely in the murder and rape cases for which exonerating DNA evidence became available? Wouldn't similar pressure have occurred in other serious crimes in which such a test was not possible? If this is a problem in advanced industrial countries, with well-resourced legal systems, what about those with less sophisticated legal systems with fewer safeguards, opportunities for review and resources? It is clear that wrongful convictions do occur and that it is unacceptable for them to end in execution. The death penalty is simply too final, given the imperfections of even the most sophisticated legal systems.

---

9   For an analysis of some of their cases, see Brandon L. Garrett, *Convicting the Innocent* (Cambridge, Massachusetts, Harvard University Press, 2011). The Innocence Project, founded by Barry Scheck and Peter Neufeld at Cardozo Law School in 1992, has done significant work on exonerations. Gradually it evolved and involved many other people and institutions in identifying and freeing the wrongfully convicted. See www.innocenceproject.org; see also Garrett's article in this book.

The question of the death penalty's deterrent effect, which is addressed in chapter 2, has attracted scholarly and political attention for centuries. Are public executions brutal relics of the past or efficient preventive measures? Does capital punishment for relatively minor crimes increase the frequency of more severe crimes because the risk to perpetrators is no greater? Does it expose crime witnesses to greater risk? The great majority of countries have stopped public executions and reduced the application of the death penalty to only the most severe crimes, but does the death penalty deter crime at all?

Government actors often feel public pressure to retain the death penalty as a crime control measure. However, there is no evidence that it is in fact a deterrent. In countries that have abolished the death penalty, this has in general not resulted in an increase in serious crime. The most comprehensive survey on the relationship between the death penalty and murder rates, which was carried out for the United Nations in 1988 and updated in 1996, found that "research has failed to provide scientific proof that executions have a greater deterrent effect than life imprisonment. Such proof is unlikely to be forthcoming. The evidence as a whole gives no positive support to the deterrent hypothesis."[10] Statistics from countries that have abolished the death penalty show that the absence of the death penalty has not resulted in an increase in serious crime.

In 2012, research from the US-based National Research Council confirmed the United Nations report's conclusions: "Research to date on the effect of capital punishment on homicide is not informative about whether capital punishment decreases, increases or has no effect on homicide rates."[11] Recent US government statistics confirm the lack of supporting evidence for the deterrent effect of capital punishment.[12]

---

10 Roger Hood, *The Death Penalty—A Worldwide Perspective* (Clarendon Press, 1996), p. 238. The fifth edition of this book, co-authored by Carolyn Hoyle and Roger Hood, who have also contributed to this volume, was published in 2015.

11 National Research Council, *Deterrence and the Death Penalty* (Washington, DC, National Academies Press, 2012).

12 According to the U.S. Department of Justice's annual FBI uniform crime report for 2012, the national murder rate remained approximately the same in 2012 as in 2011. The northeast, the region with the fewest executions, had the lowest murder rate of any region, and its murder rate decreased 3.4 per cent from the previous year. The south, which carries out the most executions of any region, again had the highest murder rate in 2012. U.S. Department of Justice, *Crime in the United States, 2012* (Washington, DC, 2013).

Most justice systems, in deciding guilt, accept the ethical principle *in dubio pro reo* (when in doubt, [decide] for the accused). By way of analogy, if there is no proof that the death penalty deters crime, why would we continue to apply it? It may be out of ignorance, or deterrence may be a fig leaf covering other motives: the desire for talionic revenge,[13] or to protect dominant social groups and their interests; in most retentionist states the death penalty disproportionately affects socially marginalised groups—migrants, racial and ethnic minorities, the poor and people with mental disabilities—some of them victims of compounded discrimination.

Chapter 3 raises concern over the disproportionate effects of the death penalty on marginalised groups in Africa, the Caribbean, India and the United States. Marginalised groups are overrepresented among the wrongfully convicted to a disturbing extent.[14] People with a mental disability or without a competent defence lawyer are more vulnerable to pressure to make a false confession, and jurors may be more prone to suspect a defendant who is different from them. Also, in too many legal systems, financial resources, or the lack thereof, determine the quality of legal representation.

From a moral perspective, the attitude and response to crimes committed by members of marginalised groups should not be to discriminate against them further, but precisely the opposite: to look for mitigating circumstances, which may have been a consequence of the discrimination they have been subjected to.

There needs to be some soul-searching and recognition of responsibility on the part of society, when members of marginalised groups are involved in crimes. To what extent have discrimination and unjust treatment of members of racial or ethnic minorities contributed to the commission of crime? How has a life of deprivation and lack of opportunity for the poor, uneducated or mentally disabled contributed to the commission of their crimes? From the perspective of justice,

---

13 Talion, or lex talionis in Latin, is a principle that perpetrators should receive as punishment the same injuries that they inflicted upon their victims. Its origins can be traced to early Babylonian law, which subsequently influenced Biblical and early Roman views on punishment. It is also reflected in later (including some current) justifications of corporal punishment.

14 See Brandon L. Garrett, *Convicting the Innocent* (Cambridge, Massachusetts, Harvard University Press, 2011), p. 235.

should there not be more questioning of individual guilt and mitigating circumstances of alleged perpetrators belonging to marginalised groups, instead of discrimination against them?

Besides the three main issues relevant for abolition or retention of the death penalty, around which the first three chapters of this book are organised, there are many other issues. The economic effect of the death penalty is one of them. In various circumstances, this may be astonishingly different. I was present at a meeting during which the top United Nations official, speaking to the leader of a developing country that carried out frequent executions after legal

> "THE EVOLUTION OF HUMAN RIGHTS HAS REDUCED STATE SOVER-EIGNTY IN MANY AREAS; THE DEATH PENALTY SHOULD BE ONE OF THEM AS WELL."
>
> —Ivan Šimonović

proceedings that were considerably below international standards, pleaded for abolition or at least a moratorium on executions. "I have no money to feed them or build them prisons," the leader responded; "a bullet is cheaper. But if you want them," he added, "you can take them back with you to New York."

International norms are clear that if the death penalty exists, those facing it should be afforded special protection and guarantees to ensure a fair trial, above and beyond the guarantees afforded to defendants in non-capital cases. This creates a paradox. The death penalty is cheaper than other forms of punishment only if its execution does not require complex legal proceedings or safeguards, such as the use of forensics and reviews. However, in such cases the likelihood of wrongful conviction is exacerbated. But if the number of safeguards is increased, the death penalty becomes the most expensive form of punishment, as the bulk of US research clearly indicates.[15]

In fact, the cost of the death penalty is so much higher than the cost of a life sentence without parole that abolitionists, especially in the United States, use this argument in their campaigns.[16] Even when the

15   For a summary of these studies, see Rudolph J. Gerber and John M. Johnson, *The Top 10 Death Penalty Myths* (Westport, Connecticut, Praeger, 2007), pp. 165-171.
16   See Death Penalty Information Center, *Smart on Crime: Reconsidering the Death Penalty in a Time of Economic Crisis* (Washington, DC, 2009).

majority of public opinion polls indicate support for the death penalty, when confronted with financial analysis that indicates that a life sentence without parole could produce savings that could instead go towards compensation of victims and their families, public opinion often tends to sway in favour of the latter option.

On the other end of the scale from the pragmatic approach are the moral and value-based arguments regarding the death penalty. Chapter 4 addresses the relationship between the death penalty and values through an article reflecting a victim's perspective, two articles that are potentially controversial, as is so often the case when values are concerned—one dealing with major religious doctrine and the other with politics, as well as two articles assessing the death penalty from the perspective of international human rights obligations

Despite the lack of evidence of deterrence, retentionist' arguments can be articulated and are indeed perceived by some as moral ones. Essentially, the reasoning is based on a "just retribution" argument—changing the perspective from utilitarian to Kantian. If crime deserves adequate punishment for moral reasons, it makes social consequences and the deterrent effect (or lack thereof) less relevant. Furthermore, even if capital punishment has negative social consequences, it should be retained because it is proportionate to some crimes—*vivat iustitia, pereat mundus* (justice should live even if the world were to die).

When discussing the death penalty from the perspective of values, it is critical to bring the victims' perspectives into the debate. Their position certainly carries important moral and political leverage. However, those perspectives at times seem to be quite different. Some family members of murder victims are among the strongest supporters of the death penalty, well organized and influential. But others are equally strongly convinced that murder cannot be countered with murder. They do not want the lives of their loved ones to be avenged with more violence, and instead of focusing on retribution, they try to set themselves free from their trauma through forgiveness, healing and restoration.[17]

---

17   In the United States they have formed an association called Murder Victims' Families for Reconciliation. Membership requirements are that a close family member has been murdered and that they oppose the death penalty. Some of their stories have been collected in Rachel King, *Don't Kill in Our Names* (Rutgers University Press, 2003).

It is also questionable whether, in practice, the death penalty helps provide closure, as it is so often argued. In most retentionist states it is gradually being reduced in scope to exclude minors, pregnant woman, people with mental disabilities and many others. For example, in the United States, prosecutors seek the death penalty in only about 2 per cent of intentional homicide cases, and the death sentence is imposed in only about half of those. Of those death sentences, about two-thirds are reversed on appeal. In the end, just about one-third of 1 per cent are executed, and this after an average delay of 12 years.[18]

Does the possibility of the death penalty psychologically prevent closure and healing—could these in fact come much sooner in cases that result in a long prison term or a life sentence without the possibility of parole? Does not the frustration of waiting in vain for a perpetrator to be executed not actually hurt those seeking revenge more than if there was no death penalty at all?

Are juries more reluctant to find defendants guilty if there is a chance that they might be executed? Does that lead to more acquittals and thus hurt victims and their families even more when they see suspects go free? Furthermore, does the death penalty affect other innocent third parties more than other penalties? Do families of convicts suffer more because of the prolonged death threat to their loved ones?[19] May some of them not also be perceived as victims?

Although the analysis of the social, economic and psychological effects of the death penalty clearly indicates its harmful effects, it can also be attacked in a Kantian moral safe-haven, detached from any measurable social effect and scientific evidence. In my view, the essence of the moral opposition to the death penalty is the argument that killing is simply wrong, whether we relate it doctrinally to a human right to life and the right not be subjected to cruel or inhuman punishment, or not.

No one can blame victims and their families for wanting revenge, including through the death penalty. In their pain and loss, they are entitled to that desire. However, laws exist to prevent individuals from

---

18   Gerber and Johnson, *The Top 10 Death Penalty Myths,* pp. 196–197 and 222.
19   Psychiatrists warn that many family members, especially those who were the primary support of a capital defendant, experience depression and symptoms associated with post-traumatic stress disorder.

pursuing vengeance and their own vision of justice. If they do anyway (if, for example, a victim kills a perpetrator) then they become perpetrators and pay the price, both legally and morally. Although we may feel empathy with such a victim seeking revenge, Nietzsche's warning—that when fighting monsters you must take care not to become one yourself—should be remembered. Killing by the state is wrong as well, potentially even worse than killing by an individual. Individuals can sometimes kill in self-defence; states have such a range of options for protecting people from a threatening individual that killing is disproportionate to the danger that person represents. An individual might kill out of passion or be criminally insane. The state, when administering the death penalty, always kills after reflection, fully aware and accepting of the consequences.

An individual who kills, whether brought to justice or not, at least pays for the violation of a fundamental moral rule through his or her guilty conscience. When a state kills, it kills through its officials, without a guilty conscience; executioners are just doing their job.[20] There is a tendency, especially in the developed retentionist countries, to carry out the death penalty in an increasingly organized, technical and bureaucratic manner, favouring teamwork and a piecemeal approach, without thorough reflection, emotion or individual responsibility.[21]

Is it acceptable that killing takes place without anyone being morally responsible for it? Is a state that kills a dangerous state? Can its right to kill be misused against enemies of the state or enemies of those in power? Is such a state, in essence, more prone to also violate other human rights? If a state can kill, can it also torture when it is deemed necessary—also without guilt on the part of the decision-makers, through professional torturers doing their job? Can it send its citizens to kill and be killed in war, not in self-defence but for some other important "national interest"?

The death penalty, and the prerogative of the state to impose and execute it, is related to our approach to contemporary state sovereignty. In the

---

20 In *If This Is a Man* (Collier Books, 1993), writing about Auschwitz, Primo Levi expressed profound amazement: "How can one hit a man without anger?" In a similar moral sense should not we ask ourselves how one can kill without guilt?

21 See Linda Ross Meyer, "The meaning of death, last words, last meals", in *Who Deserves to Die? Constructing the Executable Subject*, Austin Sarat and Karl Shoemaker, eds. (Amherst, University of Massachusetts Press, 2011).

21st century, the right to take another person's life is no longer a part of the social contract between citizens and the state. The time when Rousseau reluctantly accepted such a sacrifice as a part of the social contract, necessary to keep peace in society, has long gone. Locke believed that political power includes the right to pass laws that carry the death penalty. Not anymore. The evolution of human rights has reduced state sovereignty in many areas; the death penalty should be one of them.

But what about public opinion and democracy and the "popular sovereignty" argument in many countries, where the majority is in favour of the death penalty?[22] Even when that is the case, it does not preclude intellectual and political leaders' responsibility to push for abolition. Is it not precisely the role of leadership to influence society to become more moral? Instead of "killing for votes" and death-penalty populism, is it not their duty to share with their people relevant information, that they may not be aware of, and help change mind-sets and attitudes?[23]

Chapter 5 highlights the importance of leadership in moving away from the death penalty. To stand for abolition or even for moratorium is often not popular. To change the tide requires courageous and committed leadership and a successful information campaign. Contributions in this chapter are provided by international leaders and heads of state and government from different cultures, continents and backgrounds, each of whom contributed to moving away from the death penalty nationally and internationally. The chapter also includes an article on the relevance of public messaging and information sharing for influencing popular attitudes towards the death penalty and its abolition.

Every book, including this one, should have a conclusion or a forward-looking ending. Chapter 6 of the book includes a contribution by the secretary-general of Amnesty International dealing with statistics and trends in moving away from the death penalty.

---

22 Perhaps a little exaggerated, but with a point: "The people who know the least about how the system of death sentencing functions appear to be the ones who support it most"—Craig Haney, *Death by Design: Capital Punishment as a Social Psychological System* (New York, Oxford University Press, 2005), p. 219. The lack of information-sharing on the death penalty is especially drastic in Japan, a retentionist country with strong public support for the death penalty, which provides no official information on how many people are on death row, how and when sentenced people are selected for execution or what the costs are for the death penalty compared with the alternative punishment (see the contributions by Hoyle and Hood and Mai Sato to this volume as well as Sato's book *The Death Penalty in Japan, Will the Public Tolerate Abolition?* (Wiesbaden, Springer, 2014).

23 See Sato, *The Death Penalty in Japan.*

Let me contribute to the tracing of the way forward in moving away from the death penalty by summarizing the arguments against it and encouraging political and social leaders to act decisively towards its abolition.

In my view, the death penalty is morally, socially and politically wrong. Morally, killing is wrong. Killing on behalf of a state is wrong as well. Some may believe that the death penalty is a just and moral punishment for the most serious of crimes; victims and their families are morally entitled to long for revenge. However, the social, political and economic costs of such retribution are, in my opinion, too high:

- Despite the greatest judicial efforts, wrongful convictions are not avoidable. Capital punishment is simply too final and irrevocable, and makes it impossible to correct such mistakes. The consequences for human error are too grave.

- There is no conclusive empirical evidence that the death penalty deters crime.

- The death penalty is cheap only if it is carried out quickly. Putting in place the necessary safeguards to prevent wrongful convictions often makes legal proceedings lengthy and much more costly than the longest prison sentence.

- Long delays on death row make the death penalty a cruel punishment, unacceptable from a human rights perspective.

- Long delays in carrying out executions also postpone closure and psychological healing for victims and their families, in a way that (for example) the perpetrator's return to prison to begin a life sentence without parole does not.

- Not all victims' families support the death penalty, and even among those who do, and who desire revenge or closure through it, the great majority are left frustrated because only a small minority of perpetrators are executed.

- The death penalty is not imposed in a just and equal way. Those sacrificed on the altar of retributive justice are almost always those who are vulnerable because of poverty, minority status or mental disability.

- The use of the death penalty should no longer be perceived as an entitlement of a sovereign state, because it violates human rights. No national interest can justify human rights violations such as the death penalty or torture. International recognition and protection of human rights limit state powers in this regard.

- As long as the death penalty exists, it can be misused, for example to target particular social groups and political opponents.

This book offers solid scientific evidence that supports abolition of the death penalty. Although it is an advocacy book, mostly written and edited by committed abolitionists, it clearly distinguishes between facts and values. I encourage you to choose your stand on this issue based on solid information.

I believe that one day, people will look back and wonder how it was possible that the death penalty ever existed—just like, in most societies today, it is already hard to understand how public executions could ever have taken place. But when will it become universally accepted that the death penalty violates the most fundamental human right, the right to life? When will the day come when all states are abolitionist—when there is no death penalty anywhere, anymore?

If we were to extrapolate a curve based on current trends—reduction of the number of crimes punishable by death, moratoria on its execution, and full abolition—one could perhaps predict the number of years it may take. But of course, in society, where human action can change trends, such predictions are highly unreliable.

This is the main reason for publishing this book: it is a part of global action to encourage global abolition of the death penalty. State power has to have its limits, limits that uphold human rights.

Ivan Šimonović
Assistant Secretary-General for Human Rights

New York, 31 August 2015

"If a great country cannot ensure
that it won't kill an innocent citizen,
it shouldn't kill at all."
— *Kirk Bloodsworth*

CHAPTER 1

WRONGFUL CONVICTIONS

Chapter includes articles by an exoneree, an academic, a former prosecutor and an activist for global abolition of the death penalty. Each of them offers a different perspective. Their findings converge on this point: there are a significant number of wrongful convictions, including in capital punishment cases, and executing the innocent is simply not acceptable.

<u>Kirk Bloodsworth</u> was the first person in the United States to be exonerated— have his conviction reversed—through DNA testing. He was a young man, a former marine from a humble background, without any criminal record, when he became the victim of faulty eyewitness identification. After almost nine years (two of them on death row) trying to prove his innocence, he was finally released. Nowadays, he is a strong advocate for the abolition of the death penalty and for the rights of the wrongfully convicted.

<u>Brandon Garrett</u>, an academic who does legal research on wrongful convictions, their causes and ways to prevent them, analyses DNA-based exonerations in the United States with particular attention to death penalty cases. He documents how revelations about innocent people being sent to death row have permanently altered the death penalty debate in the United States. In his view, jurisdictions in other countries should similarly take note of the possibility of wrongful convictions.

<u>Gil Garcetti </u>is a convert. He served as a district attorney in Los Angeles County, California, for many years and sometimes sought the death penalty for those he prosecuted. However, the death penalty's disproportionate effect on minorities and the history of wrongful convictions led him to become an abolitionist. He had a major role in the Proposition 34 campaign in California, which almost succeeded in replacing the death penalty with life imprisonment without parole (it attracted 48 per cent of the vote).

<u>Saul Lehrfreund</u> discusses retentionist countries across the Caribbean, Africa and Asia in which law and practice do not provide the protections in capital punish-ment cases that are required by international human rights law. He concludes that miscarriages of justice and executions of the innocent may occur in every system and that this is a major reason that an increasing number of countries have moved away from the death penalty.

WITHOUT DNA EVIDENCE, I'D STILL BE BEHIND BARS

Kirk Noble Bloodsworth[1]

I am the first person in the United States to be exonerated from a capital conviction through DNA testing. When I was exonerated in 1993, I had spent 8 years, 11 months, and 19 days (including two years on death row) for a crime I did not commit. I am living proof that America's system of capital punishment is broken beyond repair.

In early 1984, before my life changed forever, I was just a humble waterman living in Cambridge, Maryland. I was barely 23 years old, newly married, and had just served four years in the US Marine Corps. I had never been arrested in my life. This all changed on August 9, 1984, when the police knocked on my door at 3 o'clock in the morning and arrested me for the murder of Dawn Hamilton.

In a matter of days, I became the most hated man in Maryland.

How was I, a former US Marine with no criminal record and no connection to the scene of the crime, convicted and sentenced to death for a murder I didn't commit?

On July 25, 1984, 9-year-old Dawn Hamilton was tragically raped and murdered in Baltimore County. She was playing outside with a friend in the morning when she came across two little boys fishing at a pond. A man nearby approached Dawn and offered to help her find her friend in their game of hide-and-seek. That was the last time Dawn was seen alive. Her body was found in the park that afternoon, and the evidence of the brutal crime horrified the officials at the scene.

Because of the notoriety of the crime, the police were understandably eager to find Dawn's killer and ease the community's fear. When the police department found the two little boys who had seen the suspect, the officers drafted a composite sketch of the man they were looking for.

---

1   Kirk Noble Bloodsworth, victim of wrongful conviction.

The witnesses described the suspect as 6 feet 5 inches tall, with a slim build and dirty blond hair.

At the time of the investigation, I was 6 feet tall, with a thick waist, fiery red hair and long, noticeable sideburns.

Despite the fact that I did not fit the description, an anonymous caller suggested my name to the Cambridge Police Department. In a poorly conducted police line-up, I was identified as the last man to be seen with the victim.

Eyewitness misidentification is widely recognized as a leading cause of wrongful convictions in the United States. Since 1989, DNA evidence has been used to exonerate over 200 individuals, and about 75 per cent of these cases involved inaccurate eyewitness identification.

Other faulty police procedures played a role in my wrongful conviction.

I went to the police station voluntarily. Knowing that I was innocent of this crime, I wanted to be as cooperative as possible. When I entered the interview room, a pair of girl's panties and a rock were lying on the table. I was never told why. I later found out that the items were part of an experiment that the police devised because they believed that the killer would have a strong reaction to these items related to the crime. I had no reaction. But after I left the station, I talked to my friends about what the police had done. During the trial, the police used these statements against me, claiming that I knew something that only the killer would know. I only knew because they had shown the items to me that day.

There was no physical evidence against me. I was convicted primarily on the testimony of five eyewitnesses who were later shown to be terribly mistaken. With all the fear and anger in the community surrounding Dawn's murder, it took the jury less than three hours to convict. I was sentenced to die in Maryland's gas chamber. When my death sentence was announced, the courtroom erupted in applause.

I, an innocent man, was sent to one of the worst prisons in the United States at the time, the Maryland State Penitentiary. There was not a day that passed that I didn't try to tell someone I was innocent of this crime. But, as a guard at the penitentiary told me during my first week, "Everyone in the pen is innocent, man, don't you know?" No one believed me.

Life at the Maryland State Penitentiary can only be described as hell on Earth. I still have nightmares about it. Imagine living in a cell where you can only take three steps from the back wall to the front door. I could touch the side walls with my outstretched arms. My cell was directly under the gas chamber where I was sentenced to die at the hands of the state. The guards thought it was funny to remind me of that fact. They would describe the entire procedure in detail and laugh at my fate.

Fortunately, I only had to spend two years dreading this death. A second trial reduced my punishment to back-to-back life sentences.

I spent many of my years in the penitentiary in the infamous South Wing, where men were driven mad

> ## "IF WE KILL ONE INNOCENT MAN, IT'S ONE TOO MANY."
> —Kirk Noble Bloodsworth

by the prison brawls, filth, and other horrific experiences. Prisoners kept cotton balls in their ears at night so cockroaches wouldn't lay eggs in their heads. Prisoners would scream all through the night. The conditions proved even worse for me, as I was jeered by the other prisoners as a child rapist and killer. I had to lift weights every day and adopt a rough demeanour in order to fend off constant threats.

While I fought to stay safe at the penitentiary, I spent most of my time fighting to prove my innocence to anyone who would listen. I signed every letter I sent "Kirk Bloodsworth A.I.M., An Innocent Man."

While writing countless letters to advocates, I resolved to advocate for myself through my own research. I spent long days in the prison library, reading every book I could get my hands on. The key to my freedom came in the form of a book titled *The Blooding* by Joseph Wambaugh. This book chronicled the first time a process called DNA testing was used to solve a series of homicides in England. I had an epiphany right there: "If it can convict you, it can free you."

At the time of my first trial, DNA testing was not a well-understood concept in criminal law. But when I came across this book in 1992, DNA testing in criminal cases was breaking ground. My attorney, Bob Morin, submitted a request for the evidence in my case to be tested in a lab. The prosecutor in the case almost brought my innocence claim to a halt when she sent a letter with a devastating message: The biological material in my case had been inadvertently destroyed.

But by the grace of God, the judge from my second trial had decided to store some of the physical evidence in his chambers. I cannot say for sure why he decided to do that, but I have a hunch that he knew there was more truth to be told.

One day in 1993, the truth came out. I received a phone call from my typically mild-mannered attorney. He couldn't contain his excitement. The sperm stain lifted from the victim's underpants did not match my DNA. The DNA told the truth; I was not guilty of this crime. The appeals process in capital cases can be complicated and hard to manoeuvre. I was fortunate to have supportive family, advocates and an attorney who believed in my innocence.

Had evidence for DNA testing not been available, I would still be in prison today. In the vast majority of criminal cases in the United States, DNA or other biological evidence is not available—like in the cases of Troy Davis and Carlos DeLuna, who were executed despite grave doubts about their guilt. It is difficult to overturn wrongful convictions without evidence to test. Unfortunately, it is more than likely that there are people sitting on death row right now who are in this tragic bind.

It is hard to know just how I sustained hope through this ordeal. One story in particular comes to mind. Three months before the results came back that would prove my innocence, I lost my mother. She died of a heart attack on January 20, 1993. I was escorted to the funeral home in shackles and handcuffs and was only given five minutes with my mother. This was the woman who had taught me that if I don't stand up for something, I would fall for anything. She always believed in my innocence, but she didn't live to see me vindicated.

Finally, on June 28, 1993, I walked out of the Maryland State Penitentiary a free man.

Even today, many exonerees find it hard to shake the stigma after they are released from prison. At the time of my DNA exoneration, the technology was still new and the public wasn't sure if I could be trusted. When I returned to Cambridge, Maryland, I had trouble getting a job and I was harassed by my neighbours.

It didn't help that the prosecutor, Ann Brobst, would not admit the state's mistake. Even when I was released based on clear scientific evidence, Brodst stated, "If we had the DNA evidence in 1984, Mr. Bloodsworth would not have been prosecuted, but we are not prepared to say he is innocent."

Unfortunately, it would take 10 years for Dawn's true killer to be identified. I received a phone call from Brobst in September 2003 when the state of Maryland finally found a match in the DNA database. The murderer was identified as Kimberley Shay Ruffner. Not only was his name given in a tip at the time of the original investigation, but Ruffner was a suspect in rapes in the Fells Point neighbourhood of Baltimore. He was serving time for attempted rape when the DNA match was concluded years later.

As fate would have it, Ruffner had been sleeping in the cell below me in the Maryland Penitentiary all these years. We had lifted weights together. I gave him library books. He never said a word in all that time.

When I was exonerated, the state of Maryland paid me $300,000 for lost income during the time I was wrongfully imprisoned. But I lost so much more than money in those eight years that I will never get back. While I grieve this loss, I am no longer angry, and for the past decade of my life, I have simply wanted to do something to ensure that no-one else suffers what I did. After all, if it can happen to me, it can happen to anyone.

This principle guides my work today. During my years of freedom, I have fought for wrongfully convicted people all over the United States and lobbied for reforms to the American criminal justice system, such as the Innocence Protection Act of 2003, which includes the Kirk Bloodsworth Post-Conviction DNA Testing program, providing federal funds to states for DNA testing for prisoners who claim their innocence. I have become one of many exonerees who, with the help of great advocacy organizations like Witness to Innocence, travel around the country to share our cautionary tales.

When I tell young students my story, they always say the same thing: I can't believe this could happen in America.

While people are concerned by the rate of wrongful conviction in the United States, sometimes it takes a personal story to put a real face to the issue. Now, I respectfully submit my story to you. This story is why I believe that the time is overdue for the United States to follow the lead of our partners in the international community and abolish the death penalty once and for all.

Make no mistake about it. I am not here because the system worked. I am here because a series of miracles led to my exoneration. Not every person wrongfully convicted of a capital crime is as blessed. If we kill one innocent man, it's one too many.

I certainly understand the anger and desire for justice in capital cases. When I speak at death penalty events, I sometimes carry with me the picture of the victim Dawn Hamilton. Her death was so horrific that it still moves me to tears. But the great US Supreme Court Justice Thurgood Marshall one said, "The measure of a country's greatness is its ability to retain compassion in time of crisis." Even in the midst of fear and anger, a great country must ensure that its criminal justice system is effective and accurate. If a great country cannot ensure that it won't kill an innocent citizen, it shouldn't kill at all.

For these reasons, I strongly believe that abolishing the death penalty is a necessary step for the integrity of the criminal justice system in the United States and other nations.

DNA EVIDENCE CASTS LIGHT ON FLAWS IN SYSTEM

Brandon L. Garrett[1]

In no country other than the United States has there been such a large group of people whose innocence has been clearly proven by DNA tests years after their conviction. This group of innocent people, called DNA exonerees, provides a unique opportunity to learn about what can go wrong in even the most serious criminal cases. Exoneration is an official decision to reverse a conviction based on new evidence of innocence. The most haunting feature of many wrongful convictions is that they can come to light by sheer fortuity. We may never know how many other innocent people have been convicted and punished, even for serious crimes like murder.

Accuracy may be of particular concern for very serious but diffi-cult-to-solve crimes like murder, in which the death penalty may be charged. If the culprit is not caught in the act, police may need to rely on eyewitnesses, forensics or confessions—evidence that they can get wrong, due to missteps and unsound practices early in crim-inal investigations. Once key evidence is contaminated during an investigation, it may be very difficult for subsequent trial, appeals, and post-conviction courts to detect, much less correct, the errors. What I found disturbing when reading a large set of criminal trials of DNA exonerees is that a case against an innocent person may not seem weak at the time; it may seem uncannily strong. Where very few cases can be tested using DNA, it is crucial to prevent wrongful convictions before it is too late.

Over 140 death row inmates have been exonerated since the 1970s in the United States.[2] I focused on a small group of those cases when

---

1   Brandon L. Garrett is a professor ar the University of Virginia School of Law.
2   As of this writing, the Death Penalty Information Center had a count of 144 death-row inmates who have been exonerated <www.deathpenaltyinfo.org/innocence-list-those-freed-death-row>. A 2008 study modelled a false conviction rate by examining exonerations in cap-ital cases in published work and in a work in progress. Samuel R. Gross and Barbara O'Brien, "Frequency and predictors of false conviction: Why we know so little, and new data on capital cases", *Journal of Empirical Legal Studies*, vol. 5 (2008), pp. 927 ff.

I examined what happened in the first 250 DNA exonerations in my 2011 book *Convicting the Innocent: Where Criminal Prosecutions Go Wrong*.[3] There have now been more than 300 such exonerations in the United States. Of the first 300 cases, 192 were convicted of rape, 68 of rape and murder, 32 of murder, and 8 of other crimes; 18 had been sentenced to death.[4]

Of those 18, 16 had been convicted of rape and murder and 2 of murder alone. The evidence in those cases relied heavily on confessions, which we now know to have been false, and a range of flawed forensic evidence. Eight involved detailed false confessions allegedly including inside information that only the murderer could have known. With the benefit of DNA tests, we now know those people were innocent, but they may have seemed quite guilty at the time. Absent a complete video recording of the interrogations, jurors readily believed law enforcement officials' accounts of the confessions. Three of these confessions were made by mentally disabled people who could be expected to have been highly vulnerable to police coercion and suggestion.[5]

Ten of the cases involved testimony by informants, including seven jailhouse informants, three witnesses who testified in cooperation with prosecutors, and two codefendants who alleged they were accomplices but who were also innocent and themselves wrongly convicted. These informants also claimed to have overheard, in jail or elsewhere, details that only the killer could have known. Perhaps the most chilling of those cases is that of Ron Williamson and Dennis Fritz, in which the witness testifying for the state at trial, and describing the victim having a last dance with Williamson, was later shown by DNA testing to himself have been the killer.

Eight cases involved identifications by eyewitnesses, sometimes multiple eyewitnesses, who were all mistaken about what they had seen.

---

3   Data from that research are available online at <www.law.virginia.edu/html/librarysite/garrett_innocent.htm>. A multimedia online resource about these data and ways to prevent wrongful convictions is available at <www.innocenceproject.org/Content/Getting_it_Right.php>.

4   My book examined 17 such DNA exonerations in capital cases; in 2012, Damon Thibodeaux became the 300th DNA exoneree and the 18th death row DNA exoneree in the United States. Douglas A. Blackmon, "Louisiana death-row inmate Damon Thibodeaux exonerated with DNA evidence", *Washington Post*, 28 September 2012.

5   The US Supreme Court noted the existence of one such case, that of Earl Washington Jr., in its decision in *Atkins v. Virginia*, 536 U.S. 304, 320 n. 5 (2002).

Fourteen cases involved forensic evidence, including a number with unreliable and unvalidated forensics. Ten of the cases involved hair comparisons, two involved fibre comparisons and nine involved blood typing. Two involved bite mark comparisons; perhaps most well known is the case of Ray Krone, who was convicted based on little other than a flawed bite-mark comparison.

The death penalty cases were not so different from many other DNA exoneree cases that similarly involved murders, and in which false confessions and informant testimony and flawed forensic evidence played a central role. Of the first 250 DNA exonerees, 40 had falsely confessed. I examined each of those cases in detail and found that in all but two cases, the innocent person was said to have confessed in detail. Those false confessions were all seemingly powerful because they were contaminated. While many of the interrogations were partially recorded, none was recorded in its entirety. The confessions were concentrated in the murder cases. Of the 40 false confessions that I studied, 25 involved rape and murder, 3 murder only, and 12 rape only.

EXONERATION: AN UPHILL BATTLE

Once evidence is contaminated early in a criminal investigation, post-trial procedures—like appeals and the post-appeal habeas corpus remedies that we have in the United States—may not be of much help. It is a myth that appellate judges will correct factual errors: An appellate court "knows no more than the jury and the trial judge" and has a more limited role, partially because the appellate judge is "obliged to accept the jury's verdict" and focuses on more limited questions of law rather than the reliability of facts.[6] An appellate judge, who was not present at the original trial, is highly reluctant to second-guess the jury's decision to convict. No more than 1 or 2 per cent of cases are ever reversed. Of course, the vast majority of criminal cases involve plea bargains, in which the right to an appeal or post-conviction review is usually waived. Even when an appeal can be brought, rules setting strict time limits have traditionally prevented a convict from raising new evidence of innocence (although some of those rules have been relaxed,

---

6   Jerome Frank and Barbara Frank, *Not Guilty* (Garden City, NY, Doubleday, 1957).

particularly by state statutes that permit post-conviction DNA testing), and claims of innocence remain very difficult to make.

Once the appeal is over, an indigent inmate lacks the constitutional right to a state-provided attorney. Every jurisdiction in the United States offers some type of review after the appeal is complete, usually called post-conviction or habeas review. This additional level of review may permit, in theory, litigation of claims that could not have been raised during the initial appeal. However, non-death-row inmates typically do not have lawyers to help them navigate the incredibly complex procedural barriers that limit the chances of success during such reviews.

The death-row DNA exonerees typically followed a long road from trial to exoneration. Four of them had two trials; two had three trials. Each time they were convicted again, until they finally obtained DNA testing and were exonerated. The picture was not much different for the full group of DNA exonerees, including those who were not sentenced to death, except that among the non-death-row prisoners, even fewer received any relief prior to obtaining DNA testing. Non–death-row exonerees often did not obtain lawyers after their appeal and could not get any help filing habeas petitions. They rarely challenged the faulty evidence that caused their wrongful convictions, and when they did try, they failed. The figure that follows illustrates the degree to which the first 250 DNA exonerees (those who had judges write decisions in their cases) tried to challenge the evidence presented at their trials during appeal or post-conviction review, and how few obtained conviction reversals before they were successfully exonerated using DNA testing.

Post-conviction challenges to evidence by the first 250 DNA exonerees

We now know that these people were innocent, but they did not have any luck raising claims of innocence either: Every DNA exoneree who tried to raise such a claim failed. These appeals and post-conviction challenges took time; the road to exoneration took an average of 15 years. Of the 18 death-row DNA exonerees, 8 earned reversals on appeal or post-conviction. This high reversal rate is consistent with other studies of post-conviction litigation by death row inmates, although these cases were mostly litigated before the passage of the

Antiterrorism and Effective Death Penalty Act, which now restricts the availability of federal habeas review.[7]

What is still more troubling, though, is that others were convicted again at multiple trials, until ultimately DNA evidence set them free. Rolando Cruz and Alejandro Hernandez each had two convictions reversed and three criminal trials before they were exonerated. Kirk Bloodsworth, Ray Krone, Curtis McCarty and Dennis Williams each had two trials before they were exonerated by post-conviction DNA testing. Innocent people can be wrongly convicted not only once but several times, including in capital cases.

Bloodsworth was the first person exonerated from death row in the United States based on post-conviction DNA testing. He had been sentenced to death for the Maryland rape and murder of a 9-year-old girl in 1984. Five eyewitnesses had incorrectly placed him near the crime scene. Maryland recently abolished the death penalty, in part in response to Bloodsworth's case.

Compare that case to the nationally and internationally well-known Troy Davis case, a death penalty case that similarly involved a group of eyewitnesses who had each identified Davis following eyewitness identification procedures. Although the US Supreme Court, in a rare move, granted a habeas petition filed directly with the Court and asked a judge to look into the new evidence of Davis's innocence, the Georgia Board of Pardons denied clemency, and Davis was executed in September 2011. We will never know for sure if he was innocent—there was no DNA evidence to test, or any other real forensic evidence in the case.[8]

Other prisoners have fared better, but not to the point of full exoneration: They have pled guilty in exchange for having their sentence

---

7 For a discussion of the reversal rate in capital DNA exonerations, see Brandon L. Garrett, "Judging innocence", *Columbia Law Review*, vol. 108 (2008), pp. 55 ff., 99-100 (reporting a 58 per cent reversal rate, or 7 out of 12 capital DNA exonerees with written decisions). Since that article was written, of the four additional capital DNA exonerees, Curtis McCarty received reversals, Kennedy Brewer did not, and Michael Blair and Damon Thibodeaux did not have reported decisions.

8 Brandon L. Garrett, "Eyes on an execution", *Slate*, September 20, 2011. For an example of an execution that received very little attention at the time, but regarding which grave doubts have since been raised, see James Liebman and others, "The Wrong Carlos: Anatomy of a Wrongful Execution" (Columbia U. Press: New York, NY 2014).

reduced to time served or have received partial clemency after errors came to light in their cases. This has occurred in high-profile cases like those of the West Memphis Three in Arkansas, the Norfolk Four in Virginia and Edward Lee Elmore in South Carolina.[9] There are many more exonerations that do not involve DNA testing; very few death penalty cases—or murder cases generally—have testable DNA evidence.

DEBATE AND REFORM

Exonerations in capital cases have had a broad impact on the public and policymakers and have contributed to a "new death penalty debate."[10] Revelations that innocent people were sent to death row have permanently altered the debate, regardless of whether one believes that the death penalty is justified in some circumstances. For example, in *Baze v. Rees*, US Supreme Court Justice Stevens announced his opposition to the death penalty, citing evidence from DNA exonerations:

> *Given the real risk of error in this class of cases, the irrevo-*
> *cable nature of the consequences is of decisive importance to*
> *me. Whether or not any innocent defendants have actually*
> *been executed, abundant evidence accumulated in recent*
> *years has resulted in the exoneration of an unacceptable*
> *number of defendants found guilty of capital offenses.[11]*

Justice John Paul Stevens, writing for the US Supreme Court in *Atkins v. Virginia*, noted that "a disturbing number of inmates on death row have been exonerated."[12] In contrast, Justice Antonin Scalia has argued that known exonerations represent an "insignificant

---

9   See "Kaine's full statement on 'Norfolk Four' case", *Washington Post*, 6 August 2009, available from http://voices.washingtonpost.com/virginiapolitics/2009/08/kaines_full_statement_on_ norfo.html?sidST2009080602217; Tom Wells and Richard A. Leo, *The Wrong Guys: Murder, False Confessions, and the Norfolk Four* (New York, W. W. Norton, 2008); Raymond Bonner, *Anatomy of Injustice: A Murder Case Gone Wrong* (New York, Alfred A. Knopf, 2012).

10 James Liebman, "The new death penalty debate", Columbia Human Rights Law Review, vol. 33 (2002), pp. 527 ff.; Colin Starger, "Death and harmless error: A rhetorical response to judging innocence", Columbia Law Review Sidebar, vol. 108 (February 2008), pp. 1 ff.

11 *Baze v. Rees*, 553 U.S. 35, 85-86 (2008) (Stevens, J. dissenting).

12 *Atkins v. Virginia*, 536 U.S. 304, 320 n.25 (2002).

minimum."[13] Federal district judge Jed Rakoff struck down the federal death penalty, arguing: "We now know, in a way almost unthinkable even a decade ago, that our system of criminal justice, for all its protections, is sufficiently fallible that innocent people are convicted of capital crimes with some frequency." His ruling was later reversed by the Second Circuit Court of Appeals.[14] Statewide moratoriums and abolition of the death penalty have occurred in part citing the examples of death row exonerations; the best known was the Illinois moratorium and Commission on Capital Punishment, for which

"OVER 140 DEATH ROW INMATES HAVE BEEN EXONERATED SINCE THE 1970S IN THE UNITED STATES" —Brandon L. Garrett

there was intensive study of the cases of 13 men exonerated from the Illinois death row.[15] Hearing from a death row exoneree how a wrongful execution nearly happened can have a powerful effect on legislators and the public. As noted, the death penalty was abolished in Maryland; death row survivor Kirk Bloodsworth had lobbied for the repeal in Maryland and has done so across the country. The director of Maryland Citizens Against State Executions commented, "No single individual has changed as many minds as Kirk."[16]

Looking far beyond death penalty cases, DNA testing suggests additional questions about the more mundane criminal cases. A federal inquiry conducted in the mid-1990s, when police first began to send samples for DNA testing, found that 25 per cent of these prime suspects were cleared by DNA before a trial was held.[17] Where the vast majority of criminal cases lack any DNA evidence to test, still more questions are raised concerning accuracy.

---

13 *Kansas v. Marsh*, 548 U.S. 163, 194-195 (2006) (Scalia, J. concurring). For a discussion, see Samuel R. Gross, "Souter passant, Scalia rampant: Combat in the marsh", *Michigan Law Review First Impressions,* vol. 105 (2006), pp. 67 ff.

14 *U.S. v. Quinones*, 196 F.Supp.2d 416, 420 (S.D.N.Y. 2002) rev'd *U.S. v. Quinones*, 313 F.3d 49 (2nd Cir. 2002).

15 Governor's Commission on Capital Punishment, *Report of the Governor's Commission on Capital Punishment* (Springfield, Illinois, 2002), p. 4.

16 Scott Shane, "A death penalty fight comes home", *New York Times*, 5 February 2013.

17 Edward Connors and others, *Convicted by Juries, Exonerated by Science: Case Studies in the Use of DNA Evidence to Establish Innocence after Trial* (Washington, DC, US Department of Justice, 1996), pp. xxviii–xxix, 20.

More states and local police departments are now recording interrogations and have adopted best practices for eyewitness lineups. A few have also improved quality control and standards for forensics. Those reforms are inexpensive, and they benefit law enforcement; they help to identify the guilty and clear the innocent. However, they are all being implemented at the local and state levels.

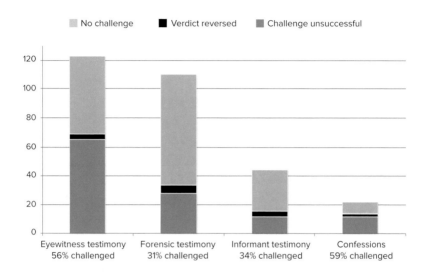

Additional reforms could improve the quality of post-conviction review. One state, North Carolina, has created an Innocence Inquiry Commission, to focus on judicial review of claims of innocence. Unlike post-conviction and habeas courts, which are sharply restricted by complex procedural barriers to relief, this Commission just investigates whether a person is innocent and should be exonerated by a three-judge panel. Other courts have made improvements on the front end by insisting that juries be carefully informed of the limitations of evidence, such as eyewitness testimony. Much more can be done, however, both to improve judicial gatekeeping to prevent wrongful convictions in the first place and to review convictions after the fact.

CONCLUSION

In the United States, because some jurisdictions happened to save crime scene evidence that could be tested years later, there has been a remarkable series of DNA exonerations, including in death penalty cases. Jurisdictions in the United States are slowly learning from these cases, and some have adopted reforms to prevent future wrongful convictions. Jurisdictions outside the United States should similarly take note. Eyewitness memory, confessions, informants and traditional forensic comparisons are not very different around the world. The same causes and practices may result in the same types of errors. Much more remains to be done to prevent wrongful convictions, in capital cases as well as other types of criminal cases. Getting it right will take a sustained commitment.

IN THE UNITED STATES, GROWING DOUBTS ABOUT THE DEATH PENALTY

Gil Garcetti[1]

The death penalty in the United States is applied through the state systems of justice and, on far fewer occasions, through the federal system. Under current federal law, each state has the authority to impose a death penalty for murders involving actions or situations that are usually referred to as "special circumstances." Likewise, any state is free to ban the death penalty. As of this writing, 18 states have banned it, and three more—Washington, Oregon and Colorado—have recently imposed moratoriums. One could also convincingly argue that the nation's largest state, California, effectively has a moratorium, given that the last execution there was in 2006.

In the 29 states that do impose the death penalty, the decision on whether to seek it is made by the county prosecutor (each state is divided into counties). California has 57 counties, and each has an elected prosecutor with the title of district attorney. Each of these district attorneys has different criteria for deciding whether to seek the death penalty in death-penalty-eligible cases. In Los Angeles, the death penalty is sought in less than 15 per cent of all eligible cases. In other California counties, this ratio is reversed. Without doubt there are cases for which, if they were tried in two counties in California, one county would seek the death penalty and the other would not.

Los Angeles County, where I have the greatest experience and familiarity, is the largest county in California and by population larger than 43 states. Because of its size, courthouses are spread throughout the county. Though the death-penalty decision-making process is centralized, whether a jury returns a verdict of death depends to a great extent on where in the county the case is tried. This has always troubled me. Why should one defendant benefit or suffer simply

---

1   Gil Garcetti was Los Angeles County District Attorney from 1992 to 2000.

because he or she is tried in an area of the county that is less likely or more likely to return a verdict of death? This concern holds for the entire state: Why should defendants benefit or suffer simply because of their county's policy regarding the death penalty or the propensity of jurors in the county to favour or oppose it?

I spent 32 years in the Los Angeles County District Attorney's office, including eight years as the elected District Attorney and four in the second-highest position, Chief Deputy District Attorney. In those capacities I oversaw the final decision-making process regarding the death penalty. In my eight years as District Attorney, I supported and implemented California's death penalty law. I left office at the end of 2000. About 10 years later, I reversed my position on the death penalty. I became convinced that it serves no useful criminal justice or societal purpose, including as a deterrent to murder; that given the number of recently exonerated death row inmates throughout the United States, there were undoubtedly people on California's death row who should not be there; that the obscene amount of taxpayers' money used to support the death penalty would be much more effectively used to keep teachers, school counsellors, and law enforcement personnel on the job; and that the current system, under which death-penalty cases often last for decades, was not fair to the families and loved ones of murder victims.

In 2011 I made my views public. My ultimate goal is to see the death penalty repealed, in California as well as the entire United States, and replaced with life in prison without the possibility of parole. Each state has a slightly different means of achieving this goal. Some, like California and Oregon, require a voter initiative,[2] while others may repeal through the state legislature. No matter the method, repeal is a difficult task, because the death penalty in the United States is a highly emotional issue, deeply political, and misunderstood by a majority of Americans.

---

2 In a voter initiative, proponents of a measure circulate a petition which, if it garners enough signatures, enables the measure to be placed on a ballot in the next election, to be voted on directly by citizens. California and 17 other states provide for state laws to be passed in this way.

THE CALIFORNIA MORATORIUM

The hard facts behind the death penalty process have begun to come to light in the United States, giving some of our political leaders, including vocal supporters of the death penalty, a reason to pause and think critically about the system. Many have publicly supported a moratorium in order to allow time for a meaningful conversation on the issue. California has since 2006 had a de facto moratorium on executions due to ongoing legal challenges to the state's lethal injection protocol. This has created an environment that has allowed us to move closer to achieving our goal of replacing the death penalty with life in prison without the possibility of parole.

California's de facto moratorium, as well as the moratoriums imposed by the governors of the states of Oregon, Washington and Colorado, have undoubtedly created an environment in which full repeal is more plausible. The positive effect of moratoriums can be seen most clearly in New Jersey, where a moratorium on executions was put in place in 2004 due to the lack of a proper lethal injection procedure. In the following years, questions about the effectiveness of the death penalty as a deterrent, cost feasibility, and, critically, the risk of sentencing innocents to death led New Jersey to repeal its death penalty in 2007. The de facto moratorium in California has similarly created an environment of scrutiny.

To fully understand the de facto moratorium in California, it is helpful to go back a few decades. After several years without a death penalty, California voters reinstated it in 1978 in an initiative process. Not many years after reinstatement, both supporters and opponents of the death penalty became very unhappy with the how it was being administered. In 2004, the California State Senate established the California Commission on the Fair Administration of Justice, a bipartisan blue-ribbon panel tasked with speeding up the death penalty process, investigating the causes of wrongful convictions and executions in the state, and recommending reforms. The resulting report made substantive recommendations for change. Even though highly respected individuals on both sides of the argument urged the legislature to adopt major changes in the administration of the death penalty, no meaningful change was adopted by the legislature.

In good part because of this failure to act, the then chief justice of the California Supreme Court and other death penalty supporters declared that there would never be the political will to change the death penalty law and that the system was broken and unfixable.

In 2005, in the court case *Morales v. Cullen*, a death row inmate challenged California's lethal injection procedure in federal court as cruel and unusual punishment prohibited by the Eighth Amendment to the US Constitution. Governor Arnold Schwarzenegger responded by agreeing to overhaul the state's lethal injection procedure. In 2006, in *Pacific News Service v. Cullen,* an inmate challenged the use of a paralytic drug during lethal injection, arguing that it violates the First Amendment rights of the press and the public by preventing witnesses from seeing what actually occurs during an execution. As a result of these legal cases, and because of a national shortage of lethal injection drugs, all of California's scheduled executions have been placed on indefinite hold. The last execution in California occurred in 2006.

"SOMEONE WHO'S VICTIM IS WHITE IS THREE TIMES MORE LIKELY TO BE SENTENCED TO DEATH THAN SOMEONE WHOSE VICTIM IS AFRICAN AMERICAN." —Gil Garcetti

In 2007, a state court ordered the California Department of Corrections and Rehabilitation (CDCR), the agency legally responsible for carrying out executions, to adopt a new lethal injection protocol while allowing for public comment and participation. A challenge to the CDCR's new protocol was advanced in 2010 based on state law in *Sims v. California Department of Corrections and Rehabilitation*. In that case, the plaintiff alleged that the CDCR violated the Administrative Procedures Act in both the process of adopting the new regulations and their substance. In May 2013, the plaintiff won the case, and the court found the state's lethal injection protocol was invalid. Since then, California has had no lethal injection protocol. If and when the state issues a new protocol, it must follow the strict guidelines of the Administrative Procedures Act and start the process of approval over again. More legal challenges to any new protocol are a certainty.

In addition to the legal challenges, the CDCR's supply of sodium thiopental, the lethal injection drug required under the regulations, has expired. The drug is no longer legally available in the United States and may not be imported under federal law. Thus, there is no legal source of the drug. Pentobarbital, another lethal injection drug used by some states, is also in short supply as the European manufacturer has cut off sales to US prisons.

REPLACING THE DEATH PENALTY WITH LIFE IN PRISON

In California, replacing the death penalty with life in prison without the possibility of parole can only be accomplished through a ballot initiative, since that is how the death penalty law was enacted. In 1978, 70 per cent of California voters passed the Briggs initiative, establishing the death penalty and specifying the criteria for eligibility. Given the current status of the death penalty in California and the general movement away from it across the nation, the goal of bringing a repeal initiative to the voters, while it may be viewed by some as audacious, is, at least in California, within reach.

California sentences more people to death than any other state. As of this writing, it has nearly 750 prisoners on death row. California led the country with 24 death sentences in 2013, 13 of them coming from just two southern counties. While more than 800 people have been sentenced to death in California since 1978, only 13 executions have been performed. Of the people sentenced to death in California in the last 30 years, only 1 per cent have been executed. Most death row inmates die of natural causes.

On a national level, the United States continues to move further away from the death penalty. Death sentences and executions are down in most states, and reported public support for the death penalty has declined significantly since the mid-1980s. California is not immune from this trend. An April 2011 poll by David Binder Research found that 63 per cent of California voters, across all parties and counties, support the governor converting all current death sentences to life in prison without possibility of parole. More Californians are realizing that the death penalty does not achieve swift and certain justice for victims' families, it is imposed discriminately at a huge cost to the state, and, most importantly, it risks executing innocent people.

The complicated and often decades-long appeals process that death row inmates are constitutionally entitled to in California and other states does not achieve swift justice for victims' families. Most appeals provide many opportunities for reversal and do not give families any kind of closure. Furthermore, the lengthy appeals process and special incarceration of death row inmates comes at a huge cost to the state. The death penalty costs 10 times as much as life in prison. If California replaced the death penalty with life in prison without the possibility of parole, the state would save $1 billion in just five years. In the midst of a severe ongoing budget crisis, a legitimate question is whether we should be investing taxpayer money in a broken death penalty that serves no worthy criminal-justice or societal purpose— or in education, mental health and law enforcement.

The death penalty in the United States has also been shown to fall disproportionately on people of colour and people of limited means. For example, data from 2011 show that someone whose victim is white is three times more likely to be sentenced to death than someone whose victim is African American, and four times more likely than someone whose victim is Latino. While only 27.6 per cent of murder victims are white, 80 per cent of prisoners executed in California have been convicted of killing whites. The location at which a murder occurs also affects the likelihood of the offender receiving the death penalty. In California, someone convicted in Alameda County, for example, is eight times more likely to be sentenced to death than someone convicted in Santa Clara County. As discussed earlier, even within the single (though large and diverse) County of Los Angeles, the death penalty is applied unequally in different locations. These stark disparities are evidence that the death penalty is being imposed discriminately, a reality that undermines a basic goal of our criminal justice system—fair and equal treatment under the law.

Finally, the death penalty comes with the unacceptable and ever-present risk of executing innocents. Between 1973 and 2011, 138 people were exonerated and released from death rows across the United States. Nationally, one person is exonerated for every 10 that are executed. The factors that commonly lead to wrongful convictions are rampant and varied: eyewitness error, false confessions, false testimony by an informant, prosecutorial misconduct and poor forensic evidence. The risk of wrongful conviction and execution can never be removed from a death penalty system.

In November 2012, California voters had the opportunity to replace the death penalty with life in prison without the possibility of parole through a voter initiative known as Proposition 34. While that proposition lost, the trend in public opinion had clearly changed. In 1978, Californians had voted overwhelmingly (70 per cent to 30 per cent) to reinstate the death penalty. But in 2012, 48 per cent of Californians voted in favour of repeal while 52 per cent voted against it (5,974,000 to 6,460,000). If about 250,000 voters had had been convinced to change their votes, there would be no death penalty in California today. The initiative failed in good part because the campaign did not reach enough voters with information. The reality of the California political system is that winning a ballot initiative, especially on a controversial issue like the death penalty, requires millions of dollars for voter education; unfortunately, the repeal campaign did not have sufficient resources.

Since Prop 34's defeat in 2012, California's death penalty repeal advocates are continuing to educate the public about the high costs of the death penalty; reshaping the California Coalition behind Proposition 34 into an ongoing advocacy campaign to promote public safety policies that reflect our shared values of safety, accountability, fairness and equality; and strengthening alliances with law enforcement, victims and labour as well as traditional supporters in the faith and civil rights communities. The ultimate goal, replacing the death penalty with life in prison without the possibility of parole, will best serve our priorities: to protect law-abiding citizens and punish those who commit society's most heinous crimes.

FEDERAL DEATH PENALTY CASES

The vast majority of death penalty cases are handled in the state courts. According to the Federal Death Penalty Resource Project, federal prosecutors tried 190 death penalty cases, involving 281 defendants, between 1988 and 2013. As of this writing there have been three federal executions; 54 federal court defendants have been sentenced to death and their appeals or writs are pending.

The movement of states toward repeal is both instructive and hopeful. Imagine the impact worldwide when California, a state with a population of over 37 million (greater than that of most countries), repeals the death penalty and replaces it with life imprisonment without the possibility of parole.

Or better yet, imagine the impact worldwide if the President of the United States declared a moratorium on the death penalty. Is this out of the question? Does the President have too many other pressing issues on his agenda? Does his previously stated position on the death penalty rule out the possibility that he would call for a moratorium in federal cases? Consider what President Obama said in May 2014: "In the application of the death penalty in this country, we have seen significant problems — racial bias, uneven application of the death penalty, you know, situations in which there were individuals on death row who later on were discovered to have been innocent because of exculpatory evidence. And all these, I think, do raise significant questions about how the death penalty is being applied."[3]

That is our opening to seek a dialogue with the President about declaring a moratorium on the death penalty while his administration studies and engages in dialogue with citizens on both sides of the issue—a dialogue that we should be confident will lead not just to a moratorium on the death penalty but to its replacement with life in prison without the possibility of parole.

AFTERWORD: HISTORIC RULING IN CALIFORNIA

On 17 July 2014, as the first edition of this publication was being produced, a historic federal district court decision was issued in the case of *Ernest Dewayne Jones v. Kevin Chappell, Warden of the California*

---

3   Peter Baker, "Obama orders policy review on executions", *New York Times, 2 May 2014, available from www.nytimes.com/2014/05/03/us/flawed-oklahoma-execution-deeply-troubling-obama-says.html?_r=0.*

State Prison at San Quentin. Federal Judge Cormac Carney concluded that California's death penalty system is dysfunctional and results in an "inordinate and unpredictable period of delay preceding their actual execution." He went on to say that "as for the random few for whom execution does become a reality, they will have languished for so long on Death Row that their execution will serve no retributive or deterrent purpose and will be arbitrary. . . . Allowing this system to continue to threaten Mr. Jones with the slight possibility of death, almost a generation after he was first sentenced, violates the Eighth Amendment's prohibition against cruel and unusual punishment." Mr. Jones has been on California's death row since April 1995.

The *Jones* decision can be appealed to the Federal Court of Appeals by the California Attorney General. If the appeal is heard and the decision of the district court is affirmed, the decision would then apply to the entire state—California's death penalty law would no longer exist. The California Attorney General could either accept the appeals court's decision or appeal it to the United States Supreme Court. The court of appeal obviously could also reverse the district court's decision. Mr. Jones would then be in the position of appealing that decision to the United States Supreme Court.

This case is historic because it appears to be the first time in the nation that a federal court judge has concluded that a specific state's death penalty law is unconstitutional because of the state's dysfunctional death penalty system. While this decision applies to this single case alone, judges and prosecutors in California can now expect the same arguments to be made in any pending death penalty case. Though judges are not required to follow a ruling by a single court, this especially well-written, exhaustive and well-documented decision is likely to persuade many judges to follow its lead and declare California's state death penalty law unconstitutional.

WRONGFUL CONVICTIONS AND MISCARRIAGES OF JUSTICE IN DEATH PENALTY TRIALS IN THE CARIBBEAN, AFRICA AND ASIA

Saul Lehrfreund[1]

International attitudes to the death penalty have evolved with the knowledge that every criminal justice system, however sophisticated, is susceptible to error and miscarriage of justice.[2] International human rights law, recognising that susceptibility, mandates that fair trial guarantees must be implemented in all death penalty cases. The understanding is that those facing the death penalty should be afforded special protection and guarantees to ensure a fair trial above and beyond those afforded in non-capital cases.

The reality is that the prevailing law and practice in far too many retentionist countries across the Caribbean, Africa and Asia do not provide the level of protection required in capital cases. Unless and until states can meet universally accepted standards, the death penalty should not be enforced. Too many countries retain the death penalty without assuming responsibility for the proper administration of criminal justice; many states fail to provide special procedural protections in capital cases.

> "…THE RISK THAT INNOCENT PEOPLE WILL BE EXECUTED CAN NEVER BE ELIMINATED…"
> —Saul Lehrfreund

UNIVERSAL STANDARDS APPLICABLE TO CAPITAL CASES

The potential for wrongful conviction and execution is precisely why international norms require such exacting standards and a heightened

---

1 Saul Lehrfreund, MBE, is co-executive director of The Death Penalty Project.
2 For a global snapshot of cases and research findings on wrongful convictions, see The Death Penalty Project, *The Inevitability of Error: The Administration of Justice in Death Penalty Cases* (London, 2014), available from www.deathpenaltyproject.org/news/1795/1795/.

level of due process in capital cases. The key question is: Are there significant gaps between the minimum conditions required in all capital cases and the law and practice in retentionist countries? If so, the only option is that the death penalty should no longer be enforced.

Two key documents laying out international standards in this regard are the International Covenant on Civil and Political Rights (ICCPR)[3] and the Safeguards Guaranteeing Protection of the Rights of Those Facing the Death Penalty.[4]

International Covenant on Civil and Political Rights

Although Article 6(1) of the ICCPR establishes that capital punishment is an exception to the right to life as long as it is not arbitrarily imposed, Article 6 requires a number of safeguards in its implementation: It may only be imposed for the most serious crimes, it cannot be pronounced unless rigorous procedural rules are followed, and it may not be imposed on pregnant women or for crimes committed before the age of 18. Article 6(2) of the ICCPR provides the following:

> *In countries which have not abolished the death penalty, sentence of death may be imposed only for the most serious crimes in accordance with the law in force at the time of the commission of the offence and not contrary to the present Covenant. . . . This penalty can only be carried out pursuant to a final judgment rendered by a competent court.*

Article 6(6) places the death penalty in its real context and assumes its eventual elimination: "Nothing in this article shall be invoked to delay or to prevent the abolition of capital punishment by any State Party to the present Covenant."

Retention of the death penalty is permitted by international law (albeit in extremely limited circumstances as discussed above), and

---

3   *International Covenant on Civil and Political Rights*, available from www.ohchr.org/EN/ProfessionalInterest/Pages/CCPR.aspx.

4   *Safeguards Guaranteeing Protection of the Rights of Those Facing the Death Penalty*, available from www.ohchr.org/EN/ProfessionalInterest/Pages/DeathPenalty.aspx.

its use does not by itself constitute cruel, inhuman or unusual punishment or torture. However, it may become an arbitrary violation of the right to life if it is imposed in circumstances that breach other rights under the ICCPR—including the right to a fair trial and the prohibition on torture, on which this paper will focus.

Article 14 of the ICCPR sets out the minimum requirements for a fair trial, which must be respected in all capital cases. The United Nations Human Rights Committee has consistently held that if Article 14 of the ICCPR is violated during a capital trial, then Article 6 (right to life) is also breached. In *Carlton Reid v. Jamaica*,[5] the Human Rights Committee held:

> *The imposition of a sentence of death upon the conclusion of a trial in which the provisions of the Covenant have not been respected constitutes . . . a violation of Article 6 of the Covenant. . . . The provision that a sentence of death may be imposed only in accordance with the law and not contrary to the provisions of the present Covenant implies that "the procedural guarantees therein prescribed must be observed, including the right to a fair hearing by an independent tribunal, the presumption of innocence, the minimum guarantees for the defence, and the right to review by a higher tribunal."*[6]

Safeguards Guaranteeing Protection of the Rights of Those Facing the Death Penalty

The restrictions on capital punishment set out in Article 6 of the ICCPR are reflected and further developed in the Safeguards Guaranteeing Protection of the Rights of Those Facing the Death Penalty (hereinafter the Safeguards), which "constitute an enumeration of minimum standards to be applied in countries that still impose capital punishment."[7]

---

5   *Carlton Reid v. Jamaica*, paragraph 11.5, Communication No. 250/1987, United Nations Doc. CCPR/C/39/D/250/1987 (1987), United Nations Human Rights Committee.

6   *Human Rights Committee, General Comment 6, Article 6 (Sixteenth session, 1982), Compilation of General Comments and General Recommendations Adopted by Human Rights Treaty Bodies*, U.N. Doc. HRI/GEN/1/Rev.1 at 6 (1994), available from http://www1.umn.edu/humanrts/gencomm/hrcom6.htm.

7   *Capital Punishment and Implementation of the Safeguards Guaranteeing Protection of the Rights of Those Facing the Death Penalty*, Report of the Secretary-General, UN Doc. E/2010/10, p. 33.

The Safeguards were adopted in 1984 by United Nations Economic and Social Council Resolution 1984/50. In 1989, they were further developed by the Council, which recommended, among other things, that there should be a maximum age beyond which a person could not be sentenced to death or executed and that people suffering from mental retardation should be added to the list of those who should be protected from capital punishment. Council Resolution 1996/15 called upon Member States in which the death penalty had not been abolished "to effectively apply the safeguards guaranteeing the rights of those facing the death penalty." The significance of the Safeguards was subsequently reaffirmed by the Commission on Human Rights in 2005 and the General Assembly in Resolutions 62/149 and 63/168. All states are bound by the international standards set out in the Safeguards, which should be considered as the general law applicable to the death penalty.

The fifth safeguard states:

> *Capital punishment may only be carried out pursuant to a final judgment rendered by a competent court after legal process which gives all possible safeguards to ensure a fair trial, at least equal to those contained in Article 14 of the ICCPR, including the right of anyone suspected of or charged with a crime for which capital punishment may be imposed to adequate legal assistance at all stages of the proceedings.*

The United Nations Special Rapporteur on Extrajudicial, Summary, or Arbitrary Executions has stated that fair trial guarantees in death penalty cases "must be implemented in all cases without exception or discrimination."[8] The Special Rapporteur has reiterated that "proceedings leading to the imposition of capital punishment must conform to the highest standards of independence, competence, objectivity and impartiality of judges and juries, in accordance with the pertinent international legal instruments."[9] International norms clearly call for those facing the death penalty to be afforded special protection and

---

8   *Extrajudicial, Summary or Arbitrary Executions: Report of the Special Rapporteur*, UN Document E/CN.4/2001/9, 11 January 2001, paragraph 86.

9   *Extrajudicial, Summary or Arbitrary Executions: Report of the Special Rapporteur*, UN Document E/CN.4/1997/60, 24 December 1996, paragraph 81.

guarantees to ensure a fair trial, above and beyond those afforded in non-capital cases (sometimes referred to as "super due process").

THE ADMINISTRATION OF JUSTICE IN CAPITAL CASES

Numerous cases in countries that still impose the death penalty in the Caribbean, Africa and Asia have failed to live up to these standards. Some of them are discussed below. In the United Kingdom, which has abolished the death penalty, several egregious wrongful convictions in murder cases helped dissipate support for its reintroduction.

The Caribbean

There are many instances of miscarriage of justice and unfair trials in capital cases in Caribbean countries. Wrongful convictions and unfair trials are all too common, and the ratio of successful appeals to the Courts of Appeal and the Judicial Committee of the Privy Council reveals that the proper administration of justice is called into question in far too many capital cases.

There are serious concerns that the common law as applied in the 19th century is not an adequate instrument for control of poorly paid, lightly disciplined police forces who are under pressure to secure results in the face of rising crime rates and criminal violence. The law as it stands does not provide an adequate basis for the exclusion of unreliable confessions, identifications and other aspects of a defective investigation. People who face the death penalty are typically tried and convicted upon confession evidence that is later challenged, given at a time when legal aid is not available. The right of access to a lawyer while in custody remains, on the whole, theoretical rather than practical, and trial and appeal lawyers are too frequently ill-equipped and/or insufficiently experienced to ensure a fair trial and often lack sufficient resources to obtain the expert assistance (medical or otherwise) needed to adequately prepare the defence.[10]

---

10 See for example the Community Legal Services Act Cap. 112A of the Laws of Barbados and decision of the Court of Appeal in Civil Appeal No. 20 of 1997 in *Hinds v. Attorney General of Barbados* (30 September 1999). On legal aid fees, see also the Poor Persons Defence Act of Jamaica.

The vast majority of prisoners in the Caribbean cannot afford to pay for legal representation and are therefore provided with an attorney through an inadequate legal aid system. The accused are often assigned a very junior member of the bar to prepare the defence, usually without any expert help, medical or otherwise.

In *R v. Bethel,*[11] the appellant's conviction for murder and his death sentence were quashed and a retrial ordered as his trial lawyer had failed to take proper instructions before the trial. The Court of Appeal of Trinidad and Tobago emphasised that whatever the time spent taking instructions, in a murder case involving the death penalty, the gravity of the charge required counsel to pursue with his client a "full and searching inquiry into the facts."

The domestic courts in the Caribbean have on a number of other occasions considered the effectiveness of legal representation and the conduct of counsel in a capital case. For example, Ann-Marie Boodram had been sentenced to a mandatory death penalty in Trinidad for the murder of her husband. Her appeal to the Court of Appeal was rejected, and she further appealed to the Judicial Committee of the Privy Council (hereinafter the Privy Council), who considered whether her trial lawyer's gross incompetence had resulted in a miscarriage of justice. In delivering the judgment of the Board, Lord Steyn held:

> *In the present case [her trial lawyer's] multiple failures, and in particular his extraordinary failure when he became aware on 17th February, 1998 that he was engaged on a retrial to enquire into what happened at the first trial, revealed either gross incompetence or a cynical dereliction of the most elementary professional duties. . . . it is the worst case of the failure of counsel to carry out his duties in a criminal case that their Lordships have come across. The breaches are of such a fundamental nature that the conclusion must be that the defendant was deprived of due process. . . . The conclusion must be in this exceptional case the defendant did not have a fair trial.*[12]

---

11   *R v. Bethel*, Unreported, 23 March 2000, Court of Appeal of Trinidad and Tobago, Republic of Trinidad and Tobago.

12   *Boodram v. the State*, paragraph 40, 1 Criminal Appeal Reports 12 (2002), Judicial Committee of the Privy Council, Republic of Trinidad and Tobago.

Another death penalty case from Trinidad (*Dookran and another v. the State*)[13] concerned the investigation and collection of the evidence by the police and the conduct of the trial itself. It revealed that the law and practice as it stands does not guarantee the level of protection required by international norms in the investigation, prosecution and trial of a capital case.

In 1997, Chitrah Dookran and her mother, Malharri Dookran, were convicted of the murder of Chanardai Dookran-Bissoon, who was Chitrah's sister and Malharri's daughter. A third defendant, Devon Cunningham (the alleged hit man), was acquitted whilst Chitrah and Malharri were sentenced to death. Both were unrepresented when taken into police custody, and the case centred on incriminating statements they allegedly gave to the police. Chitrah claimed her statement was involuntary and preceded by threats and promises by a police officer whom the prosecution never called as a witness, but the trial judge still admitted her statement into evidence. The Court of Appeal held that Chitrah's statement should not have been admitted into evidence before the jury, but nevertheless held that there had been no miscarriage of justice. The Privy Council disagreed and held that the approach of the Court of Appeal was fundamentally flawed as they could not be satisfied that a reasonable jury would have inevitably convicted her had the statement not been admitted into evidence. This was a clear miscarriage of justice, and Chitrah's conviction was quashed and she was released from death row.

Malharri, who was elderly and of low intelligence and who had a history of being battered by her husband, contended at trial that she was kept in custody without food for over 14 hours before her statement was taken. She alleged that the investigating police officer made her take off her glasses and threatened to bang her head against a wall before she eventually put her cross (X) on the statement that the police officer had written out for her. The trial judge admitted Malharri's statement into evidence in spite of the allegations of physical abuse and coercion by the police and evidence indicating Malharri was especially vulnerable due to her low intelligence and history of domestic abuse.

---

13 *Dookran and another v. the State*, UKPC 15 (2007), Judicial Committee of the Privy Council, Republic of Trinidad and Tobago.

Having already quashed Chitrah's conviction and death sentence, the Privy Council held that they could not "avoid a residual feeling of unease about whether justice has been done in Malharri's case."[14] The appeal was allowed, and Malharri was also released from death row.

In many capital cases from the Caribbean, individuals who are sentenced to death have subsequently been found to be suffering from mental illness and/or an intellectual disability that affected the safety and lawfulness of their convictions and death sentences. This is especially so in countries with inadequate mental health services. The reality is that the death penalty is regularly imposed on people with significant mental disorders, contrary to recognised norms and procedural requirements. There are many examples of defendants being wrongly sentenced to death by virtue of the fact that inadequate or no medical evidence was produced at trial.

In 2012, on the strength of fresh psychiatric evidence, the appeal of Shorn Samuel,[15] a prisoner under sentence of death in Saint Vincent and the Grenadines, was allowed by the Eastern Caribbean Court of Appeal. The Court found that new medical evidence demonstrated that Mr. Samuel was suffering from a severe mental disorder at the time of the murder, which substantially diminished his responsibility for the offence. Mr. Samuel's conviction for murder was therefore quashed, and a conviction of manslaughter was substituted by reason of diminished responsibility. The death sentence was reduced to life imprisonment.

In 2012, the appeal of Sheldon Issac,[16] a prisoner under sentence of death in Saint Kitts and Nevis, was determined by the Eastern Caribbean Court of Appeal. The last hanging in Saint Kitts and Nevis had taken place in 2008, and Mr. Isaac and his three co-defendants were at real risk of execution. The Privy Council granted all four defendants stays of execution pending the determination of their appeals. Psychiatric and psychological evidence was presented to the Privy

---

14 Ibid., paragraph 36

15 *Shorn Samuel v. the Queen*, Criminal Appeal No. 22 of 2008 (2012), Eastern Caribbean Court of Appeal, Saint Vincent and the Grenadines.

16 *Sheldon Issac v. Director of Public Prosecutions*, Criminal Appeal No. 19 of 2008 (2012), Eastern Caribbean Court of Appeal, Saint Kitts and Nevis.

Council demonstrating that Mr. Isaac was severely brain-damaged and should never have stood trial. The Privy Council remitted the case to the Eastern Caribbean Court of Appeal for review, and the Court of Appeal accepted the evidence that he was severely mentally disordered and concluded that he was unfit to stand trial. The Court rejected a retrial as inappropriate and unnecessary. The system of criminal justice in Saint Kitts and Nevis clearly failed in this capital case: The investigating authorities, the prison service, the lawyers and the trial judge all failed to recognize that Mr. Isaac was so severely mentally disordered that he was unfit to stand trial. As a result, he was tried, convicted, sentenced to death and very nearly executed, contrary to international standards and norms.

In 2005, the UN Commission on Human Rights urged all states that maintain the death penalty "not to impose the death penalty on a person suffering from any mental or intellectual disabilities or to execute such a person."[17] The reality, though, is that a large proportion of prisoners under sentence of death have never been properly examined by a psychiatrist or psychologist, resulting in many prisoners who are mentally disordered or impaired facing the death penalty in the Caribbean and beyond.

Africa

I am not aware of any academic research into innocence and miscarriages of justice in capital cases in Africa, but there are concerns that many of the features identified in Caribbean death penalty cases also prevail in African retentionist countries. A few of these are described below.

Malawi's criminal justice system, like that of many Commonwealth Caribbean countries, is based on English common law. An obvious difference is that capital murder trials are held in the High Court before a single judge who determines guilt and imposes a sentence, not before a jury. Although Malawi's Criminal Procedure Code provides for the right of trial by jury, jury trials in homicide cases were discontinued in 2009 by executive fiat, a decision justified at least in part by their cost.

---

17 Office of the High Commissioner of Human Rights, Human Rights Resolution 2005/59, "The question of the death penalty", paragraph 7(c), available from http://ap.ohchr.org/documents/alldocs.aspx?doc_id=11140.

Article 42 of the Malawi Constitution provides that indigent defendants facing criminal charges are entitled to free legal aid "where the interests of justice so require." In practice, however, legal aid is provided only in homicide cases as there are so few lawyers to serve the entire country.

> *Malawi has struggled for years with a tremendous backlog of homicide cases causing severe prison overcrowding throughout the country . . . . Bail is rarely granted in such cases, and homicide trials are frequently suspended, meaning many accused persons spend several years awaiting trial. These "remand" prisoners typically will not speak to a lawyer until the day of trial, when a Legal-Aid advocate will interview them briefly. The defence rarely calls witnesses or conduct any investigation; in most cases counsel simply cross-examines the prosecution's witnesses based on a thin file containing witness statements and a post-mortem examination. . . . Under Section 11 of the Supreme Court of Appeals Act, each individual convicted of homicide has the right to appeal to the Malawi Supreme Court. In practice, however, the right to appeal is often frustrated by the lack of an effective case-management system and the failure of Legal-Aid attorneys to track cases on appeal. Case files often go missing. . . . As of January 2012, no appeals had been filed for 11 of the prisoners sentenced to death from 2005 to 2009. In several of these cases, the courts appear to have lost all court records relating to the conviction, including the trial transcript and exhibits.[18]*

Clearly, the requisite fair trial standards cannot be applied to every death-penalty case in countries that lack the resources to ensure due process. Thus, there is a great risk of innocent people being sentenced to death. The law, as applied in countries such as Malawi, does not protect against mistakes leading to the wrong person being convicted and sentenced to death.

In **Uganda**, Edmary Mpagi spent over 18 years on death row, accused of killing a man who was later found to be alive. In 1982, he was

---

18 Sandra Babcock and Ellen Wight McLaughlin, "Reconciling human rights and the application of the death penalty in Malawi: the unfulfilled promise of Kafantayeni v. Attorney General", in *Capital Punishment: New Perspectives*, Peter Hodgkinson, ed. (Farnham, United Kingdom, Ashgate Publishing, 2013), p. 193

convicted, together with his cousin, of murder and sentenced to death, after what has been called "fabricated evidence, coerced testimony and a generally slipshod trial."[19] Mpagi met with his state-appointed lawyer only twice before the trial, and no translator was provided even though neither he nor his cousin had any working knowledge of English.[20] Prison conditions were reportedly cruel, degrading and inhumane. Mpagi's cousin died in prison in 1985 after the prison authorities refused to provide him with medical attention, stating that they could not waste time or money on a condemned prisoner who was due to be executed.[21] In 1989, the Attorney General established that Mpagi was innocent and wrongly convicted; however, it was not until 2000, 11 years later, that Mpagi received a presidential pardon and was released.

In **Sierra Leone**, "MK" was the longest serving woman on death row. She was arrested in 2003 and charged with the murder of her stepdaughter, convicted in 2005, and received the death penalty, which was mandatory at the time in Sierra Leone. MK's case highlights many of the serious human rights concerns that can occur in capital cases. From her arrest until shortly before trial, she received no legal advice or assistance. MK, who is illiterate, thumb-printed a confession which was later used against her at trial. The state did not provide MK with a lawyer until the commencement of the trial. This lawyer met with MK three times before the trial, each meeting lasting no longer than 15 minutes.

Following her trial, MK again did not have access to a lawyer, and she did not have the knowledge or resources to file an appeal against her conviction within the stipulated 21-day time limit. MK filed an appeal to the Court of Appeal 10 months after her conviction with the assistance of a state-provided Prison Welfare Officer. The Court of Appeal rejected the appeal, holding that the time period for filing appeals cannot be extended even for those facing the death penalty.

---

19 Foundation for Human Rights Initiative, *Towards the Abolition of the Death Penalty in Uganda*, *the Civil Society Coalition on the Abolition of the Death Penalty in Uganda* (2008).

20 Mpagi Edward Edmary, "Mpagi Edward Edmary", *Our Friends in Prison*, available from www. ourfriendsinprison.weebly.com/lifestory-of-mpagi-edward-edmary.html.

21 Ibid.

In 2010, MK received legal assistance from AdvocAid, a Sierra Leonean non-governmental organisation, and her case was re-listed in the Court of Appeal. In March 2011, after she spent six years on death row, MK's conviction was overturned in a landmark decision by the Court of Appeal, and she was released immediately. The Court found that the procedural irregularities—lack of legal advice and assistance, lack of resources to file an appeal—were fundamental, and therefore rendered MK's trial a nullity.

Asia

An authoritative recent United Nations report[22] stated: "In many countries in Asia, specifically in death penalty cases, the right to a fair trial was impeded by laws which denied due process. Even in countries where due process safeguards exist in principle, they were not applied in practice." The Anti-Death Penalty Asia Network has reported that

> *courts continue to rely on "confessions" extracted through torture as evidence in criminal trials—despite the international ban on torture and on the use of such confessions. Laws impose mandatory death sentences for crimes such as drug trafficking, and place the burden of proof on the accused, depriving them of the right to be presumed innocent until and unless proven guilty according to law. Access to a lawyer before, during and after trial is often denied, and in some countries the independence of the judiciary is not assured. Some states have established special courts which sentence people to death after hasty proceedings.*[23]

There have been 11 executions in Taiwan since 2013, in spite of growing public disquiet about the death penalty with the knowledge that there is a real danger the state could execute someone in error following an unfair trial.[24] In January 2011, Taiwan's Ministry of

---

22   *Moratorium on the Use of the Death Penalty*, Report of the Secretary-General (3 August 2012), UN Doc. A/67/22, paragraph 34.

23   Anti-Death Penalty Asia Network, *When Justice Fails, Thousands Executed in Asia After Unfair Trials* (Amnesty International ASA 01/023/2011), p. 6.

24   For more information on the death penalty in Taiwan, see The Death Penalty Project, *The Death Penalty in Taiwan: A Report on Taiwan's Legal Obligations under the International Covenant on Civil and Political Rights* (London, 2014), available from www.deathpenaltyproject.org/ news/1750/dpp-launches-report-on-the-death-penalty-in-taiwan/.

Justice admitted that Chiang Kuo-ching had been executed in error in 1997, for the rape and murder of a five-year-old girl committed 15 years previously. After a campaign by Chiang's parents, the Military Supreme Court Prosecutor's Office filed an extraordinary appeal with the Military Supreme Court to reopen the case in 2010. The authorities acknowledged that Chiang's confession was the result of torture by military investigators, including being subjected to a 37-hour interrogation, exposed to strong lights, threatened with an electric prod and deprived of sleep while being forced to undergo strenuous physical activities.[25] The authorities accepted that the trial court had ignored Chiang's allegations of torture and his pleas of innocence and that his conviction had been rushed through by the military court.[26] In September 2011, a military court formally acquitted Chiang, and in October 2011, Taiwan's Ministry of Defence agreed to pay US$3.4 million in compensation to Chiang's relatives. President Ma Ying-Jeou publicly apologised to Chiang's mother and conceded that the authorities had "acted wrongly" in the case.[27]

In many retentionist countries in Asia, prisoners facing the death penalty have little or no access to a lawyer following arrest and when preparing for trial or appeal.

> *Many of those sentenced to death in Afghanistan do not have proper legal representation at the time of their trial. In fact, defence lawyers in Afghanistan are normally not even present in the trial court but must submit a written rebuttal of the charges against their client to the court. In Indonesia even though the Criminal Procedure Code guarantees the right to be assisted by a lawyer, in practice there are documented cases of defendants who do not have access to a lawyer. In China, the authorities may block or make it very difficult for defence lawyers to meet with their clients, gather evidence and access case documents.*

---

25 Taiwan Alliance to End the Death Penalty, "Doubts raised over soldier's execution" (30 January 2011), available from www.taedp.org.tw/en/story/1875.

26 Amnesty International, *Death Sentences and Executions 2013*, p. 5. See also Amnesty International, *China: Against the Law: Crackdown on China's Human Rights Lawyers Deepens* (2011), available from www.amnesty.org/en/library/info/ASA17/018/2011/en.

27 The National, "Taiwan 'child rapist' cleared 14 years after his execution" (2 February 2011), available from www.thenational.ae/news/world/asia-pacific/taiwan-child-rapist-cleared-14-years-after-his-execution.

> *Lawyers defending clients involved in politically sensitive cases have been subjected to intimidation and excluded from proceedings. Others have had charges filed against them for advising their clients to withdraw forced confessions or for trying to introduce evidence that challenges the prosecution's case.*[28]

In Japan, there are no legal provisions requiring the effective assistance of defence counsel. Indeed, Japanese courts tend not to find problems even when defence counsel's assistance is clearly ineffective and inappropriate.[29] In some cases, death sentences have been imposed and finalised despite insufficient assistance from a defence lawyer, but there have been no cases in which a death sentence has been overturned because of the ineffective assistance of counsel.

A minimum fair trial guarantee that needs to be respected in all capital cases is the right of appeal. In the Caribbean, the availability of an automatic appeal has saved many innocent lives, as the appellate courts have on numerous occasions overturned capital convictions. However, in a number of Asian countries there is no mandatory right of appeal, thus increasing the risk that wrongful convictions will not be remedied.

China now provides for more than one appeal, but there are concerns that the review process before the Supreme People's Court does not meet the minimum requirements of Article 14 of the ICCPR because the present procedures are insufficient to meet developing human rights standards. All appeals must be governed by the principles and safeguards of Article 14, and in order to ensure an effective right of appeal, the convicted person should be granted effective access to the review process with adequate legal representation in an open, public hearing.

In Japan, appeal to a higher court against a death sentence is not automatic despite repeated recommendations by the UN Committee

---

28 Anti-Death Penalty Asia Network, *When Justice Fails*, p. 24.

29 The Death Penalty Project, *The Death Penalty in Japan: A Report on Japan's Legal Obligations under the International Covenant on Civil and Political Rights and an Assessment of Public Attitudes to Capital Punishment* (2013), pp. 7-8, available from www.deathpenaltyproject.org/ legal-resources/research-publications/the-death-penalty-in-japan/.

against Torture and the UN Human Rights Committee.[30] The government of Japan insists that a mandatory appeal system is unnecessary because most defendants do exercise their right to appeal. But the numbers are troubling. Of the first 15 death sentences imposed by lay judge panels in Japan, three (20 per cent) were finalised after defendants withdrew their appeals. Moreover, people sentenced to death in Japan who withdraw their appeals tend to be executed more quickly than non-volunteers (people who withdraw their appeals seldom file requests for retrial or pardon either).

In South Korea and parts of Pakistan, there is no mandatory requirement for appeal to a higher court in death penalty cases, and in North Korea there is no possibility of appeal at all.[31]

Japan also fails to conform to universally agreed standards for special protection and fair-trial guarantees beyond those offered in non-capital cases.[32] Capital punishment is not treated as a different form of punishment in Japan despite claims to the contrary. As a result, there are few special procedural protections accorded to suspects and defendants in potential capital cases.[33] Since Japan's lay judge system started in 2009, the courts have become more restrictive about what evidence can be introduced at trial. The change is largely motivated by the desire to minimise the burden felt by citizens who serve as lay judges, and the courts have become more likely to demand that expert testimony be presented in extremely abbreviated forms. As a result, a defendant's psychological condition and developmental problems are seldom considered by the lay judge tribunals as carefully as they should be.[34] Furthermore, Japan does not require unanimity (of all judges and lay judges on a panel) or even a super-majority (agreement by six or more of the nine

---

30 Paragraph 20, CAT/C/JPN/CO/1, 3 August 2007; paragraph 17, CCPR/C/JPN/CO/5, 30 October 2008.

31 Anti-Death Penalty Asia Network, *When Justice Fails,* p. 31.

32 International Federation for Human Rights, *The Death Penalty in Japan: The Law of Silence* (2008), available from www2.ohchr.org/english/bodies/hrc/docs/ngos/FIDHJapan94.pdf; Amnesty International, *Death Sentences and Executions 2012,* available from www.amnesty.org/en/library/asset/ACT50/001/2013/en/bbfea0d6-39b2-4e5f-a1ad-885a8eb5c607/act500012013en.pdf. See also Taiwan Alliance to End the Death Penalty, "Doubts raised over soldier's execution".

33 David T. Johnson, "Capital punishment without capital trials in Japan's lay judge system", *Asia Pacific Journal,* vol. 8, issue 52 (27 December 2010), pp. 1-38, available from www.japanfocus.org/-David_T_-Johnson/3461.

34 The Death Penalty Project, *The Death Penalty in Japan,* pp. 21-22.

people on a panel) before the death penalty can be imposed. A bare "mixed majority"—five votes, with at least one from a professional judge—is enough to condemn a person to death. "It is difficult to square Japan's mixed majority rule with the claim often made by Japanese officials that the country is extremely 'cautious' (*shincho*) about capital punishment."[35]

The combination of the lack of effective judicial control over the use of lengthy pretrial detention, the failure to require jury unanimity for a death sentence, the lack of effective mandatory appeals and the need for a fair and functioning process of executive mercy places Japan in breach of its international obligations with regard to the death penalty. Japan is one of the wealthiest nations in Asia, with a sophisticated and well-resourced legal system, but is yet another example of a country that fails to implement capital punishment in accordance with universally accepted safeguards. Miscarriages of justice will inevitably occur, and when the death penalty is imposed, it results in an irreversible injustice.

---

35   Ibid p. 22. See also David T. Johnson, "Progress and problems in Japanese capital punishment", in *Confronting Capital Punishment in Asia: Human Rights, Politics, Public Opinion, and Practices*, Roger Hood and Surya Deva, eds. (Oxford, Oxford University Press, 2013), p. 176.

The United Kingdom

Many lessons can be learned from the United Kingdom, where the death penalty was in effect abolished in 1965.[36] Between 1966 and 1993, there were 13 attempts in Parliament to reintroduce the death penalty for certain categories of murder. These attempts ended after a shocking series of miscarriages of justice in cases concerning particularly heinous crimes. The most notable were those of the Birmingham Six and the Guildford Four, all wrongfully convicted of murder through terrorist bombings, and Stefan Kisko, a man of limited intelligence, wrongfully convicted of a child sex murder. "All would certainly have attracted the death penalty had it been available. This persuaded many who had previously supported the reintroduction of capital punishment to change their minds."[37]

The last execution in the United Kingdom was carried out in 1964, but it was not until 1999 that the United Kingdom ratified Protocol No. 6 to the European Convention on Human Rights and Protocol No. 2 of the ICCPR, thus marking by international treaty its final rejection of capital punishment.

> *There have been no campaigns since then, in the press, by pressure groups, or in parliament to seek to reinstate the death penalty. Even the families of the victims of the most appalling types of crime, like the abduction and sexual murder of children, have expressed themselves generally as satisfied by a sentence of life imprisonment, with a guaranteed lengthy period of custody.[38]*

This rejection of capital punishment has been further strengthened by a series of cases where the courts have posthumously reviewed the murder convictions of individuals who were executed. In 1998,

---

36 In 1965, the death penalty for murder was suspended for a period of five years (to expire on 31 July 1970) unless both houses of Parliament determined that it should not expire by affirmative resolutions. In reality this was the end of capital punishment for murder in the United Kingdom, and in 1969, the House of Commons endorsed the 1965 Act.

37 Roger Hood, "Abolition of capital punishment in the United Kingdom", paper presented at the workshop Global Survey on Death Penalty Reform, Beijing, 25-26 August 2007, p. 13. See also Roger Hood and Carolyn Hoyle, *The Death Penalty: A World-wide Perspective,* 4th ed. (Oxford, Oxford University Press, 2008), pp. 42-47.

38 Ibid, p. 14.

the Court of Appeal found that the conviction of Mahmoud Hussein Mattan, who was hanged in Cardiff Prison on 8 September 1952, should be quashed. In delivering judgement, Lord Justice Rose stated that the case had wide significance and demonstrated that "capital punishment was not perhaps an appropriate culmination for a criminal justice system which was human and therefore fallible."[39]

CONCLUSION

A precondition, under international law, for imposing the ultimate penalty is that the investigation, prosecution and trial have been conducted with impeccable fairness and propriety. All too often, capital trials fall short of these standards. But even when procedural guarantees are improved and the protection of law is provided to all individuals, wrongful convictions and miscarriages of justice will still occur. The likelihood of wrongful convictions can be decreased, but the risk that innocent people will be executed can never be eliminated altogether as there is no perfect justice system.

---

39   *R v. Mattan*, All England Official Transcripts 676 (1998), Court of Appeal, United Kingdom.

"The empirical research conducted over the past few decades demonstrates that no matter what politicians argue or the public believe, neither deterrence nor public opinion should be seen as barriers to abolition."

—*Carolyn Hoyle and Roger Hood*

CHAPTER 2
MYTH OF DETERRENCE

Chapter focuses on deterrence and the death penalty. Three academics, based on results of their own as well as those of other researchers during the last fifty years assessing the deterring effects of the death penalty.

Drawing on studies in diverse countries including Australia, Canada, Trinidad and Tobago, the United States, as well as a number of Asian and European countries, well-known academics <u>Carolyn Hoyle and Roger Hood</u> demonstrate that there is no clear evidence that the death penalty has a deterrent effect on crime. Popular support for the death penalty depends heavily on belief in its deterring power; the best way to counter this belief is through better information. Leaders should not hide behind public opinion statistics but should lead the move away from the death penalty. In a number of countries, since the death penalty has been abolished, more and more citizens have come to regard it as cruel and obsolete.

<u>Jeffrey Fagan</u>, a Columbia Law School Professor, warns that deterrence remains deeply embedded in the social and political culture in States that execute. Moving away from the death penalty should be based on information: five decades of research have shown that scientific evidence supporting the belief in deterrence is unreliable. Using examples regarding the death penalty for drug offences and terrorism, he demonstrates how, and why, assumptions of its deterring effects are wrong. States that execute in the face of uncertainty about its deterrent effects are implicated in taking lives without a measurable return beyond vengeance or retribution.

DETERRENCE AND PUBLIC OPINION

Carolyn Hoyle and Roger Hood[1]

DECLINING USE OF THE DEATH PENALTY

At the end of 2013, the number of countries that were "actively retentionist" (had carried out at least one judicial execution within the past 10 years and had not subsequently declared a permanent moratorium on executions) had fallen to just 39, 20 per cent of the world's countries. Only seven of these countries have executed 10 or more citizens every year for the past decade (2003 to 2012), and not all of them because they believe that it is a necessary deterrent to crime: China, Iran, Iraq, North Korea (probably), Saudi Arabia, Yemen and the United States.

The use of capital punishment in retentionist countries has also been declining. Whereas 37 countries carried out a judicial execution in 1998, only 21 did so in 2012. With very few exceptions, such as Iran, Iraq, and Saudi Arabia, the number of executions per year appears to be falling almost everywhere.

Singapore, which in the mid-1990s had the world's highest execution rate per head of population—carrying out 74 executions in 1994—has reduced the number drastically, executing only a few people in the last five years. Malaysia, which executed between 13 and 15 people a year between 1970 and 2000, has carried out very few executions since the turn of the millennium, despite retaining a mandatory death penalty for certain offences. Thailand and Indonesia now also carry out only sporadic or occasional executions.

Pakistan, which executed at least 135 people in 2007 and 36 in 2008, has since adopted a policy not to carry out executions (although one did occur under military jurisdiction in November 2012). India had no executions between 2004 and November 2012; since then, two

---

1   Carolyn Hoyle and Roger Hood are the authors of *The Death Penalty: A Worldwide Perspective. This paper draws on their research for the book's fifth edition (Oxford University Press, 2014).*

people convicted of murders committed during terrorist attacks have been executed.

These examples don't demonstrate that executions are coming to an end in these countries, but they do suggest a commitment to progressive restriction—to using the ultimate penalty only in the most egregious cases.

On the other hand, there has been considerable resistance to the political movement to force change ever since the Second Optional Protocol to the International Covenant on Civil and Political Rights was adopted by the United Nations General Assembly in 1989. Attempts since 1994 by abolitionist nations at the United Nations General Assembly to press for a resolution calling for a worldwide moratorium on the imposition of death sentences and executions were still being resisted by 41 countries (on the grounds that there is no international consensus that the death penalty is a violation of human rights) when the resolution was debated at the General Assembly in December 2012. This is significantly fewer than the 66 countries that opposed such a resolution in 2005. Indeed, opposition has weakened at each subsequent vote since 2007, though powerful countries such as Japan, China, India and the United States have consistently voted against the resolution.

RESISTANCE TO CHANGE

Across abolitionist jurisdictions, and within supranational and national bodies that oppose the death penalty, abolition is now established as a matter of principle, with the doctrine of inalienable human rights—specifically the right to life and the right not to be subjected to cruel, inhuman and degrading punishment—drawn on to provide the absolute justification for abolition. However, governments in many retentionist countries argue that total prohibition is not yet established as a human rights norm. They cling to their sovereign right to determine their own laws and criminal justice practices, often drawing on public support for the death penalty, and in particular belief in its deterrent effect.

In the past decade, various countries—including some that are abolitionist de facto, such as South Korea, Jordan and Algeria—have rejected bills to abolish the death penalty, with the public faith in its deterrent effect cited as a reason for caution. Deterrence is the main argument, or at least a powerful secondary argument alongside retribution, of many governments that support capital punishment, such as those of China, Japan, Indonesia, Singapore and a number of countries in the Middle East and Africa. In Iraq, the authorities in 2010 at its United Nations Universal Periodic Review stated that "because of the exceptional circumstances in Iraq and the prevalence of terrorist crimes targeting the right to life, the death penalty had been maintained as a means of deterrence and to provide justice to the families of victims."[2]

CAPITAL PUNISHMENT AND THE HOMICIDE RATE

Because it would be morally repugnant to conduct random experiments in the use of capital punishment, it remains difficult, if not impossible, to find empirical data on the deterrent effects of the threat of capital punishment that would utterly persuade a committed proponent of the death penalty to change his or her mind. Indeed, as far as some crimes punishable by death in several countries are concerned—such as importing or trading in illegal drugs, economic crimes, or politically motivated violence—there simply is no reliable evidence of the deterrent effects of executions. Nor have any empirical studies investigated the impact of capital punishment when used on a more extensive scale as an exemplary punishment in law-and-order campaigns, such as have occurred in China and Iran. Consequently, almost all the studies available for review are concerned with the deterrent effect of capital punishment on the murder rate in the United States.[3]

That said, the evidence should lead any dispassionate analyst to conclude that it is not prudent to accept the hypothesis that capital punishment, as practiced in the United States, deters murder to a marginally greater

---

2   *Report of the Working Group on the Universal Periodic Review, Iraq* (2010), UN Doc. A/HRC/14/14.

3   For a review of deterrence studies in the United States, Singapore and Hong Kong, see Ethan Cohen-Cole, Jeffrey Fagan and Daniel Nagin, "Model uncertainty and the deterrent effect of capital punishment", American Law and Economics Review, vol. 7, no. 2 (2008), pp. 335-369; Franklin Zimring, Jeffrey Fagan and David T. Johnson, "Executions, deterrence and homicide: A tale of two cities", Journal of Empirical Legal Studies, vol. 7 (2010), pp. 1-29, at p. 24.

extent than does the supposedly lesser punishment of life imprisonment. A 2012 report by the Committee on Deterrence and the Death Penalty of the National Research Council in the United States, which reviewed evidence published over 34 years, offered the same conclusion:

> *Research to date on the effect of capital punishment on homicide is not informative about whether capital punishment decreases, increases, or has no effect on homicide rates. Therefore the Committee recommends that these studies not be used to inform deliberations requiring judgments about the effect of the death penalty on homicide and . . . should not influence policy judgments about capital punishment.*[4]

One rather unsophisticated way of considering deterrence is to analyse homicide rates before and after the death penalty is abolished. This at least can show whether countries that abolish capital punishment inevitably experience more murders, as those who support the deterrent argument claim. In Australia, where the last executions occurred in the mid-1960s, the reported murder rate has, a few fluctuations aside, fallen. Prior to the abolition of the death penalty in Canada, the reported homicide rate had been rising, yet in 2003, 27 years after abolition, the rate had fallen to 1.73 per 100,000 population, 43 per cent lower than it was in 1975 (3.02 per 100,000), the year before abolition.[5] The sharp decline following abolition was a potent argument used by the Canadian prime minister in 1987 when opposing the reintroduction of capital punishment.[6] The rate has continued to fall. In 2012 it was 1.56 per 100,000 population, its lowest level since 1966.

Although not designed to study the relationship between abolition of the death penalty and homicide rates, a 2011 study by the United Nations Office on Drugs and Crime of global trends in homicide showed that although the homicide rate rose initially after abolition

---

4   Daniel S. Nagin and John V. Pepper, eds., Deterrence and the Death Penalty (Washington, DC, National Academies Press, 2012), p. 3.

5   Susan Munroe, "Abolition of capital punishment in Canada: Canadian murder rate stays low without capital punishment", About.com (updated 31 October 2010), available from http://canadaonline.about.com/od/crime/a/abolitioncappun.htm.

6   Speech in the Canadian House of Commons, 22 June 1987, by the Right Honourable Brian Mulroney, Prime Minister of Canada, Commons Debates, p. 7477.

of the death penalty in Eastern European countries, it declined quite sharply after the mid-1990s, and this decline has not been reversed. Thus, the homicide rate in five countries of Central and Eastern Europe (the Czech Republic, Hungary, Moldova, Poland and Romania, all of which abolished the death penalty in the 1990s) declined by 61 per cent from 4.5 to 1.6 per 100,000 between 2000 and 2008, declining especially in respect to male victims. The study concluded that "virtually all countries [in Europe] where there has been a strengthening of the rule of law [and no death penalty] have also experienced a decline in the homicide rate."[7]

In Trinidad and Tobago, which has a very high homicide rate, academics have not been able to establish any relationship between trends in the execution and murder rates.[8] Taiwan's informal moratorium on executions, which lasted from 2006 to 2010, provided an opportunity to examine whether the withdrawal of the threat of execution led to an increase in violent crimes reported to the police. Analysis by the Taiwan Alliance to End the Death Penalty showed that in fact the violent crime rate per 100,000 of the population fell during these four years from 62.9 in 2005 (when there were three executions) to 53.6 the following year and 29.3 in 2009.[9]

In 2009, Richard Berk, a distinguished statistician, concluded that over the past 20 years no progress had been made towards determining whether or not executions had a deterrent impact and that no further progress would be made in the next 20 years.[10] Given the data available for analysis and the statistical and econometric techniques that can be employed, as well as the methods employed for selecting and controlling for all other factors that might be associated with the murder rate and execution rate over

7   United Nations Office on Drugs and Crime, *2011 Global Study on Homicide: Trends, Contexts, Data (Vienna, 2011)*, p. 33.

8   David F. Greenberg and Biko Agozino, "Executions, imprisonment and crime in Trinidad and Tobago", British Journal of Criminology, vol. 52 (2012), pp. 113-140 and 117-118; Roger Hood and Florence Seemungal, A Rare and Arbitrary Fate: Convictions for Murder, the Mandatory Death Penalty and the Reality of Homicide in Trinidad and Tobago, report prepared for the Death Penalty Project (Oxford: University of Oxford Centre for Criminology, 2006), pp. 15-22.

9   A Blow to Human Rights: Taiwan Resumes Executions: The Death Penalty in Taiwan, 2010 (Taipei: Taiwan Alliance to End the Death Penalty, 2011), p. 15.

10   Richard Berk, "Can't tell: Comments on 'Does the death penalty save lives?'", Criminology and Public Policy, vol. 8, no. 4 (2009), pp. 845-851.

time and across jurisdictions, contradictory findings and interpretations seem to be inevitable.[11] Articles in the *Journal of Quantitative Criminology*, published in 2013, came to similar conclusions, making clear that the recent literature on deterrence in the United States was "inconclusive as a whole, and in many cases uninformative",[12] primarily because of methodological problems. As another article in the journal concluded: "It is thus immaterial whether the studies purport to find evidence in favour or against deterrence. They simply do not rise to level of credible evidence on deterrence as a behavioural mechanism."[13]

Although there must have been instances in which people refrained from murder out of fear of execution, this in itself is an insufficient basis on which to conclude that the existence of the death penalty and the (often remote) threat of execution will lead to a lower rate of murder than would be the case without it. The issue is not whether the death penalty deters some (if only a few) people where the threat of a lesser punishment would not, but whether, when all the circumstances surrounding its use are taken into account, it is associated with a marginally lower *rate* of the death-penalty-eligible kinds of murder than the next most severe penalty, life imprisonment.

The reason one must weigh all its effects is that capital punishment has several drawbacks to counter its supposedly obvious advantages. For example, offenders threatened with death could have an added incentive to kill witnesses to their crimes. Furthermore, it may be much less easy to convict people when the punishment may be death than when it is less draconian. In other words, *severity* of punishment may run counter to the more effective *certainty* of punishment. Evidence to support this comes from England, Wales and Canada,

---

11 See Ethan Cohen-Cole, Jeffrey Fagan and Daniel Nagin, "Model uncertainty and the deterrent effect of capital punishment", American Law and Economics Review, vol. 7, no. 2 (2008), pp. 335-369. These authors used a model-averaging method across different studies and concluded, "not that there is no deterrent effect present, but rather that inferences on its magnitude are so imprecise as to make representation of strong claims impossible" (p. 364).

12 Aaron Chalfin, Amelia M. Haviland and Steven Raphael, "What do panel studies tell us about a deterrent effect of capital punishment? A critique of the literature", Journal of Quantitative Criminology, vol. 29 (2013), pp. 5-43, at pp. 5 and 8.

13 Kerwin Kofi Charles and Steven N. Durlauf, "Pitfalls in the use of time series methods to study deterrence and capital punishment", Journal of Quantitative Criminology, vol. 29 (2013), pp. 45-66, at pp. 45-46 and 65.

where since abolition of the death penalty it has proven easier to obtain convictions for murder rather than the less serious offence of manslaughter. In fact, the proportion convicted of murder among all those convicted of a homicide in England and Wales increased from 28 per cent in 1965 (the year that capital punishment was abolished) to 63 per cent in 2005/2006.[14] The same has been true in Canada, where the conviction rate for first-degree (capital) murder, rather than second-degree murder or a lesser charge, has doubled from under 10 per cent when execution would result, to about 20 per cent "now they [juries] are not compelled to make life-and-death decisions."[15]

PUBLIC OPINION WORLDWIDE

Support in the United States for executions is decreasing. According to Gallup polls, public support fell from 80 per cent in 1994 to 60 per cent in October 2013. In November 2012, California held a plebiscite to decide whether the death penalty should be abolished and replaced by life imprisonment without parole. It was defeated by a margin of only 6 percentage points (53 per cent to 47 per cent). The risk of innocent people being executed; the cost of obtaining a conviction for capital murder, holding a prisoner on death row and providing a lengthy appeals process;[16] and the rising use of the primary alternative—life in prison without the prospect of parole—are all factors in the declining level of public support. The proportion of supporters of capital punishment who say that they favour it because of its deterrent effect has dropped remarkably in recent years.

A number of public opinion polls in the United States have shown the same trend, but what of other retentionist nations? This section

14 Kevin Smith, ed., Kathryn Coleman, Simon Eder and Philip Hall, "Table 1.02: Offences initially recorded as homicide by outcome, 1999/00 to 2009/10", in Homicide, Firearm Offences and Intimate Violence 2009-10, Home Office Statistical Bulletin 01/11 (2011).

15 Mark Warren, The Death Penalty in Canada: Facts, Figures and Milestones (London, Amnesty International, 2005).

16 A recent study of the cost of the death penalty in Colorado showed that capital proceedings require six times more days in court and take considerably longer to resolve than life-without-parole cases. Justin Marceau and Hollis Whitson, "The cost of Colorado's death penalty", *University of Denver Criminal Law Review*, vol. 3 (2013), pp. 145 ff. And a report of the California Commission on the Fair Administration of Justice found that the additional cost of confining an inmate to death row—as compared to a maximum-security prison for a life-without-parole sentence—is $90,000 per year per inmate. California Commission on the Fair Administration of Justice, *Report and Recommendations on the Administration of the Death Penalty in California* (2008), available from www.ccfaj.org/documents/reports/dp/official/FINAL%20REPORT%20 DEATH%20PENALTY.pdf.

will look at surveys from Asia and the Caribbean, where governments have claimed that public opinion would be hostile to abolition.

Japan

Statements from the judiciary and the executive in Japan justify retention of capital punishment on the grounds that a democratic government cannot ignore strong public support for it without endangering public confidence in, and support for, the law. In this, they draw on an official government survey on the death penalty that has been conducted since 1956, approximately every five years. In the most recent survey, conducted in 2009, 86 per cent of respondents favoured retention. In 2010 the minister of justice said that this high level of support should be respected as an expression of "the voice of the people."[17]

There is a great deal of secrecy around the death penalty in Japan. Until 2007 the Japanese government did not announce the names of prisoners and the crimes they had committed after executions. And as a powerful Amnesty International report pointed out, death-sentenced prisoners and their family members are not informed of execution dates. The inmate is only informed of the execution a few hours before it takes place.[18]

What is more, there is still no official information on how and when prisoners under sentence of death are selected for execution, how they are treated on death row, or what the cost of the death penalty is compared to life imprisonment. At the time of writing, Japan had 157 people on death row in solitary confinement[19]—which is probably double the number at the turn of the millennium, as the number of death sentences has risen. This kind of information is only available informally through those who are involved in the execution process, and through somewhat speculative secondary sources. The government does not ensure the publication of accurate information on the process or outcomes. This has led scholars to state that "the secrecy

---

17 *Yomiuri newspaper, 2010, cited in* Mai Sato, The Death Penalty in Japan: Will the Public Tolerate Abolition? (Wiesbaden, Springer, 2014), p. 25.

18 Amnesty International, *"Will This Day Be My Last?" The Death Penalty in Japan (July 2006), AI Index: ASA 22/006/2006.*

19 *Death Penalty Worldwide (updated 12 November 2013), available from www.deathpenaltyworldwide.org/country-search-post.cfm?country=Japan.*

that surrounds capital punishment in Japan is taken to extremes not seen in other nations" and that the public only has very abstract ideas about the punishment.[20] This inevitably poses the question: on what grounds does the public support the death penalty?

A recent study by Mai Sato argued that, although the Japanese assertion that retaining capital punishment is a democratic obligation may be theoretically coherent, it requires reliable evidence that the public feel so strongly in favour of retaining the death penalty that to abolish it would undermine the legitimacy of the criminal justice system.[21] In other words, the Japanese government's case is defensible only if the surveys on which it relies accurately capture public attitudes on the subject. Sato tested this through three rigorous surveys of public opinion and found that the government's interpretation of its survey—and its contention that it reliably reflected the views of the public as a whole—was seriously flawed. Her findings suggest that opposition to abolition is neither as strong nor as unalterable as the government claims. With more information and greater transparency about how the death penalty system works in practice, and reliable evidence on whether the execution rate has any deterrent effect on the murder rate, a more accurate sense of the Japanese public's support for the death penalty would emerge. This suggests that retention of the death penalty in Japan is not so central to popular trust in the criminal justice system that abolition would result in the erosion of political and judicial legitimacy.

Malaysia

In Malaysia, death is the mandatory penalty for murder, trafficking in certain amounts of narcotics, and discharging a firearm during the commission of various crimes, even if no one is hurt. There is a growing debate on whether the mandatory death penalty should be replaced by a discretionary system where it is used only in exceptional circumstances, or abolished altogether. In a recent public opinion survey of 1,535 Malaysian citizens on this issue,[22] a large majority said they were

---

20 David Johnson, "When the state kills in secret: capital punishment in Japan" *Punishment and Society, vol. 8, issue 3 (2006), pp. 251-285, at p. 251.*

21 Mai Sato, The Death Penalty in Japan: Will the Public Tolerate Abolition? (Wiesbaden, Springer, 2014).

22 Roger Hood, *The Death Penalty in Malaysia (London, The Death Penalty Project, 2013).*

in favour of the death penalty (either mandatory or discretionary): 91 per cent for murder, 74-80 per cent for drug trafficking (depending on the drug concerned), and 83 per cent for firearms offences. Concerning the mandatory death penalty, 56 per cent said they were in favour of it for murder, but only 25-44 per cent supported it for drug trafficking and 45 per cent for firearms offences.

When asked what sentences they themselves would impose on a series of hypothetical cases, all of which were subject to a mandatory death sentence, respondents gave markedly different answers than they had given to the more theoretical questions. For none of four hypothetical drug trafficking cases did more than 30 per cent choose the death penalty. Only 8 per cent chose death for all the cases they judged. Only 1.2 per cent thought that the death penalty was the appropriate punishment for all 12 hypothetical cases of murder, drug trafficking and firearms offences, showing decisively that the vast majority favoured discretionary use of the death penalty.

These findings suggest that there would be little public opposition to abolition of the mandatory death penalty. Public support for the death penalty for drug trafficking and firearms offences, as well as for murder, was not nearly as strong as had been assumed, so may not be a definite barrier to complete abolition.

Trinidad

Another study recently surveyed 1,000 residents of Trinidad, focusing on support for and use of the mandatory death penalty for murder under current Trinidadian law.[23] It found that a large majority of Trinidadians are in favour of the death penalty, but only a minority (close to a quarter) favour it being mandatory for all murders. Trinidadians also favoured discretionary use of the death penalty in cases involving violent robbery or drug or gang killing, preferring to take into account mitigating factors such as age and previous good character. When faced with three murder scenarios, only 1 in 5 survey respondents thought that the death penalty was the appropriate punishment for all three crimes. The majority of

---

23 Roger Hood and Florence Seemungal, *Public Opinion Survey on the Mandatory Death Penalty in Trinidad (London: The Death Penalty Project, 2011).*

those who favoured the death penalty in one of these scenarios gave justice as the reason; only 1.3 per cent based their decision primarily on deterrence.

The high level of support for the death penalty was contingent on it being enforced with no possibility that an innocent person could be executed. If this were proven to have happened, only 35 per cent of those interviewed said they would continue to support capital punishment—as was the case in Malaysia, where support fell to just 33 per cent with the risk of an innocent person being executed.

China

The consensus among the authorities in China is that the public will not yet tolerate abolition. Thus, it is argued that the attempts now being made to reform the death penalty, through

> "...THERE MUST BE LIMITS TO THE POWER THAT THE STATE CAN BE PERMITTED TO EXERCISE..."
> —Carolyn Hoyle and Roger Hood

due process safeguards and progressive restriction of its application, must proceed slowly and carefully, for fear of a public backlash and collapse of confidence in the government and the criminal justice system. It is true that some judicial decisions not to impose the death penalty are met with a flurry of online criticism. But a recent analysis[24] argued that the scholarly debate on the death penalty in China often ignores contemporary survey evidence when claiming that the strength of the Chinese public's support for capital punishment is a barrier to abolition, and that even liberal intellectuals who favour reducing the use of the death penalty have tended to blame popular support for harsh penalties for the slow pace of capital punishment reform.

The 2007-2009 survey referred to in that article demonstrated a low level of interest and knowledge; a relatively high proportion of

---

24 Børge Bakken, "Capital punishment reform, public opinion, and penal elitism in the People's Republic of China", in *Confronting Capital Punishment in Asia: Human Rights, Politics, and Public Opinion*, R. Hood and S. Deva, eds. (Oxford, Oxford University Press, 2013), pp. 187-204.

respondents had no firm opinion on the subject of the death penalty.[25] When asked whether they favoured or opposed the death penalty, 58 per cent of almost 4,500 respondents in three provinces were definitely in favour, not a very high proportion when compared with the experience of European countries when they abolished capital punishment. While only 14 per cent said they opposed capital punishment, as many as 28 per cent said they were unsure. When asked whether China should speed up the process of abolishing the death penalty, only 53 per cent were opposed to doing so; 33 per cent were unsure. This hardly indicates the kind of fervent support for capital punishment that would make abolition politically impossible.

Almost three-quarters of survey respondents said they were either "not very interested" or "not interested at all" in the subject; only 1.3 per cent said they had "a lot of knowledge," and less than a third said they had "some knowledge" of the death penalty law and its administration. Many were concerned about wrongful convictions, and only a quarter said that they would support the death penalty if it were proven that innocent people had been executed. Almost 70 per cent thought that the death penalty was not equitably administered, being more likely to be imposed on poor and powerless people than on rich people, officials or relatives of officials.

When respondents were asked whether they would support the death penalty if various alternatives were available, a substantially lower proportion definitely opposed abolition. If the death penalty were replaced by life imprisonment *with* the possibility of parole, only 38 per cent said they would still favour the death penalty. If the alternative maximum sentence was the harsh penalty of life with no possibility of parole and an obligation to make restitution, less than a quarter said they would oppose abolition, and half definitely favoured it.[26] Meanwhile, a survey of a sample of 455 criminal justice professionals (including judges, prosecutors, police and legislative and judicial administrative staff) in Wuhan found that 91 per cent

---

25 Dietrich Oberwittler and Shenghui Qi, *Public Opinion on the Death Penalty in China: Results from a General Population Survey Conducted in Three Provinces in 2007/09 (Freiburg, Max Planck Institute, 2009).*

26 Dietrich Oberwittler and Shenghui Qi, *Public Opinion on the Death Penalty in China: Results from a General Population Survey Conducted in Three Provinces in 2007-08, Research Survey on the Death Penalty in China, 2007-9 (London, Great Britain-China Centre, 2009), p. 29.*

favoured the death penalty, though for the more serious crimes, rather than for nonviolent offences.[27]

It seems likely that it is the intellectual, legal and administrative elites that are slowing the pace of reform in China, not the masses, and it is the legal practitioners and political leaders who need to embrace the human rights objections to capital punishment.

DETERRENCE AND PUBLIC OPINION: NO BARRIERS TO ABOLITION

The empirical research conducted over the past few decades demonstrates that no matter what politicians argue or the public believe, neither deterrence nor public opinion should be seen as barriers to abolition. At the seminars and meetings that we have attended in China, people who work within the criminal justice system often say that the public will not tolerate abolition while the crime rate is high, for fear it will lead to further rises in serious crimes, especially drug trafficking and corruption. The evidence on deterrence discussed above suggests that this is not likely to be the case. Furthermore, the public opinion studies we have reviewed for the forthcoming fifth edition of *The Death Penalty* suggest that there is no immutable relationship between rising levels of homicide and increased support for the death penalty. Much will depend on the extent to which citizens believe in the general deterrent power of executions, their faith in alternative punishments, and the ability of the political system to tackle the roots of the problem through social reforms and a criminal justice approach that increases the certainty, rather than the severity, of punishment. In none of the countries that we have studied do the data suggest that there would be disastrous consequences for public order and respect for the law if the death penalty were abolished and replaced by a (humane) sentence of life imprisonment.

The experience of nearly all abolitionist countries is that opinions change and support for capital punishment withers as it comes to be seen as a thing of the past. Analysis of support for the death penalty

---

27   R. Hood, "Introduction", in *Research Survey on the Death Penalty in China, 2007-9, available from www.gbcc.org.uk/files/documents/dp2introduction.pdf.*

across 17 countries[28] came to two interesting conclusions. First, it found that "residence in a retentionist nation significantly increases the odds of an individual supporting the death penalty." This suggests that people on the whole support what has been the norm in their culture. Second, each year of abolition lowered the odds that an individual would support the death penalty by 46 per cent.[29] Clearly, as the example of Europe shows, when the death penalty has been abolished, more and more citizens come in time to regard it as a cruel and outdated punishment. Abolition can lead to previously unimagined changes in opinion by creating a different climate for the discourse on the limits of state punishment. France provides an obvious example of this. François Mitterrand stood for election in 1981 on a manifesto that included abolition of the death penalty despite 63 per cent of the general public being in favour of it. He was elected president, and after abolition he was re-elected. This showed that the public was ready to accept leadership on this issue; subsequently, France has become one of the leading nations to protest against capital punishment around the world.

Opinions about capital punishment also differ in different sectors of the population—which may be related to their social status, their political or religious beliefs and how well they are informed about the issue, including what the effects of abolition might be. Ultimately, public opinion on the death penalty—essentially an expression of superficial sentiment by the electorate, who may or (as is more usual) may not be aware of all the facts and arguments relating to the issue—should not be allowed to determine an issue which many, indeed now the majority of countries, believe must be dealt with on the basis of a principled interpretation of human rights.

CONCLUSION

Those governments that still favour capital punishment in principle or believe that it is necessary pay insufficient attention to human rights protections, such as due process safeguards to reduce the risk of executing those who are innocent or otherwise wrongly

---

28 Steven Stack, "Public opinion on the death penalty: analysis of individual-level data from 17 nations", International Criminal Justice Review, vol. 14 (2004), pp. 69–98.

29 Ibid., pp. 87–88.

convicted. They may be presented with convincing evidence of the abuses, discrimination, mistakes and inhumanity that inevitably accompany capital punishment in practice—as have been revealed by social scientists, legal theorists and human rights lawyers—but they don't tend to recognize the importance of such knowledge, because their concern is with upholding state power and maintaining social control, rather than with the rights of all citizens to be protected from the state as far as their life, liberty and just and humane treatment are concerned. They argue that the death penalty is a general deterrent, not because the academic studies show this to be the case, but because, despite the evidence to the contrary, they believe it can be deduced from human nature.

But ultimately a human rights perspective must reject the utilitarian justification that nothing less severe can act as a sufficient deterrent to those who contemplate committing capital crimes. This is not only because the social science evidence does not support the case for deterrence but also because those who care about human rights would reject the deterrence rationale even if it could be proven.

Those retentionist countries that rely on the deterrent justification should face the fact that if capital punishment were used to try to obtain its maximum possible deterrent effect, it would have to be enforced mandatorily, or at least with a high degree of probability, on a substantial scale across most categories of homicide, and swiftly. This would increase the probability of innocent or wrongfully convicted people, and people whose crimes had sufficient mitigating circumstances, being executed. As mentioned above, too-vigorous enforcement may also backfire, resulting in fewer convictions for murder and thus a decline in the certainty of punishment on which the deterrent theory relies.

One wonders, therefore, whether those states that do retain the death penalty for some limited class of murders and murderers, imposed in a somewhat haphazard and arbitrary way on only a few of those who are death-eligible, can really claim that such a policy is justified by its deterrent effects. Looked at this way, the balance of evidence clearly favours the abolitionist position.

Furthermore, abolitionists who have embraced the view that all citizens have a right to life argue that the issue cannot be left to public opinion, not only because that opinion may not be fully informed as to the consequences of capital punishment, but also because the appeal to human rights is based on the protection of all citizens from cruel and inhumane punishment, whatever crimes they may have committed. Some countries have attempted to stigmatise opposition to the death penalty as a form of cultural imperialism, an attack on national sovereignty and an attempt to turn a domestic criminal justice issue into a human rights issue. This implies that if it is one it cannot also be the other. In our opinion this is a false antithesis. Whatever system of criminal justice a country may choose, there must be limits to the power that the state can be permitted to exercise over people accused and convicted of crimes, however serious: limits defined by universal human rights principles that apply to all citizens of the world.

DETERRENCE AND THE DEATH PENALTY IN INTERNATIONAL PERSPECTIVE

Jeffrey Fagan[1]

Many states that retain the death penalty do so with the belief that executions deter the targeted crime. While some states execute solely on the basis of retribution or a belief in a moral imperative based on the harm of the crime, many others cling to the theory that executions prevent further crimes by deterring other people from committing them. Whether the death penalty is reserved for murder or also applied to drug crimes or terrorism, belief in its deterrent power remains deeply embedded in the social and political culture in states that execute. Leaders in those states, as well as large segments of their populations, endorse this view. But rarely do those states or their citizens reflect on the evidence that supports those beliefs or the theory that underpins them. Were they to explore the deep body of empirical evidence and the core elements of the theory itself, their belief in deterrence might well be shaken.

THE MEANING OF DETERRENCE

The core ambition of deterrence is to make threats credible to the point where they influence behavioural choices. In the case of capital punishment, retentionist states wish to signal to those contemplating murder, or any other death-penalty-eligible offense, that there is a substantial risk of dying at the hands of the state if they commit the crime and are caught and convicted. The premise is that a would-be offender, knowing about the threat of execution, would forego the act because the cost (death) is unacceptably high and well in excess of any benefits from the crime. It assumes a rational actor whose risk-reward calculus would lead to the avoidance of a capital crime and whose perceptions of risk are well calibrated to

---

1 Jeffrey Fagan is the Isidor and Seville Sulzbacher Professor of law at Columbia Law School, professor of epidemiology at the Mailman School of Public Health, Columbia University, and senior research scholar at Yale Law School.

the likelihood of execution. It also assumes that risks are substantial and observable.

This proposition leaves many practical and empirical questions unanswered. How would we know about murders or other death-eligible crimes that are contemplated but abandoned because of the threat of the death penalty? How many murders have been averted, and how many would have to be averted to show a deterrent effect? Is execution the reason for the abandonment of a capital crime? What about other punishment threats, like death in prison through an irreversible life sentence? What ratio of executions to capital crimes would present evidence of deterrence? How many executions are needed to signal a credible deterrent?

These questions are not simply policy matters, for they also give weight to moral arguments about execution. Proponents of capital punishment suggest that evidence of deterrence morally justifies execution.[2] States that fail to execute knowing that lives may be saved through deterrence violate their moral requirements to protect people from serious harms including death. If there is a life-life trade-off from execution, even if one life is saved for another taken by execution, then by this argument, states are moral agents that are required to impose capital punishment to save the lives of innocents, regardless of any other consideration of the culpability of the accused; the risks of wrongful execution of the innocent in this framework are viewed as part of a "risk-risk" trade-off.[3]

Much turns, then, on the evidence of deterrence. Not only are there practical consequences of deterrence and execution, but state legitimacy is also implicated by its obligation to protect and save lives. Deterrence is a central justification for capital punishment in many retentionist countries, and their use of execution is linked to their state legitimacy.[4] Whatever moral reservations a state or its agents may have about execution would, under this argument, be

---

2 Cass Sunstein and Adrian Vermeule, Is capital punishment morally justified? Acts, omissions and life-life tradeoffs. 58 *Stanford Law Review* 703 (2005).
3 Cass Sunstein and Adrian Vermeule, "Is capital punishment morally justified?, at p. 705. The risks of wrongful execution of the innocent in this framework are viewed as part of a "risk-risk" tradeoff.
4 Roger Hood and Carolyn Hoyle, *The Death Penalty in Worldwide Perspective* (Oxford, UK, Oxford University Press, 2014).

neutralized by the evidence of lives saved. The strength of this evidence, then, carries weight beyond the practical and policy matter of capital punishment. In this view, the moral legitimacy of the state depends in part on its willingness to fulfil its obligation to save lives. Countries like Japan argue that popular support for capital punishment, including cultural belief in its deterrent value, is reciprocally tied to the legitimacy of the government itself. [5]

But what if the evidence for deterrence is weak, speculative and inconclusive? Then this logic would be turned on its head. States that execute in the face of uncertainty about execution's deterrent effects are implicated in taking lives without a measurable return beyond vengeance or retribution. Those states then lose the moral grounding of life-life trade-offs, and in fact, create risks that reverse the statistical and moral justification for taking lives. The deaths of people who are innocent, or lacking in the requisite culpability for execution, become moral casualties of execution. The costs to state legitimacy are potentially severe, with the risk of spill-over effects such as deteriorating respect for the law.[6] Much rides, then, on the evidence for deterrence.

THE EVIDENCE ON THE DEATH PENALTY'S VALUE AS A DETERRENT

Whether the offense is murder, a drug-related crime or terrorism, the scientific evidence for deterrence is unreliable, inconclusive and, in many instances, simply wrong. This has been the conclusion across a wide range of studies over five decades. While there are no experiments on execution, nor can there be for obvious moral and ethical reasons, some studies have examined the effects of moratoria on capital punishment. Other studies have compared places that practice capital punishment with carefully matched places that have abolished or suspended executions and found no differences in murder rates or other capital-eligible crimes, regardless of the number of executions in the retentionist places.

---

5 See for example Mai Sato, *The Death Penalty in Japan: Will the Public Tolerate Abolition?* (Wiesbaden, Germany, Springer, 2014); David T. Johnson and Franklin E. Zimring, "Development without abolition: Japan in the 21st century", chapter 3 in *The Next Frontier: National Development, Political Change, and the Death Penalty in Asia* (New York, Oxford University Press, 2009).

6 Sharon Dolovich, "Legitimate punishment in liberal democracy", *Buffalo Criminal Law Review*, vol. 7 (2004), pp. 307-442

A. Murder

From 1972 to 1976, there was a moratorium on capital punishment in the United States, inspired in part by growing doubts about its deterrent effect on murder.[7] Executions resumed following publication of research claiming that the death penalty did in fact deter homicides—in fact, that each execution deterred as many as eight homicides.[8] But that evidence was strongly contested, and a 1978 panel of the National Academy of Sciences found little evidence that claims of deterrence were accurate.[9] Still, belief in deterrence was politically and culturally popular, even if scientific evidence didn't support it.[10] The belief in deterrence persisted for over two decades, despite the fact that murder rates rose dramatically in the 1980s just as executions were increasing.

Two factors undermined those beliefs. First, while the murder rate began declining sharply in the second half of the 1990s, at the same time that executions rose sharply, the decline in the murder rate continued after executions declined sharply in 2000. Second, a large body of statistical evidence emerged showing that the claims of deterrence advanced in the early 2000's were deeply flawed. My own research showed that the decline in murders starting in 1996 was no greater in states that continued to sentence and execute murderers than in states that did not.[11] This included states with a formal moratorium and states with a de facto moratorium such as California, Illinois and Pennsylvania, which had large numbers of condemned prisoners but almost no executions. In those places, despite the absence of executions, murder rates declined sharply.

---

7 *Furman v. Georgia*, 408 U.S. 238, 315 (1972) (Marshall, concurring).

8 Issac Ehrlich, The deterrent effect of capital punishment: A question of life and death", *The American Economic Review*, vol. 65, pp. 397-417 (1975).

9 For a summary, see Brian A. Forst, "Capital punishment and deterrence: Conflicting evidence", Journal of Criminal Law and Criminology, vol. 74, pp. 927-942 (1983). See, also, Lawrence R. Klein, Brian Forst, & Victor Filatov, "The Deterrent Effect of Capital Punishment: An Assessment of the Estimates", pp. 336-60 in Alfred Blumstein, Jacqueline Cohen and Daniel Nagin (eds), *Deterrence and Incapacitation: Estimating the Effects of Criminal Sanctions on Crime Rates*. Washington, DC: National Academy of Sciences (1978)

10 Samuel R. Gross, Public opinion on the death penalty: It's getting personal", Cornell Law Review, vol. 83 (1998): pp. 1448-1479

11 Jeffrey Fagan, Franklin E. Zimring, and Amanda Geller. "Capital punishment and capital murder: Market share and the deterrent effects of the death penalty." *Texas Law Review, vol.* 84 pp. 1751 - 2134 (2005).

A recent intensive review of the evidence on deterrence by the US National Academy of Sciences in 2012 concluded that there was no reliable evidence of deterrence based on its failure to once we consider its deterrent effects beyond the effects of the next most severe punishment, life in prison without the possibility of parole; other research commissioned by the panel reached much the same conclusion.[12] These analyses noted that there was no credible evidence of deterrence, owing to the failure to establish, if not the impossibility of establishing, the necessary conditions for making sufficiently strong causal conclusions.

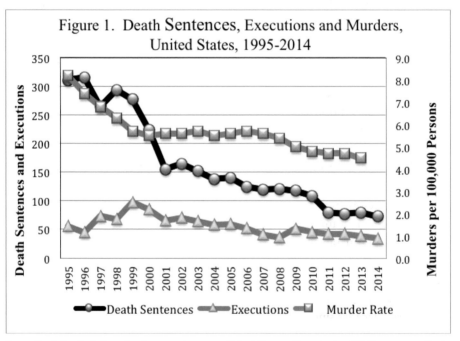

Figure 1. Death Sentences, Executions and Murders, United States, 1995-2014

Sources: Death Penalty Information Center, various years. Federal Bureau of Investigation, U.S. Department of Justice, Uniform Crime Reports, various years.

The panel's findings confirmed what was evident from observable trends in the United States that showed no plausible evidence of executions' deterrent effect. Murders rose from 1985-1996, as states ramped up executions. Figure 1 shows that murders have been declining across the United States in retentionist, moratorium and

---

12 Daniel S. Nagin and John V. Pepper, eds., *Deterrence and the Death Penalty* (Washington, DC, National Academy of Sciences, 2012); Aaron Chalfin, Amelia M. Haviland, and Steven Raphael, "What do panel studies tell us about a deterrent effect of capital punishment? A critique of the literature", *Journal of Quantitative Criminology*, vol. 29 (2013), 5-43.

abolitionist states since 1999, when executions reached their peak. Starting that year, murder rates, death sentences and executions have all declined at the same time and at the same pace. The homicide rate in the United States has declined since 1996; death sentences peaked in 1998, and executions in 1999. The murder rate throughout the decade starting in 2000 and into the current decade was unaffected by the changes in the risk of a death sentence or execution.

Further evidence of the absence of deterrent effects from execution can be seen in recent abolition events in several US states—Connecticut, Illinois, Maryland, New Jersey, New Mexico and New York. These states allow comparisons of murder rates before and after the cessation of the threat of execution.[13] Over the several years following abolition in New Jersey in 2007, Illinois in 2011, and New Mexico in 2009, there appears to be no evidence of an increase in murders following the abolition of capital punishment. In fact, homicides in Chicago, Illinois, reached a 50-year low in 2014, long after the last execution in the late 1990s.[14]

Evidence from other countries shows similar trends. Following the abolition of capital punishment in eastern Europe in the early 1990s, homicide rates declined.[15] Studies in Trinidad and Tobago showed no change in homicide rates despite increases in executions.[16] Homicide rates in Taiwan declined during a sharp reduction in executions from 2005-2009. A study comparing Singapore, where executions for murder have been common, with Hong Kong, where executions were banned, showed no difference in the murder rates over nearly three decades since the cessation of executions in Hong Kong.[17]

13 Death Penalty Information Center, "Recent legislative activity", www.deathpenaltyinfo.org/recent-legislative-activity.

14 Jeremy Gorner, Chicago ends 2014 with fewer homicides, but shooting victims up 14 percent," Chicago Tribune, June 3, 2-15, at http://www.chicagotribune.com/news/ct-chicago-crime-year-end-met-20150101-story.html. Total homicides in Chicago were the lowest since 1965.

15 United Nations Office of Drugs and Crime, 2011 Global Study on Homicide: Trends, Contexts and Data (Vienna, Austria, UNODC, 2011), p. 33. Homicide declined by 61% from 2000 to 2008 in the Czech Republic, Hungary, Moldova, Poland, and Romania.

16 David Greenberg and Biko Agozino, "Executions, imprisonment, and crime in Trinidad and Tobago", British Journal of Criminology, vol. 52, no. 113 (2012). See, generally, Hood and Hoyle, The Death Penalty in Worldwide Perspective, p. 389.

17 Franklin E. Zimring, Jeffrey Fagan, and David T. Johnson, "Executions, deterrence, and homicide: a tale of two cities", Journal of Empirical Legal Studies, vol. 7 (2010), 1-29.

B. Drug crimes

The death penalty for drug smuggling is authorized in 33 countries, including the Palestinian Authority.[18] All but four of these (Cuba, South Sudan, Sudan and the United States) are in Asia or the Middle East. Executions overall are rare in those four. The United States authorizes capital punishment for drug crimes only if committed in federal jurisdiction or charged under federal law, and then only for high-volume drug importation. In some countries, the death sentence is mandatory for drug trafficking over a specified amount, yet executions for drug crimes are uncommon.[19] There are no reliable cross-national data on the number of executions for drug offenses, although some recent multiple executions have shed light on the practice across the world.[20]

States that authorize executions for drug offenses invoke two rationales: that drug offenses fall under the international-law principle of the "most serious crimes"[21] and that executions deter, and thus are essential to controlling, drug crime. The deterrence rationale is based on arguments that drug crimes cause numerous deaths, some arguing that there are more drug-related deaths than deaths from murder or other intentional killing. Accurate assessment of both claims—the seriousness of drug crimes and the deterrent effect of the death penalty—is essential.

---

18 Patrick Gallahue, *The Death Penalty for Drug Offences: A Global Overview* (London, UK, Harm Reduction International, 2011). See also Hood and Hoyle, *The Death Penalty in Worldwide Perspective,* 160.

19 Hood and Hoyle, *The Death Penalty: A Worldwide Perspective,* appendix 1. The nations with this provision are China, Indonesia, Iran, Iraq, Malaysia, Pakistan, Saudi Arabia, Singapore, Viet Nam, Yemen, and Thailand. In Singapore, the parliament passed the Misuse of Drugs Amendment Act, which allowed for a discretionary sentence of life imprisonment plus caning to be substituted for the mandatory death penalty if the defendant could prove that the trafficker was a paid courier and not a reseller, and with substantial cooperation in the prosecution of the major trafficker (Hood and Hoyle, *The Death Penalty,* 161, note 60).

20 Indonesia executed six people for drug offenses in January 2015 and another eight people in April 2015. See, for example, Sara Kaplan and Sarah Larimer, "'Bali Nine' leaders executed by firing squad in Indonesia", *Washington Post,* 29 April 2015, available from www.washingtonpost. com/news/morning-mix/wp/2015/04/28/bali-nine-leaders-in-indonesia-could-face-death-by-firing-squad-wednesday/. In 2011, Amnesty International reported that Iran had executed 448 people for drug offenses. See Amnesty International, *Addicted to Death: Executions for Drug Offences* (London, Amnesty International, 2011). Under Iran's Anti-Narcotics Law, death is a mandatory sentence for anyone found in possession of more than 5 kg of hashish or opium or more than 30 g of heroin, codeine, methadone, or morphine.

21 See for example William A. Schabas, *The Abolition of the Death Penalty in International Law,* 3rd ed. (Cambridge, UK, Cambridge University Press, 2002), p. 373.

Consider the case of the Indonesian government, which has claimed, in justification of its recent escalation of executions of drug traffickers, that illegal drugs caused 40-50 deaths per day and that 2.6% of its population, or nearly 4.5 million people, used drugs.[22] In contrast, the World Health Organization estimated that 1.5 million people in Indonesia used any drugs.[23] The government numbers in Indonesia are disputed, however, by local experts, who argued that there were flaws in the research design and a lack of transparency in disclosing the evidence.[24] The methods themselves are questionable: imprecise wording of survey questions that confuses use with addiction, setting arbitrary thresholds for assigning a respondent to the status of addict, relying on imprecise wording to determine which users died because of drugs or how their deaths were related to drugs, and failing to consider that trafficking itself is often a cause of death owing to the legal status of drugs.[25]

Evidence for or against these claims is crucial not only to assess the soundness of a government's rationale for executing drug offenders, but also to determine if drug problems are responsive to executions, in the manner of sound empirical research on deterrence and murder.[26] In the matter of drug trafficking, the causal claims remain global, and a one-size-fits-all explanation is applied to all drugs and a range of putative causal mechanisms. Governments claiming that executions are necessary to deter drug crimes rarely if ever define the precise causal mechanism through which drugs cause deaths, leaving open any one factor or combination of factors: drug overdose, infectious disease transmitted via drug paraphernalia, murder resulting from drug selling, adverse psychological reactions to banned substances. It has not been established which if any of these pathways is sensitive to the threat of execution, rendering the search for deterrence a moot point.

---

22 Claudia Stoicescu, "Indonesia uses faulty stats on drug 'crisis' to justify death penalty", *The Conversation*, 4 February 2015, available from http://theconversation.com/indonesia-uses-faulty-stats-on-drug-crisis-to-justify-death-penalty-36512.

23 World Health Organization, "Country profile: Indonesia", *Atlas of Substance Abuse Disorders*, available from www.who.int%2Fsubstance_abuse%2Fpublications%2Fatlas_report%2Fprofiles%2Findonesia.pdf.

24 Melissa Davey, "Data used by Indonesia to justify drug laws is 'questionable', say experts", *The Guardian*, 4 June 2015, citing a letter from health experts in Indonesia challenging the accuracy of the government's claims; Stoicescu, "Indonesia uses faulty stats".

25 See for example Jeffrey Fagan, "Interactions among drugs, alcohol, and violence", 72 *Health Affairs*, vol. 72 (1993), pp. 65-79.

26 John J. Donohue III, "Empirical evaluation of law: the dream and the nightmare", American Law and Economic Review, vol. 17, no. 1 (spring 2015), doi:10.1093/aler/ahv007.

No empirical research supports the claim that the threat of execution, or even of a lengthy prison term, deters drug use or drug trafficking.[27] The types of evidence that are available to test the deterrent effects of executions on murder are not available to test deterrence of different forms of drug offenses. The types of empirical tests themselves are likely to differ. There are many reasons for this, but perhaps the most important is that there is no reliable way to count or even estimate the number of people who are involved in drug trafficking.[28] We also lack reliable evidence on the number of people using drugs, which would be an indirect estimate of drug availability, or the elasticity in drug prices under different forms of sanction threats.[29] There are other challenges to research in this area, including the diversity of drugs that are trafficked and the differences from one place to another in the resources devoted to drug enforcement. Comparisons therefore are complicated.

Analyses of market dynamics in response to punishment actions provide an alternative to the direct measure of criminal activity. Economic theory suggests that market dynamics and parameters will be sensitive to executions, incarceration and other forms of harsh punishment.[30] Under a theory of deterrence, drug traffickers would exact higher prices for drugs owing to greater risk and scarcity under threats of harsh punishment. Also, production and importation are likely to be lower in places where the risks of punishment from drug trafficking are greater. Producers and traffickers are likely to offset the greater risks of punishment by increasing prices in places that execute drug offenders. Also, if executions for drug crimes are a deterrent, availability of drugs will decline over time as executions for drug crimes increase.

To see if drug prices or availability are higher in such countries, we can compare both availability and prices for heroin, cocaine or other

---

27 David Skarbek, "Prisonomics: lessons from America's mass incarceration", 34 *Economic Affairs*, vol. 34 (2014), 411; John F. Pfaff, "The durability of prison populations", *University of Chicago Legal Forum* 73 (2010), 73-116.

28 Carol V. Petrie, John V. Pepper, and Charles F. Manski, eds., *Informing America's Policy on Illegal Drugs: What We Don't Know Keeps Hurting Us* (Washington, DC, National Academies Press, 2001).

29 See Jonathan P. Caulkins and Peter Reuter, "How drug enforcement affects drug prices, *Crime and Justice: A Review of Research*, vol. 39, pp. 213-71 (2012). See, also, Stoicescu, "Indonesia uses faulty stats"; Davey, "Data used by Indonesia". As the critiques of the Indonesian studies suggest, drug crimes and drug trafficking are particularly difficult to measure, owing not only to the inconsistencies in definitions or metrics but also to the inability of states to agree on the mechanisms to generate these data. See Petrie et al., *Informing America's Policy on Illegal Drugs*.

30 Jonathan P. Caulkins and Peter Reuter, *id.*.

banned substances such as ecstasy (MDMA) with prices in nearby similar countries that do not execute people convicted of drug trafficking. While many countries authorize the use of the death penalty for drug offenses, only a few actually carry out executions. These include China, Iran, Malaysia, Saudi Arabia, Singapore, Viet Nam and, more recently, Indonesia.

MAP: Global seizures of heroin and morphine, 2010 (countries and territories reporting seizures* of more than 100kg)

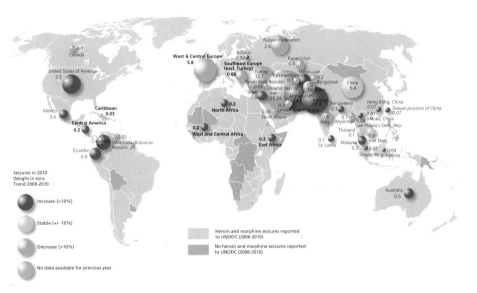

Source: UNODC annual report questionnaires data supplemented by other sources.
Note: The boundaries and names shown and the designations used on this map do not imply official endorsement or acceptance by the United Nations. Final boundary between the Republic of Sudan and the Republic of South Sudan has not yet been determined.

Evidence suggests that executions do not appear to have a deterrent effect in these countries or the surrounding regions. Instead, there has been a steady increase in drug seizures over the past decade, a sign of increased availability and trafficking, even in the face of executions in the countries that are nearest to the producing areas and supply routes. Data from the 2012 U.N. World Drug Report show that in the regions where drug executions are most frequent, availability (as indicated by drug seizures) has either remained stable or increased compared to the previous reporting period.[31] For example, prices in

31 United Nations Office on Drugs and Crime, World Drug Report, 2012, available at http://www. unodc.org/unodc/data-and-analysis/WDR-2012.html

China, Malaysia, Thailand and Viet Nam have either remained stable or increased as executions have been carried out.

Again, deterrence would predict that a strong risk of punishment, including death, associated with drug trafficking would result in higher prices to compensate for those risks. In other words, a trafficker facing the risk of execution would be likely to charge more for the commodity than a trafficker whose risks are lower, in turn lowering the amount of drugs imported and available for seizure. Without a deterrent threat, drugs presumably would flood a market and prices would be driven down. This is simple economic theory that applies for many commodities, based on scarcity and the costs of producing and distributing the banned product. Yet, current data from the 2012 U.N. Report on Drugs and Crime suggest that even in the face of the threat of execution, seizures remain high, suggesting an uninterrupted flow of drugs.[32]

Overall, the lessons of execution for drug offenses are lost on a person who is involved in drug trafficking. Research in the United States has shown that even the prospect of the harshest punishments, including death, have no deterrent effect. Drug offenders are strongly motivated by both economic interests and the personal thrills of their lifestyle, and the exaggerated value of these rewards colours their risk–reward calculations.[33] They see the risk of detection and punishment as remote and the rewards of drug offenses as well worth any price. Were there a deterrent effect, drug prices would be higher in places that more frequently execute drug offenders. There is no evidence that this is the case. Drug prices appear to be disconnected from punishment risks, including the risks of execution. Moreover, imprisoned or executed traffickers are often quickly replaced in a market that is deeply integrated at a macro level into both national and regional economies.[34]

---

32 United Nations Office on Drugs and Crime, World Drug Report, 2012, pp. 27-32.

33 Patricia A. Adler, *Wheeling and Dealing: An Ethnography of an Upper-Level Drug Dealing and Smuggling Community* (New York, Columbia University Press, 1993); Volkan Topalli, Richard Wright, and Robert Fornango, "Drug dealers, robbery and retaliation, vulnerability, deterrence and the contagion of violence", *British Journal of Criminology*, vol. 42 (2002), 337-351.

34 Thomas Fuller, "Profits of drug trade drive economic boom in Myanmar", *New York Times*, 6 June 2015.

C.   Terrorism

Assessing the likelihood that the death penalty would deter terrorism presents additional empirical and theoretical challenges.[35] First, the data on deterrence and terrorism present many of the same challenges as the data on deterrence and drug crimes. Defining terrorism in a way that facilitates reliable cross-national comparisons is the major challenge, and it is multiplied by the difficulty of obtaining precise estimates at the national level.[36] For example, recent estimates of terrorist activity in the U.S. since the September 11, 2001 domestic attacks include incidents of deadly force, property destruction, and "material support" for terrorist organizations operating internationally.[37]

In the case of terrorism, execution can be a perverse incentive.[38] The logic of deterrence rests on the assumption that criminals are rational and act in their own self-interest, and that their goals are elastic and sensitive to both cost and reward. For most people, death by execution would be a fate worth avoiding. But many terrorists view execution as a form of principle or martyrdom. For those who commit acts of terrorism motivated by religious beliefs, execution offers martyrdom and rewards in the afterlife. Thus, executions of terrorists could well inspire rather than deter terrorist violence.

For terrorists and other criminals, a lifetime of incarceration and deprivation can be a far harsher punishment than execution in the spotlight of public and political attention. British philosopher John Stuart Mill characterized a life sentence as a "living tomb":

> *What comparison can there really be . . . between consigning a man to the short pang of a rapid death, and immuring him in a living tomb, there to linger out what*

---

35 Bruno S. Frey and Simon Luechinger, "How to fight terrorism: alternatives to deterrence", *Defence and Peace Economics,* vol. 14 (2003), pp. 237-249.

36 Gary LaFree, Nancy A. Morris, and Laura Dugan, "Cross-national patterns of terrorism comparing trajectories for total, attributed and fatal attacks, 1970-2006", *British Journal of Criminology,* vol. 50 (2010), pp. 622-649.

37 Scott Shane, "Homegrown radicals more deadly than Jihadis in the U.S.", *New York Times.* June 24, 2015, at http://securitydata.newamerica.net/extremists/deadly-attacks.html

38 For example, Laura Dugan and Erica Chenoweth, in "Moving beyond deterrence: the effectiveness of raising the expected utility of abstaining from terrorism in Israel" (*American Sociological Review,* vol. 77 [2012], pp. 597-624), argued that increasing the rewards for abstaining from terrorism may discourage terrorist acts more than raising the likelihood and severity of punishment.

*may be a long life in the hardest and most monotonous toil,
without any of its alleviation or rewards—disbarred from
all pleasant sights and sounds, and cut off from all earthly
hope.......?"[39]*

Decades later, a committee of the British Parliament concluded in
1930 that the relative physical and psychological pains of execution are far preferable to the slow decay of body and spirit of life
imprisonment:

> "A further alternative is to lengthen the sentence
> to the limit of life itself. . . . This is a death sentence
> where the inevitable end is reached by the imper-
> ceptible stages of institutional decay instead of by
> one full stroke."[40]

RETHINKING THE THEORY OF DETERRENCE

The logic of deterrence rests on the principle that persons people
committing these crimes have motivations that influence their consideration of the possibility of death as a consequence of their act. There is
strong and consistent social science evidence that persons contemplating murder tend to heavily undervalue the risks of punishment. They
regard punishment as a distant possibility, and not one to be taken seriously.[41] In some instances, the rewards and gratification from murder
outweigh any risks of death, or even the certainty of death itself.[42]
Even in places with frequent and well-publicized executions, there
is no scientific evidence that executions deter homicides marginally
more than do lengthy incarceration prison sentences.[43]

---

39 John Stuart Mill, *Collected Works*, vol. 28 (London, Routledge, 1868), pp. 266-272.
40 Sir Alexander Paterson, *Report of the Committee on Capital Punishment* (1930), pp. 484-487.
41 See, for example, Kenneth Polk, *When Men Kill: Scenarios of Masculine Violence* (New York, Cambridge University Press, 1994).
42 This can be observed both in the high number of people who commit suicide after killing
   before being arrested by police, and also in the acts of terrorism that result in certain death by
   the attacker. See, Scott Eliason, "Murder-suicide: a review of the recent literature", Journal of the
   American Academy of Psychiatry and the Law Online, vol. 37 (2009): 371-376.
43 Randi Hjalmarsson, "Does capital punishment have a 'local' deterrent effect on homicides?"
   American Law and Economics Review, vol. 11 (2009), pp. 310-334.

A recent review of the empirical research on deterrence[44], concluded that three preconditions of decision-making by criminal offenders are necessary for deterrence to be effective:

1. Knowledge—Do offenders know and understand the implications of the law? Do they know which actions are criminalized and what will mitigate their culpability?

2. Rationality—If so, will they allow that understanding to determine their conduct?

3. Perceived net cost—If so, are they likely to choose compliance as the more beneficial option? Is the punishment worth avoiding? This in turn requires assessment of three concurrent probabilities: (a) the probability of being caught and convicted, (b) the likely severity of a sentence, and the marginal increases in severity for each level of punishment, and (c) the delay in reaching the final stage of the most severe punishment.

The third precondition raises the most difficult challenges: assuming rationality in both perception and weighing of risks associated specifically with execution. In most instances, the risks are remote: Few murderers are caught, even fewer sentenced to death, and still fewer actually executed.[45] In the case of drug trafficking, its apparent high volume suggests that perceptions of risk are realistically low.

For both murderers and drug traffickers, with detection and punishment uncertain if not unlikely, and with the payoffs of drug trafficking well exceeding conventional returns, the net cost hurdle is likely to defeat deterrence. Empirical research has shown that the calculus drug offenders apply in their decision making renders deterrence simply a component of their task to be managed and avoided. But it hardly changes how net costs are evaluated.

There also are personal rewards that alter the rationality of decision making. Economic necessity, emotional rewards and other non-rational

---

44 Paul Robinson and John Darley, "Does the criminal law deter?" *Oxford Journal of Law,* 24 (2004), p. 173.
45 See, for example, Scott Phillips and Alena Simon, "Is the modern American death penalty a fatal lottery? Texas as a conservative test", *Laws,* vol. 3 (2014), pp. 85-105, doi:10.3390/laws3010085.

"MANY TERRORISTS VIEW EXECUTION AS A FORM OF MARTYRDOM."

—Jeffrey Fagan

considerations make severe penalties unlikely to deter many acts of murder, drug trafficking or terrorism. Several ethnographic studies of decision making by drug traffickers have shown the remoteness of detection and punishment in their thinking. Both in the United States and elsewhere, even with the death penalty for major drug crimes, there is no evidence that severe punishments—either death or life in prison without parole—have affected the price, availability or demand for drugs. Even when there is a small probability of detection and punishment, these factors are diminished in the calculus of deterrence among active offenders.[46] Risks tend to be underestimated and rewards inflated by many criminal offenders,[47] defeating the ability of deterrence to overcome the "perceived net cost" hurdle of rational decision making.

IS THE DEATH PENALTY AN EFFECTIVE CRIME CONTROL MEASURE?

Deterrence is an effective crime control measure for crimes such as tax evasion, minor property crimes and vehicular offenses.[48] There also is some evidence that rapid criminal justice responses to marital violence can be an effective deterrent, but only for some types of offenders.[49] In general, deterrent effects are weakest for the most serious crimes.[50] We have no expectation that executions will deter homicides in the United States, and limited evidence that they do so elsewhere.

---

46 For basic expressions of the principles of discounting and risk, see Daniel Kahneman and Amos Tversky, "Prospect theory: an analysis of decision under risk", *Econometrica: Journal of the Econometric Society,* vol. 47, no. 2 (March 1979), pp. 263-291; Amos Tversky and Daniel Kahneman, "Advances in prospect theory: cumulative representation of uncertainty", *Journal of Risk and Uncertainty,* vol. 5 (1992), pp. 297-323. See, generally, Derek B. Cornish and Ronald V. Clarke, eds., *The Reasoning Criminal: Rational Choice Perspectives on Criminal Offending,* 2nd ed. (New Brunswick, New Jersey, Transaction Publishers, 2014).

47 See, for example, Taku Yokoyama and Taiki Takahashi, "Mathematical neurolaw of crime and punishment: the qexponential punishment function, *Applied Mathematics,* vol. 4 (2013), pp. 1371-1375, doi:10.4236/am.2013.410185; for a review, see Richard H. McAdams, *Present Bias and Criminal Law* (John M. Olin Program in Law and Economics Working Paper No. 562, 2011).

48 Daniel Nagin, "Deterrence in the 21st century: a review of the evidence", in *Crime and Justice: An Annual Review of Research,* M. Tonry, ed. (Chicago, University of Chicago Press) (2014).

49 Christopher D. Maxwell, Joel H. Garner, and Jeffrey A. Fagan, "The preventive effects of arrest on intimate partner violence: research, policy and theory", *Criminology & Public Policy,* vol. 2 (2002), pp. 51-80.

50 Nagin, "Deterrence in the 21st century".

The conditions to establish deterrence for drug traffickers would be infeasible for most sovereign governments, for several reasons. First, drug traffickers are not easy to apprehend. In the countries that carry out executions for drug offenses, the vast supply of drugs stands in contrast to the few arrests that are made for drug trafficking. Despite the threat of execution, drugs remain available, large seizures occur regularly, and few arrests are made. These arrests often are widely publicized, partially establishing the conditions for deterrence, yet there seem to be no measurable effects on the supply or price of drugs in these countries.

Second, to increase the risks of apprehending and convicting drug traffickers, significant investments in police and prosecution agencies would be necessary above the current levels of investment, in turn detracting from the enforcement of other crimes. Police efficiency would also have to improve markedly, the number of arrests for drug offenses would have to increase significantly, and corruption would have to be eliminated. These reforms would strain legal institutions and weaken other areas of public security. In addition, deterrence requires efficiency in conducting trials to reduce the time so that drug offenses are temporally connected to arrests. Procedural rights would be compromised under these conditions, challenging the legitimacy of governments and courts. The central role of the drug economy in some states also would pose a barrier to creating the conditions necessary for deterrence, with institutional incentives off-setting if not surpassing the demand for punishment and control of drug trafficking.[51]

---

51 Fuller, "Profits of drug trade drive economic boom in Myanmar".

"They took us to trial, and the evidence was the Stephen King novels that I read, the music I listened to and the clothes that I wore. They found us guilty, and I was sentenced to death."
—Damien Echols

CHAPTER 3
DISCRIMINATION

This chapter contains articles by geographically diverse authors showing that, all over the world, the death penalty disproportionately targets members of marginalised groups. Discrimination can be based on various characteristics—including racial, ethnic and cultural identity or mental disability—but poverty almost always plays a role.

<u>Damien Echols</u> and <u>Stephen Braga</u> both describe the so-called West Memphis Three murder case. He was one of the suspects and the only one sentenced to death. Damien Echols writes about growing up in poverty and social isolation, feeling different from other kids, and the comfort he received from the books, music, and all-black clothes that others judged him for. At the age of 18, he was wrongfully convicted and sentenced to death. He describes the horrors of death row and of life in the prison where he spent 18 years.

<u>Stephen Braga</u>, who was his lawyer during an advanced stage of the proceedings, describes how, based on the West Memphis Three's appearance and taste for heavy-metal music, they were accused of being satanists, and how this, as well as their inability to afford a better defence, led to a wrongful conviction. When a documentary movie on the trial revealed its shortcomings, growing public support for the West Memphis Three, including financial donations, made it possible to hire first-rate lawyers on their behalf, and they won their freedom.

<u>Stephen Bright</u>, an academic, analyses the unequal application of the death penalty in the United States. He finds that the likelihood of receiving the death penalty relates not only to the crime committed but also to the social and economic status of the accused. Almost all who are sentenced to death are poor, and half are members of a racial minority; many did not have a proper defence. Many have suffered from a mental disability or were victims of childhood abuse. Lawyers who were intoxicated or asleep during trial, were absent during crucial testimony, did not know their client's name, said nine words during sentencing or missed the deadlines for appeals have contributed to their clients' convictions and ultimately their executions.

<u>Usha Ramanathan</u>, an activist, writes about poverty, women's rights, terrorism and the death penalty in her native India, where events such as the 2008 attack on Bombay and recent brutal crimes against women may have

led to resurgence in support for the death penalty. She points to the dangers that inflamed public passions can pose to fair trials, as well as the way that high-profile trials can further inflame divisive emotions, and describes how many women's groups reject the notion that the death penalty should be imposed in their name for the crime of rape.

Alice Mogwe, executive director of DITSHWANELO, the Botswana Centre for Human Rights, examines the status of the death penalty in Botswana, in the context of the African human rights architecture. The death penalty remains on the books in Botswana and is mandatory for murder unless there are extenuating circumstances. She examines the barriers faced by poor people and members of ethnic and linguistic minorities in Botswana's justice system—including inadequate representation, lack of translation services in this multilingual country and secrecy surrounding the clemency process—and supports the call by the African Commission on Human and People's Rights for a moratorium on the death penalty.

Innocent Maja, a lawyer and a lecturer at the University of Zimbabwe, analyses the extent to which Zimbabwe has implemented the United Nations General Assembly resolution on the moratorium on the use of the death penalty. Although there is no official moratorium, Zimbabwe has not carried out an execution since 2004. The country's 2013 Constitution severely limits the circumstances in which a death penalty could be imposed, and there is currently no death penalty law on the books that meets those criteria. But shortcomings in the legal system—from the paucity of legal aid for indigent defendants to appalling conditions for death-row prisoners—as well as the fact that Zimbabwe has paused and resumed executions before, call for a more final and formal end to the death penalty.

Arif Bulkan, an academic from Trinidad and Tobago, analyses the application of the death penalty in the Commonwealth Caribbean. While the death penalty has not been abolished there, its use has been limited by a series of appeals-court rulings focusing on how it is carried out—for example, limiting how long a prisoner can be kept on death row, making the pardons process more accessible and transparent, enabling petitions to international treaty bodies, and challenging mandatory sentencing. Despite these limits, severe problems in the legal system—including failure to assess defendants' mental and psychological status, the poor quality of legal aid for indigent prisoners, and a low clearance rate in murder investigations—combine to make the pattern of death sentences that still do occur tragically arbitrary and useless as a deterrent.

THE TERRORS OF PRISON FADE SLOWLY

Damien Echols[1]

When I first arrived on death row, the guards decided they were going to welcome me to the neighbourhood. So they took me to the part of the prison they call The Hole. It's a very small, dark, filthy place that's in complete isolation. And for the next 18 days they beat the hell out of me. They used to come in at about twelve or one o'clock in the morning, and they would chain me to the bars of the cell and beat me with nightsticks. They beat me so badly at one point that I started to piss blood. I still wake up at night sometimes dreaming that I'm pissing blood again.

They starved me. They tortured me.

Eventually word of what they were doing started to leak out into the rest of the prison. Other prisoners started to hear about it. So they went to a deacon from the Catholic Church, who used to come to prison to bring Catholic inmates communion, and they told him what was going on. And he went to the warden's office, and he told the warden, "I know what you're doing to this guy. I know you're killing him. And if it doesn't stop, I'm going to go public."

So that night they took me out of The Hole and put me back in a regular prison cell. The other prisoners told me later that they had expected to see me carried out in a body bag any day. And I think the only reason they didn't murder me is because they realized they were being watched.

When I was a kid my family was beyond dirt poor. When we finally moved into a trailer park with running water and electricity, we thought we were really moving up in the world. I used to take refuge in books and music. Reading became a sanctuary for me. It allowed me to escape the world I lived in for a little while.

---

1   Damien Echols spent 18 years on death row for a crime he did not commit.

I'd read Stephen King novels over and over and listen to bands like Iron Maiden. I started dressing in black all the time because it was like a security blanket for me. It made me feel a little safer in an unsafe and scary world. I didn't have many friends; in fact, my only real friend was a skinny blonde kid with a mullet named Jason Baldwin, and Jason was with me the night I was arrested.

> "NOTHING IN THIS CONFESSION MADE ANY SENSE WHATSOEVER, BUT IT DIDN'T MATTER TO THEM."
>
> —Damien Echols

Jason, my sister, my girlfriend and I were sitting in the living room watching movies when the cops started hammering on the door. And when I opened the door, they were pointing guns at me. They swarmed into the house like ants. They stampeded over everything and pawed through every possession my family owned. They put Jason and me in handcuffs, threw us into the backs of cop cars, and took us to jail.

I spent all night in a cell about the size of a closet. I wasn't allowed to go to the bathroom, wasn't given so much as a drink of water. Every so often a cop would come in and ask me if I had anything to tell him, or if I was ready to make my confession yet. This went on all night, until the next day when we were given an arraignment hearing.

At this hearing the judge told me that I was being charged with three counts of capital murder, accused of killing three children as part of a satanic sacrifice. He said someone had confessed, but he refused to read the confession in the courtroom. Instead, I was put in a broom closet somewhere in the back of the jail and given a transcript of the confession.

I was only 18 years old, in complete shock and trauma, and suffering from sleep deprivation. My life had just been destroyed. But even so, I could see that there was something wrong with that document. It made no sense. It was like some sort of bizarre patchwork Frankenstein thing that they had stitched together.

It turned out that they had picked up a mentally handicapped kid in our neighbourhood and coerced him into making a confession, and then he was led to implicate Jason and me. Nothing in this confession made any sense whatsoever, but it didn't matter to them. I was put in a cell. I kept thinking, surely someone's going step in and put a stop to this. Surely, someone is going to rectify the situation. They can't put you on trial and prove you've done something you haven't done. It seemed to me that science would say that's impossible.

But they did.

They took us to trial, and the evidence was the Stephen King novels that I read, the music I listened to and the clothes that I wore. They found us guilty, and I was sentenced to death—not once, not twice, but three times. The judge read these death sentences in this really bored, monotone voice, like it was just another day at the office for him.

People asked me later, "What were you feeling when he was sentencing you to die?" It's almost impossible to describe. If you've ever been beaten, when you're punched in the head, you don't register pain. You see a bright flash of light, hear a loud noise, and you're completely disoriented, you have no idea where you even are for a few minutes. That's what it was like when he was reading those death sentences; it was like being repeatedly punched in the head.

They sent me to death row. I was in a cell for about a week before I noticed a shadow on the wall. It was from a man who had already been executed who was in the cell before I got there. He had stood against the wall and traced around himself with a pencil really, really lightly, and then lightly shaded it in. I didn't even see it for about the first week—but after I saw it, I couldn't un-see it. So for years I slept on a dead man's mattress, stared at a dead man's shadow, and lived in the cell with ghosts.

People filed appeal after appeal on my behalf, all before the same judge who sentenced me to death. He denied them all. Even when new DNA evidence came in that excluded me and the other two guys from the crime scene, the judge still said: "This is not enough."

Then we were allowed to appeal to the Arkansas Supreme Court, and by that time public awareness and interest in the case had been building. There'd been documentaries, books, and countless newspaper and magazine articles and TV shows. So the Arkansas Supreme Court justices knew they were being watched. In the end, the only thing they really cared about was winning the next election. So they ruled that all of the new evidence would be heard, and the prosecutors realized that meant there was going to be another trial.

So a deal was hammered out—an Alford Plea. What an Alford Plea means is that I plead guilty, and I walk out of the courtroom, and I can still publicly maintain my innocence, but I can't sue the state.

People have asked me what I was thinking about the day that I went into court knowing that I could very well go home that day. And the truth is, I wasn't thinking anything. By that time I was so tired and beat down that all I wanted to do was rest. I was dying. My health was deteriorating rapidly. I was losing my eyesight. I knew I wasn't going to make it much longer.

The prosecutor said that one of the factors in his making this deal was the fact that the three of us together could have collectively sued the state for $60 million. I knew they could have had me stabbed to death for $50 any day of the week. It happens in prison all the time. So I knew if I didn't take that deal, one way or another I would never live to see the outside of those prison walls. So I took it.

I've been out of prison now for almost two years. I lived in terror every single day for the first year or so, but it's getting better. I'm still scared sometimes, but I'm trying to fight my way through it. And I know that I will eventually be free from fear and anxiety. I'll do it, and I'll be free, because if there's one thing that I learned from 18 years in prison, it was how to fight.

DAMIEN ECHOLS AND THE WEST MEMPHIS THREE CASE: A SEARCH FOR MOTIVE RUN AMOK

Stephen L. Braga[1]

On a beautiful spring afternoon in 1993, three young boys disappeared from their neighbourhood in West Memphis, Arkansas, around dinnertime. The next day their bodies were found, naked, bound and in horrific condition, submerged in a creek in the woods. Fear and panic quickly swept through the community, along with rumours about the murders, including that a satanic cult was to blame.

Shortly thereafter, three local teenagers—Damien Echols, Jason Baldwin and Jessie Misskelley—were charged with the murders. Echols's own lawyer called him the "weird" kid in town because of the way he dressed and acted, which—along with his first name—played right into the sensational nature of the allegations. Agreements were reached to film the teenagers' trials and surrounding circumstances for a documentary, with defence lawyers, prosecutors and even the victims' families playing leading roles. Less than a year later, the three teenagers were convicted in two separate trials. Baldwin and Misskelley were sentenced to life in prison without the possibility of parole; Echols was sentenced to death by lethal injection.

Questions arose almost immediately about the validity of the teenagers' convictions. The evidence seemed thin, and the alleged motive was almost impossible to believe. Public release of the documentary *Paradise Lost* spread those questions worldwide. Journalists, researchers, supporters and new counsel for the three teenagers began to re-examine every aspect of the case. What they found was deeply disturbing at every level, but perhaps nothing was more troubling than the facts surrounding the prosecution's purported proof of the alleged motive for the murders.

---

1   Stephen Braga is a professor at the University of Virginia School of Law and counsel for Damien Echols, whose essay also appears in this volume.

As the United States Supreme Court has noted, "when identity is in question, motive is key."[2] Identity was the issue in this case. There was no question that the three young boys had been brutally murdered; the only question was who did it. To convince the jury that the West Memphis Three were the perpetrators of these crimes, the prosecutors had to establish a motive for why they would kill three young boys with whom they had no prior relationship.

The motive associated with the prosecution theory at trial was clearly explained by prosecutor John Fogelman during his closing argument to the jury:

That's the only thing that matters, in relation to motive. The testimony in this case was that these murders—when you take the crime scene, the injuries to these kids, the testimony about the sucking of blood—and do you remember there was testimony about that—in the satanic areas that blood is a life force, there is a transference of power from drinking of blood—when you take all of that together, the evidence was that this murder had the trappings of an occult murder. A satanic murder.

To establish this theory of motive, the prosecution used questionable science, flawed forensic science and the testimony of a prison informant, and played on the rampant fear and prejudice in the community at the time. The jury bought it, hook, line and sinker.

THE EXPERT TESTIMONY

The questionable science came in the form of testimony from Dale Griffis, a purported expert in satanic and occult behaviour. After the trials, the institution from which Griffis received his master's and PhD degrees (without ever attending a class or taking a test) was shut down by the state of California. During his testimony, Griffis conceded that he had only previously worked on one criminal case involving an alleged satanic motive, and that motive was not too hard to figure out since a pentagram had been carved into the victim's body.

---

2   House v. Bell, 547 U.S. 518, 540 (2006).

Given this background, it was hardly surprising that Griffis's testimony about the West Memphis murders was a collection of generalizations. According to Griffis, the wearing of black clothing, such as Damien favoured, was a sign of occult beliefs, as was listening to heavy metal bands like Led Zeppelin. The reading of books about magic and horror, such as the Stephen King novels Damien was fond of, was also a sign of an occult mindset, he said, as was writing dark fantasy poetry. The fact that the murders happened on the night of a full moon was yet another indicator of occult activity, as was the location of the murders in a wooded area. In perhaps the most outrageous aspect of his testimony, Griffis responded to the judge's question about whether the fact that there were three victims was relevant to his analysis by stating that it was because 666 was the number for the Devil and if that number was divided by two the result was 333. Twenty years later, it is hard to do anything but laugh at such ridiculous testimony, but at the time of Echols's trial it was deadly serious.

The only specifics Griffis relied on for his conclusions about the murders were (1) forensic evidence that a knife was used to emasculate one victim and to create ritualistic patterned wounds on all three victims, and (2) testimony by prison informant Michael Carson that Jason Baldwin admitted details of the crime to him while they were incarcerated together. Neither piece of evidence was accurate.

THE FLAWED FORENSICS

With great flourish during his closing argument, prosecutor John Fogelman performed a demonstration with a large serrated knife and a grapefruit in order to convince the jury that the knife had made the allegedly serrated pattern wounds on the victims' bodies. In his rebuttal closing argument, prosecutor Brent Davis added that the knife was used in the genital mutilation of one of the victims. The knife had been found in the lake behind Jason Baldwin's home, which made it all the more suspicious to the prosecutors and incriminating to the jury. The prosecutors' claims about the knife being used to inflict the victims' injuries was based on the testimony of the state's forensic pathologist, Frank Peretti.

However, subsequent re-examination by several of the country's leading forensic pathologists found Peretti's testimony to be completely wrong. Each of these experts, evaluating the evidence independently, concluded that the injuries suffered by the victims were caused by post-mortem animal predation rather than by a knife. Thus, the injuries with the alleged serrated-knife patterns and the emasculation of one victim were caused by animals attacking the young boys' bodies in their watery grave, not by a knife used as part of a satanic ritual killing. The unanimity of these experts is as striking as their findings, which leave no room for doubt that the forensic arguments used to convict the West Memphis Three and to sentence Damien Echols to death were wholly unfounded.

How could the state's forensic pathologist have been so wrong? Peretti had failed the board examination for forensic pathologists twice, yet Arkansas law permitted him to keep his state job. Arkansas law, like that in many states, provided little funding for criminal defence attorneys to hire their own experts in court-appointed criminal cases. So the system enabled a weakly (if at all) qualified expert with the imprimatur of a state title to impress the jury more than whatever the defence could come up with on a limited budget.

Everyone recognizes that money can make a difference in the effectiveness of a criminal defence, but the West Memphis Three case provides a particularly dramatic example of the human tragedy that can result. At trial with limited resources, Damien Echols was unable to effectively counter the state forensic pathologist's evidence that a knife had been used to commit the murders. After the trial, with the financing of numerous well-to-do supporters, Echols was able to retain the world's best forensic pathologists to testify, in unison, that the state's expert was completely wrong and that no knife had been used in the crimes. The case for adequate defence funding in criminal justice systems around the world could hardly be made more clear. It can literally be a matter of life and death.

THE PRISON INFORMANT

In another of the trial's dramatic moments, the prosecutors called inmate Michael Carson to the stand to recount statements allegedly made to him by Jason Baldwin about the murders while the two men were briefly incarcerated together. Carson said that Baldwin had told him about sucking blood from a victim, which is what Griffis relied on for the blood-related element of his conclusion that the crime had an occult aspect. Griffis conceded on cross-examination that if Michael Carson's testimony was false, then there was no other evidence in the case to connect Baldwin to the occult.

Although the jury accepted Carson's testimony as credible, it too turned out to be false on later re-examination. Prison informants make notoriously unreliable witnesses, as Brandon Garrett's landmark book *Convicting the Innocent* makes clear.[3] Carson proved to be even more unreliable than most. As Carson himself explained in the movie *West of Memphis*,[4] he was a heavy drug user at the time of his testimony, could not distinguish between reality and fantasy, and had no idea what he was doing or why. To this day, Carson is not certain whether Baldwin ever made the statements he testified about at trial, and he has publicly apologized to Baldwin.

FEAR AND PREJUDICE

Like Salem, Massachusetts, during the witch hysteria of the late 1600s and New York City in the 1980s at the time of the Central Park jogger's brutal beating and rape (for which five defendants were wrongfully convicted), rural Arkansas was terrified by the West Memphis murders. Who could possibly have committed such unthinkably heinous acts? Adding allegations of satanic activity with ritualistic knife murders and the drinking of blood into the investigation of these murders was like tossing a Molotov cocktail of prejudice into the mix. Who could be impartial, dispassionate and analytical, who would not be afraid in the face of such a panoply of evil? Due process disappears when such fear and prejudice creep into the system to warp people's judgment.

Regrettably, fear and prejudice did not merely creep into the West Memphis Three case—they were injected into the case by prosecutors

---

3   Brandon Garrett, *Convicting the Innocent: Where Criminal Prosecutions Go Wrong* (Cambridge, Massachusetts: Harvard University Press, 2011).
4   Amy Berg (director), *West of Memphis* (Sony Pictures Classics, 2012).

and law enforcement authorities. In *West of Memphis*, Steve Jones, an Arkansas State Criminal Justice official who searched for and found the victims' bodies, recalled a pretrial conversation with prosecutor Fogelman in which, in response to Jones's inquiry, Fogelman told him that the case was not satanic and was "just a murder." Unfortunately, Jones told no one at the time about this.

"TERRIBLE TRAGEDIES INVOLVING SENSATIONAL CRIMES TOO OFTEN MAKE BAD LAW."

—Stephen L. Braga

During the subsequent trials, the prosecutors used the satanic characterization of the case whenever and wherever they could. Such appeals to jurors' "passions and prejudices" have long been outlawed precisely because of their power to distract the jury from an impartial evaluation of the evidence and encourage an emotional response to what they have heard. Yet those arguments were allowed to be made in this case and proved damning.

Many other errors were committed during the trial. But on the basis of the errors relating to motive alone, the defendants never had a chance. In the juror's minds, the weird kid with the bad attitude, dressed in black, listening to violent metal music and reading counterculture books, simply had to be the ringleader of these horrible crimes—because it could not possibly have been a regular member of the community. Or could it?

A FRESH LOOK AT MOTIVE

As part of the post-trial efforts to free the West Memphis Three, the Echols defence team retained forensic profiling expert John Douglas, the former head of the FBI's Behavioral Science Unit. Douglas reviewed the crime without meeting any of the defendants because he did not want personal relationships to play a role in his analysis. Douglas could not have been more emphatic in rejecting the prosecution's theory that the crimes fit a satanic-murder pattern. As Douglas explained, in the early 1990s, the FBI was flooded with claims of satanic crimes due to fears and rumours running rampant at the time. According to Douglas, the FBI examined all of them and found that none of them constituted satanic crimes. Rather, they were all attributable to more traditional motives for criminal activity.

As Douglas saw it, the murders of which the West Memphis Three were accused were also explainable by a far more typical motive and were likely committed by someone who had a personal relationship with one or more of the victims and whose actions were triggered by some cause arising from that relationship. Yet in their rush to judgment to solve this crime under the mistaken notion of a satanic motive, the West Memphis police ignored a number of leads and suspects which would have more naturally fit into Douglas's profile for the killer or killers.

CONCLUSION

An old adage tells us that "hard cases make bad law." Terrible tragedies involving sensational crimes too often make bad law as well. One need look no further than this case, or that of the Central Park Five, to see evidence of this, although there are many other examples as well. When authorities use aggressive tactics to rush to judgment to quell community fear in such notorious cases, and when those fearful community members wind up serving as jurors reviewing evidence of unspeakable horror, mistakes happen and wrongful convictions result. Fortunately for the Central Park Five, New York had no death penalty at the time of their wrongful convictions. Arkansas did have the death penalty, and Damien Echols came within weeks of being executed for a crime he did not commit.

The finality of the death penalty is its strongest point for those who believe in it—and its weakest point for those who oppose it. After watching a documentary on the Central Park Five, commentator George Will summarized the conservative case against the death penalty: "Its finality leaves no room for rectifying mistakes."[5] This is not just a liberal Democratic issue. It is a social justice issue.

---

5   George Will, "'Central Park Five' tells of a gross miscarriage of justice", *Washington Post*, 12 April 2013.

As an empirical matter, we must acknowledge that mistakes happen in an imperfect criminal justice system run by fallible human beings. Those mistakes include wrongful convictions imposing the death penalty. For example, the work of the Innocence Project demonstrates that 18 of the first 300 prisoners exonerated after wrongful convictions on the basis of scientifically unimpeachable DNA evidence had been on death row. Eighteen people might have been executed even though they were demonstrably innocent. The case of Damien Echols is yet another instance.

The best judicial system in the world cannot guarantee 100 per cent accuracy. The risk of inaccuracy creates the very real possibility that an innocent man or woman might be executed. No civilized society, operating under any modern notion of the rule of law, can condone such a possibility. We likewise cannot ignore it. The only sensible and just approach in the face of such facts is a worldwide moratorium on the death penalty.

IMPOSITION OF THE DEATH PENALTY UPON THE POOR, RACIAL MINORITIES, THE INTELLECTUALLY DISABLED AND THE MENTALLY ILL

Stephen B. Bright[1]

The death penalty is imposed in the United States upon the poorest, most powerless, most marginalized people in the society. Virtually all of the people selected for execution are poor, about half are members of racial minorities, and the overwhelming majority were sentenced to death for crimes against white victims. Many have a significant intellectual disability or suffer from a severe mental illness. Many others were the victims of brutal physical, sexual and psychological abuse during childhood and lived on the margins of society before their arrests. Some are innocent. They are subject to discretionary decisions by law enforcement officers, prosecutors, judges and jurors that are often influenced by racial prejudice. Because of their poverty, they are often assigned lawyers who lack the skills, resources and inclination to represent them capably in capital cases.

One does not need to look far for illustrative examples. As of this writing, the state of Georgia plans to execute Warren Hill, an African American man, despite the fact that he is intellectually disabled.[2] The United States Supreme Court has held that the Constitution does not allow the execution of a person who is intellectually disabled (once called "mentally retarded"),[3] but Georgia requires that a person facing death prove intellectual disability beyond a reasonable doubt. Although four experts testified at the hearing on the issue that Hill was not intellectually disabled, they all later changed their

---

1   Stephen Bright is president and senior counsel of the Southern Center for Human Rights in Atlanta, Georgia, and Harvey Karp visiting lecturer at Yale Law School.
2   It has been delayed in doing so while the state's supreme court considered and rejected his challenge to the secrecy of its lethal injection procedures. *Owens v. Hall*, 758 S.E.2d 794 (Ga. 2014).
3   *Atkins v. Virginia*, 536 U.S. 304 (2002) (using the term "mental retardation").

opinions when they reviewed additional information about him. As a result, all nine experts who have examined Hill have found that he is intellectually disabled.

Nevertheless, the state and federal courts have held that they are powerless to prevent a patently unconstitutional execution.

Before the Supreme Court held that the mentally retarded could not be executed, a Florida court found that Freddie Lee Hall had been "mentally retarded his entire life."[4] But after the Supreme Court's decision, the Florida courts held that he is not retarded and could be executed because of an IQ score above 70.[5] However, the United States Supreme Court held that Florida could not treat an IQ score above 70 as final and conclusive and, instead, must consider other evidence of intellectual disability. Other states have fashioned their own definitions of intellectual disability. The Texas Court of Criminal Appeals held that someone with the severe mental limitations of Lennie in John Steinbeck's Of Mice and Men (1973) would be exempt from the death penalty, but not others who were diagnosed by psychologists as intellectually disabled.[6] This definition allowed Texas to execute Marvin Wilson in 2012, even though he had an IQ of 61, which is below the first percentile in human intelligence, sucked his thumb, and could not tell the difference between left and right.[7]

Glenn Ford, a black man, was released in March 2014 after 30 years on death row in Louisiana's notorious Angola Prison for a crime he did not commit.[8] As a result of his poverty, Ford was assigned two lawyers to represent him at his capital trial. The lead attorney was

---

4   *Hall v. Florida, 134 S.Ct. 1986, 1991 (2014).*

5   Ibid.; Andrew Cohen, "Supreme Court case may stop states that still execute mentally disabled", *The Atlantic*, 28 February 2014, available from www.theatlantic.com/health/archive/2014/02/supreme-court-case-may-stop-states-that-still-execute-the-mentally-ill/283969/.

6   *Ex parte Briseno, 135 S.W.3d 1, 6 (Tex. Crim. App. 2004).*

7   Andrew Cohen, "Of mice and men: the execution of Marvin Wilson", *The Atlantic, 8 Aug 2012, available from www.theatlantic.com/national/archive/2012/08/of-mice-and-men-the-execution-of-marvin-wilson/260713/.*

8   Andrew Cohen, "Freedom after 30 years on death row", *The Atlantic*, 11 March 2014, available from www.theatlantic.com/national/archive/2014/03/freedom-after-30-years-on-death-row/284179/; Andrew Cohen, "Glenn Ford's first days of freedom after 30 years on death row", *The Atlantic*, 14 March 2014, available from www.theatlantic.com/national/archive/2014/03/glenn-fords-first-days-of-freedom-after-30-years-on-death-row/284396/; Andrew Cohen, "The meaning of the exoneration of Glenn Ford", *Brennan Center*, 13 March 2014, www.brennancenter.org/analysis/meaning-exoneration-glenn-ford.

an oil and gas lawyer who had never tried a case, criminal or civil, before a jury. The second attorney had been out of law school for only two years and worked at an insurance defence firm on slip-and-fall cases. As often happens in capital cases, the prosecutors used their peremptory strikes to keep blacks off the jury. Despite a very weak case against him, Ford, virtually defenceless before an all-white jury, was sentenced death.

Ford is just one of many people who were found guilty beyond a reasonable doubt in capital and non-capital cases but were actually not guilty at all. States have already executed innocent people—like Carlos DeLuna and Cameron Todd Willingham in Texas[9]—and will continue to do so as long as they have the death penalty.

Missouri executed John Middleton in July 2014, despite questions about his guilt and his mental competence. United States Appeals Court Judge Kermit Bye, dissenting from a decision vacating a stay granted by a lower court, stated, "Missouri is positioned to execute a man who may very well be incompetent. That fact simply cannot be denied or overstated. But, for some reason, that fact has been ignored."[10] Florida executed John Ferguson, a black man, who suffered from schizophrenia, in 2013 even though he believed that he was the Prince of God and that after execution, he would be resurrected and return to earth in that capacity. The federal Court of Appeals in Atlanta treated this as nothing more than an unusual religious belief:

> *While Ferguson's thoughts about what happens after death may seem extreme to many people, nearly every major world religion—from Christianity to Zoroastrianism—envisions some kind of continuation of life after death, often including resurrection. Ferguson's belief in his ultimate corporeal resurrection may differ in degree, but it does*

---

9   James S. Liebman, *The Wrong Carlos: Anatomy of a Wrongful Execution* (New York, Columbia University Press, 2014); and "The wrong Carlos", available from www3.law.columbia.edu/hrlr/ltc/; David Grann, "Trial by fire: did Texas execute an innocent man?", *The New Yorker*, 7 September 2009, available from www.newyorker.com/reporting/2009/09/07/090907fa_fact_grann?printable=true.

10   Chris McDaniel, "After delays, Missouri carries out sixth execution this year", St. Louis Public Radio, 16 July 2014, available from http://news.stlpublicradio.org/post/after-delays-missouri-carries-out-sixth-execution-year.

not necessarily differ in kind, from the beliefs of millions
of Americans.[11]

The court warned against treating unusual religious beliefs as proof of mental illness. But religious delusions and obsessions are frequent manifestations of mental illness. This was just an effort by judges to gloss over the fact that Florida and other states are executing people who are out of touch with reality.

POVERTY AND POOR LAWYERING

Georgia plans to execute Robert Wayne Holsey, an African American, even though he was represented at his trial by a lawyer who drank a quart of vodka every night of trial and was preparing to be sued, criminally prosecuted, and disbarred for stealing client funds.[12] Holsey's other court-appointed lawyer had no experience in defending capital cases and was given no direction by the alcoholic lawyer in charge of the case except during trial, when she was told to cross-examine an expert on DNA and give the closing argument at the penalty phase.[13] The lawyers failed to present mitigating evidence that might well have convinced the jury to impose life imprisonment instead of death: Holsey was intellectually limited and as a child had been "subjected to abuse so severe, so frequent, and so notorious that his neighbours called his childhood home 'the Torture Chamber.'"[14]

Holsey was by no means the first person sentenced to death at a trial where he was represented by a drunken lawyer. Ronald Wayne Frye, executed by North Carolina, was represented by a lawyer who drank 12 shots of rum a day during the penalty phase of the trial.[15] And there are other cases of intoxicated lawyers, drug-addicted lawyers, lawyers who referred to their clients with racial slurs in front of the jury, lawyers who slept through testimony (three people were

---

11 *Ferguson v. Secretary*, 716 F.3d 1315, 1342 (11th Cir. 2013).

12 Marc Bookman, "This man is about to die because an alcoholic lawyer botched his case", *Mother Jones, 22 April 2014, available from www.motherjones.com/politics/2014/04/alcoholic-lawyer-botched-robert-wayne-holsey-death-penalty-trial?page=2.*

13 Ibid.

14 *Holsey v. Warden*, 694 F.3d 1230, 1275 (11th Cir. 2012) (Barkett, J., dissenting).

15 Jeffrey Gettleman, "Execution ends debatable case", *Los Angeles Times, 31 August 2001, available from http://articles.latimes.com/2001/aug/31/news/mn-40577.*

sentenced to death in Houston at trials in which their lawyers slept[16]), lawyers who were not in court when crucial witnesses testified, and lawyers who did not even know their client's names.[17]

There are lawyers who never read their state's death penalty statute, lawyers who filed one client's brief in another client's death penalty appeal without changing the names, and lawyers who missed deadlines that cost their clients review of their cases.

James Fisher Jr. spent 26 1/2 years in the custody of Oklahoma—most of it on death row—without ever having a fair and reliable determination of his guilt. The lawyer assigned to represent him tried his case *and 24 others*, including another capital murder case, during September 1983.[18] The lawyer made no opening statement or closing argument at either the guilt or sentencing phase and uttered only nine words during the entire sentencing phase.[19] On appeal, the Oklahoma Court of Criminal Appeals pronounced itself "deeply disturbed by defence counsel's lack of participation and advocacy during the sentencing stage," but it was not disturbed enough to reverse the conviction or sentence.[20]

Nineteen years later, a United States Court of Appeals set aside the conviction and death sentence, finding that Fisher's lawyer was

---

16 Even though George McFarland's lawyer was snoring, the presiding judge took no action, saying, "The Constitution does not say that the lawyer has to be awake." John Makeig, "Asleep on the job: slaying trial boring, lawyer said", *Houston Chronicle*, 14 August 1992, p. A35. McFarland's conviction and death sentence were twice upheld by the Texas Court of Criminal Appeals. *Ex parte McFarland*, 163 S.W.3d 743 (Tex. Crim. App. 2005); *McFarland v. State*, 928 S.W.2d 482 (Tex. Crim. App. 1996). Carl Johnson was executed even though his lawyer, Joe Frank Cannon, slept during parts of trial. David Dow, "The state, the death penalty, and Carl Johnson", *Boston College Law Review,* vol. 37, no. 4 (1 July 1996), pp. 691-711. Cannon also slept during the trial of Calvin Burdine. The Texas Court of Criminal Appeals upheld the conviction and sentence, but the federal court of appeals set aside the conviction, holding, over a bitter dissent, that a sleeping lawyer is absent from trial and thus a denial of counsel. *Burdine v. Johnson*, 262 F.3d 336 (5th Cir. 2001) (en banc).

17 See Stephen B. Bright and Sia M. Sanneh, "Fifty years of defiance and resistance after Gideon v. Wainwright", *Yale Law Journal,* vol. 122, no. 8 (2013), pp. 2150-2174, available from www.yalelawjournal.org/essay/fifty-years-of-defiance-and-resistance-after-gideon-v-wainwright; Kenneth Williams, "Ensuring the capital defendant's right to competent counsel: it's time for some standards!", *Wayne Law Review*, vol. 51 (2005), pp. 129-162; Jeffrey L. Kirchmeier, "Drink, drugs, and drowsiness: the constitutional right to effective assistance of counsel and the Strickland prejudice requirement", *Nebraska Law Review*, vol. 75 (1996), pp. 425, 455-462; Bruce A. Green, "Lethal fiction: the meaning of 'counsel' in the Sixth Amendment", *Iowa Law Review*, vol. 78 (1993), pp. 433 ff.

18 *Fisher v. Gibson*, 282 F.3d 1283, 1293 (10th Cir. 2002).

19 Ibid., p. 1289.

20 *Fisher v. State*, 739 P.2d 523, 525 (Okla.Crim.App.1987).

"grossly inept," had "sabotaged" Fisher's defence by repeatedly reiterating the state's version of events, and was disloyal by "exhibiting actual doubt and hostility toward his client's case."[21] The Court of Appeals would not reach the same result today, because Congress has severely restricted its power to review state court judgments and grant habeas corpus relief.[22] Today, Fisher would probably be executed. And Robert Holsey's death sentence would almost certainly have been set aside if the federal courts had considered his case before the restrictions were adopted.

James Fisher was assigned another bad lawyer for his retrial in 2005. The lawyer was drinking heavily, abusing cocaine and neglecting his cases.[23] The lawyer physically threatened Fisher at a pretrial hearing and, as a result, Fisher refused to attend his own trial.[24] He was again convicted and sentenced to death, but this time Oklahoma's highest criminal court recognized the disgraceful incompetence of his lawyer and set the conviction aside.[25] Prosecutors agreed to Fisher's release in July 2010, provided that he be banished from Oklahoma forever.[26]

> "THE DEATH PENALTY
> IS ONE OF AMERICA'S
> MOST PROMINENT
> VESTIGES OF SLAVERY
> AND RACIAL OPPRESSION."
> —Stephen B. Bright

Juan Balderas was sentenced to death in Houston in March 2014. He was represented by Jerome Godinich, an attorney who missed the statute of limitations in two federal habeas corpus cases five years

---

21 Ibid., pp. 1289, 1300, 1308.
22 The Antiterrorism and Effective Death Penalty Act, adopted in 1996, restricts federal review of convictions and death sentences imposed in the state courts in many ways. Among its provisions is one that provides that habeas relief may not be granted unless the state court's decision "was contrary to, or involved an unreasonable application of, clearly established Federal law, as determined by the Supreme Court of the United States" 28 U.S.C. § 2254(d)(1) (2006). The Supreme Court has held that a "state court's determination that a claim lacks merit precludes federal habeas relief so long as 'fairminded jurists could disagree' on the correctness of the state court's decision." *Harrington v. Richter*, 131 S. Ct. 770, 786 (2011), quoting *Yarborough v. Alvarado*, 541 U.S. 652, 664 (2004). The Court added in Richter: "If this standard is difficult to meet, that is because it was meant to be" (ibid.).
23 *Fisher v. State*, 206 P.3d 607, 610-11 (Okla. Crim. App. 2009).
24 Ibid., p. 610.
25 Ibid., pp. 612-613.
26 Dan Barry, "In the rearview mirror, Oklahoma and death row", *New York Times*, 10 August 2010, available from www.nytimes.com/2010/08/11/us/11land.html.

earlier, depriving his clients of any review of their cases by inde-pendent, life-tenure federal judges.[27] Both clients were executed. Yet, despite such gross malpractice, the Texas Bar took no action, nor did the Texas Court of Criminal Appeals. The trial court judges in Hous-ton continued appointing Godinich to defend poor people accused of crimes, including in capital cases. He has been the lawyer in as many as 350 criminal cases at one time.

Micah Brown was sentenced to death in May 2014, represented by Toby Wilkinson, who filed appellate briefs in two capital cases in 2006 that contained gibberish, repetitions, and rambling arguments. In one case, Wilkinson clearly lifted passages from one of his previous cases so that in places the brief discussed the wrong crime and used the wrong names. In the other case, Wilkinson included portions of letters sent to him by his client.[28] No matter how egregiously lawyers handle a capital case, Texas judges keep appointing them to represent others.

Lawyers have missed the statute of limitations in at least seven other cases in Texas. In 2014, the federal courts refused to consider an appeal in the case of Louis Castro Perez, who was sentenced to death in Texas, because his lawyer without telling Perez or other counsel on the case did not file a notice of appeal.[29] One judge dissented, pointing out that the lawyer's failure to file a notice of appeal was "an egregious breach of the duties an attorney owes her client" and that Perez had made a strong showing that he may have been sentenced to death in violation of the Constitution.[30] In Florida, lawyers assigned to represent condemned inmates have missed the statute of limitations in 34 cases, depriving their clients of any review of their cases by federal courts.[31]

Many people are sentenced to death and executed in the United States not because they committed the worst crimes, but because they had the misfortune to be assigned the worst lawyers. Over 100 people

---

27 Lise Olsen, "Lawyers' late filings can be deadly for inmates", *Houston Chronicle,* 22 March 2009, available from www.chron.com/news/houston-texas/article/Slow-paperwork-in-death-row-cases-ends-final-1736308.php.

28 Maro Robbins, "Convict's odds today may rest on gibberish", *San Antonio Express-News*, 24 August 2006.

29 *Perez v. Stephens*, 745 F.3d 174 (5th Cir. 2014).

30 Ibid., pp. 182, 187, 191-92 (Dennis, J., dissenting).

31 *Lugo v. Secretary, 750 F.3d 1198, 1216-18, 1222-26 (11th Cir. 2014) (Martin, J., dissenting) (listing the 34 cases).*

sentenced to death in Houston, Harris County, Texas, have been executed in the last 40 years. The reason is no secret: Harris County judges appoint incompetent lawyers to represent people facing the death penalty[32] and, after they are sentenced to death, the condemned are assigned equally bad lawyers to represent them in post-conviction proceedings. There is not even the pretence of fairness.[33]

United States Supreme Court Justice Ruth Bader Ginsburg has said, "I have yet to see a death case, among the dozens coming to the Supreme Court on eve of execution petitions, in which the defendant was well represented at trial."[34] United States Circuit Judge Boyce Martin has pointed out that defendants with "decent lawyers" often avoid death sentences, while those assigned bad lawyers are sentenced to death.[35]

It is disturbing how commonly courts and prosecutors are willing to overlook the gross incompetence of counsel when it occurs, and how doggedly they try to defend the death sentences that result. Trial judges, who are elected in most states, are often the ones who appointed the incompetent lawyers. And they appoint them in case after case, as Texas judges have done with Jerome Godinich and Toby Wilkinson. Prosecutors have no incentive to demand that their courtroom adversaries be qualified and effective. The poor quality of counsel in capital cases is well known, but very little, if anything, is being done about it in many states.

---

32 For example, one lawyer repeatedly appointed by judges in Houston had 20 clients sentenced to death due largely to his failure to "conduct even rudimentary investigations." Adam Liptak, "A lawyer known best for losing capital cases", New York Times, 17 May 2010, available from www.nytimes.com/2010/05/18/us/18bar.html?_r=0. Houston judges repeatedly appointed Ron Mock, despite his poor performance in capital cases. Sara Rimer and Raymond Bonner, "Texas lawyer's death row record a concern", New York Times, 11 June 2000, available from www.nytimes.com/2000/06/11/us/texas-lawyer-s-death-row-record-a-concern.html. Sixteen people represented by Mock were sentenced to death. Andrew Tilghman, "State bar suspends troubled local lawyer," Houston Chronicle, 12 February 2005. Another favourite was Joe Frank Cannon, who was known for trying cases like "greased lightning" and not always being able to stay awake during trials; 10 people represented by Cannon were sentenced to death. Paul M. Barrett, "Lawyer's fast work on death cases raises doubts about the system", Wall Street Journal, 7 September 1994.

33 Stephen B. Bright, "Death in Texas: not even the pretense of fairness", The Champion, vol. 23 (July 1999), pp. 1-10, available from http://library.law.yale.edu/sites/default/files/death_in_texas_champion_99.pdf; Stephen B. Bright, "Elected judges and the death penalty in Texas: why full habeas corpus review by independent federal judges is indispensable to protecting constitutional rights", Texas Law Review, vol. 78 (2000), pp. 1805-1837, available from http://library.law.yale.edu/sites/default/files/electedjudges.pdf.

34 Ruth Bader Ginsburg, "In pursuit of the public good: lawyers who care", lecture at the District of Columbia School of Law, 9 April 2001, available from www.supremecourt.gov/publicinfo/speeches/viewspeeches.aspx?Filename=sp_04-09-01a.html.

35 Moore v. Parker, 425 F.3d 250, 268 (6th Cir. 2005) (Martin, J., dissenting).

RACIAL DISCRIMINATION

The death penalty is one of America's most prominent vestiges of slavery and racial oppression.[36] It was essential to the institution of slavery. Michigan abolished the death penalty in 1846, and other northern states repealed their death statutes or restricted the use of the death penalty before the Civil War. But that could not be done in the South—in states that had a captive population. After the Civil War, the death penalty continued to be imposed on African Americans; some crimes were punishable by death depending upon the race of the offender and the victim. Slavery was perpetuated through the system of convict leasing: Black people were arrested on minor charges—such as loitering, not having proper papers, or theft, and then leased to the railroads, coal mines and turpentine camps.[37]

Today, the courts remain the part of American society least affected by the civil rights movement of the mid-20th century. Many courtrooms in the South today look no different than they did in the 1950s. The judge is white, the prosecutors are white, the court-appointed lawyers are white, and, even in communities with substantial African American populations, the jury is often all white. It is well known and well documented that a person of colour is more likely than a white person to be stopped by police, to be abused during that stop, to be arrested after the stop, to be denied bail when brought to court, and to receive a severe sentence, whether it is jail instead of probation or the death penalty instead of life imprisonment without the possibility of parole.[38]

The two most important decisions made in every death penalty case are made by prosecutors: whether to seek the death penalty and whether to

---

36 See Stephen B. Bright, "Discrimination, death and denial: the tolerance of racial discrimination in the infliction of the death penalty", *Santa Clara Law Review*, vol. 35 (1995), pp. 433-483, available from http://library.law.yale.edu/sites/default/files/discrimination_death.pdf.

37 Douglas A. Blackmon's *Slavery by Another Name: The Re-Enslavement of Black Americans from the Civil War to World War II (New York, Doubleday, 2008)* describes how slavery was perpetuated until World War II in Alabama through convict leasing; David M. Oshinsky's *Worse than Slavery: Parchman Farm and the Ordeal of Jim Crow Justice (New York, Free Press, 1996)* describes convict leasing in Mississippi and other southern states.

38 See, for example, Amy E. Lerman and Vesla M. Weaver, *Arresting Citizenship: The Democratic Consequences of American Crime Control (Chicago, University of Chicago Press, 2014)*; Cynthia E. Jones, "'Give us free': addressing racial disparities in bail determinations", *New York University Journal of Legislation and Public Policy*, vol. 16 (2013), pp. 919 ff; Michelle Alexander, *The New Jim Crow: Mass Incarceration in the Age of Colorblindness (New York, Free Press, 2010)*.

resolve the case through a plea bargain for a sentence less than death. Those decisions are often influenced by race. Some people who are intellectually disabled or mentally ill reject plea offers with little or no understanding of what they are doing and are later sentenced to death at trial.

Prosecutors continue to use their discretionary strikes to prevent or minimize the participation of members of racial minorities on juries. A Supreme Court decision purportedly preventing such discrimination by requiring prosecutors to give race-neutral reasons for their strikes is widely regarded as a farce. After calling the process a "charade," one court described it as follows: "The State may provide the trial court with a series of pat race-neutral reasons .... [W]e wonder if the reasons can be given without a smile. Surely, new prosecutors are given a manual, probably entitled, 'Handy Race-Neutral Explanations' or '20 Time-Tested Race-Neutral Explanations.'"[39] And, indeed, just such a "cheat sheet" of pat race-neutral reasons to justify the strike of any minority jury member came to light in North Carolina. A one-page handout titled "Batson Justifications: Articulating Juror Negatives" containing a list of reasons a prosecutor could give for strikes of minorities was distributed at the Conference of District Attorneys' statewide trial advocacy course called "Top Gun II."[40] A North Carolina court found that a prosecutor had used reasons from the list to justify striking African Americans in four capital cases.[41] The court also found that in capital cases in North Carolina, "prosecutors strike African Americans at double the rate they strike other potential jurors."[42] The probability of such a disparity occurring in a race-neutral process is less than one in ten trillion.[43] The court found a history of "resistance" by prosecutors "to permit greater participation on juries by African Americans." It continued:

---

39   *People v. Randall*, 671 N.E.2d 60, 65 (Ill. App. 1996). A judge discusses the reluctance of judges to find that prosecutors intentionally discriminated and then lied about it by giving pretextual reasons for their strikes—the finding the Supreme Court requires to prohibit a strike motivated by race—in Mark W. Bennett, "Unraveling the Gordian knot of implicit bias in jury selection: the problems of judge-dominated voir dire, the failed promise of Batson, and proposed solutions", *Harvard Law & Policy Review*, vol. 4 (2010), pp. 149 ff.

40   *State v. Golpin*, Cumberland Co., NC, Superior Nos. 97 CRS 42314-15, 98 CRS 34832, 35044, 01 CRS 65079, at 73-74, ¶¶ 68-72 (Dec. 13, 2012), available from https://www.aclu.org/files/assets/rja_order_12-13-12.pdf.

41   Ibid., pp. 74-77, ¶¶ 72-79.

42   Ibid., pp. 112-201, ¶¶ 171-393. The Court found that prosecutors statewide struck 52.8 per cent of eligible black venire members and 25.7 per cent of all other eligible venire members. Ibid., p. 153, ¶ 254.

43   Ibid.

That resistance is exemplified by trainings sponsored by the North Carolina Conference of District Attorneys where prosecutors learned not to examine their own prejudices and present persuasive cases to a diverse cast of jurors, but to circumvent the constitutional prohibition against race discrimination in jury selection.[44]

The Supreme Court has held that states must minimize the risk of race coming into play in the decisions that lead to imposition of the death penalty.[45] But this raises the question of how much racial bias is acceptable in the process through which courts condemn people to die. With the long history of slavery, lynchings, convict leasing, segregation, racial oppression and now mass incarceration that has a much greater impact on racial minorities, surely states should eliminate any chance that racial prejudice might play a role. But there is only one way to do that: by eliminating the death penalty.

DEATH FOR PEOPLE WITH INTELLECTUAL LIMITATIONS AND MENTAL ILLNESSES

There are other equally troubling questions. How much uncertainty is acceptable with regard to executing people of low intelligence and people who are mentally ill? Are juries able to measure precisely the degree of culpability of an intellectually disabled person? Are they able to discern whether people are so intellectually disabled (or "mentally retarded") that they are exempt from the death penalty,[46] or not quite intellectually disabled enough, so that it is acceptable to execute them? Is a jury capable of determining whether profoundly mentally ill people are so impaired that their culpability is reduced, so that they should be spared the death penalty, or so dangerous that they should be executed?

Different people on different juries make those decisions, but it is impossible for them to make them consistently or to know which ones are reaching the right conclusions. Intellectual disability cannot be precisely measured. Psychiatrists and psychologists do not fully

---

44 Ibid., pp. 4–5.
45 *McCleskey v. Kemp*, 481 U.S. 279 (1987); *Turner v. Murray*, 476 U.S. 28, 37 (1986).
46 *Atkins v. Virginia*, 536 U.S. 304 (2002) (holding that execution of the intellectually disabled, then called the "mentally retarded," violates the Eighth Amendment).

understand mental illness and often disagree with regard to its existence, severity and influence on behaviour. Capital cases are often influenced by the passions and prejudices of the moment, which distort the decision-making process.

As a result, there are many intellectually disabled and mentally ill people on death rows throughout the country. Among them is Andre Lee Thomas, sentenced to death in Texas. He suffers from schizophrenia and psychotic delusions and has gouged out both his eyes.

After engaging in bizarre behaviour and attempting suicide, Thomas stabbed and killed his wife and two children, acting upon a voice that he thought was God's telling him that he needed to kill them using three different knives so as not to "cross contaminate" their blood and "allow the demons inside them to live." He used a different knife on each one and carved out the children's hearts and part of his wife's lung, which he had mistaken for her heart, and stuffed them into his pockets. He then stabbed himself in the heart which, he thought, would assure the death of the demons that had inhabited his wife and children.

After being hospitalized for his chest wound, he was taken to jail, where he gave the police a calm, complete and coherent account of his activities and his reasons for them. In jail, five days after the killings, Thomas read in the Bible, "If the right eye offends thee, pluck it out." Thomas gouged out his right eye. After being sentenced to death and sent to death row, he gouged out his left eye and ate it.[47]

Scott Panetti, sentenced to death in Texas, suffered from schizophrenia, fragmented personality, delusions and hallucinations for which he was hospitalized numerous times before committing the crimes for which he was sentenced to death. He was unable to overcome his mental illnesses even though he took medication that could not have been tolerated by a person not suffering from extreme psychosis. One day, he dressed in camouflage, drove to the home of his estranged wife's parents and shot and killed them in front of

---

47   Marc Bookman, "How crazy is too crazy to be executed?", *Mother Jones*, 12 February 2013, available from www.motherjones.com/politics/2013/02/andre-thomas-death-penalty-mental-illness-texas; *Ex Parte Andre Lee Thomas*, 2009 Westlaw 693606 (Tex. Crim. App. March 18, 2009) (Cochran, J., concurring).

his wife and daughter. He was found competent to stand trial and allowed to represent himself. He wore a cowboy suit during trial and attempted to subpoena Jesus Christ, John F. Kennedy, and a number of celebrities, some dead and some alive. His behaviour at trial was described as bizarre, scary and trance-like, rendering his trial "a judicial farce."[48]

Since his trial in 1995, the courts have debated whether Mr. Panetti understands the relationship between his punishment and the crimes he committed, just as courts often wrestle with whether mentally ill people are capable of participating in a trial, cooperating with their lawyers and making decisions in their cases. Some experts testify that they are capable, and other experts testify they are not. The prosecution will always present an expert who says the person is malingering, even in cases in which, long before any criminal act, there was bizarre behaviour, paranoia, delusions, treatment with psychotropic drugs, hospitalizations, electroshock therapy, suicide attempts or self-mutilation. Judges, if they are free from political influences in deciding the issue, try to comprehend the incomprehensible and parse legal concepts when dealing with manifestations of mental disorders. But at best, their rulings are "a hazardous guess."[49]

The more fundamental question is why people like Andre Lee Thomas and Scott Panetti, who are undoubtedly profoundly mentally ill, are subject to the death penalty. Of course they committed horrendous crimes, took innocent lives that left others suffering and scarred for life, and must be isolated to protect society. But through no fault of their own, they are tormented souls suffering from devastating afflictions that leave them unable to think and reason like people who are not so afflicted. That is greater punishment that any court can impose.

The intellectually disabled and mentally ill are at an enormous disadvantage in the criminal courts. Some have no family support, and others have families afflicted with the same limitations or disorders that they have. Their court-appointed lawyers may know nothing about their disabilities, have no idea how to interact with them, and

---

48 *Panetti v. Quarterman*, 551 U.S. 930, 936–37 (2007).
49 *Ford v. Wainwright*, 477 U.S. 399, 412 (1986), quoting *Solesbee v. Balkcom*, 339 U.S. 9, 23 (1950) (Frankfurter, J., dissenting).

know nothing about how to conduct an investigation of the disability or which experts to consult. In many cases, they do not have adequate resources for expert consultation or testing.

The Alabama lawyers who represented Holly Wood, who was convicted of the murder of his ex-girlfriend, did not present his limited intellectual functioning as a reason he should be spared the death penalty. It would not have been difficult. Special education teachers who had Mr. Wood in their classes at the local school would have testified that his IQ was probably "low to mid 60s," that Wood was "educable mentally retarded or trainable mentally retarded,"[50] and that, even at the time of his trial, he could read only at the third-grade level and could "not use abstraction skills much beyond the low average range of intellect."[51] Alabama executed Mr. Wood, a black man, in 2010.

CONCLUSION

The United States promises equal justice for all in its Constitution and its pledge of allegiance and above the entrance to its Supreme Court. Yet poverty, race and mental impairment influence the selection of those who will be subject to what Justice Arthur Goldberg called the "greatest conceivable degradation to the dignity of the human personality."[52] Finality—not justice—has become the ultimate goal of the American legal system. Processing cases in as little time as possible—not competent representation, equal justice or protection of the most vulnerable—is the concern of most courts, even in cases where life and death are at stake. Technicalities and procedural rules made up by the Supreme Court and Congress now prevent enforcement of the Bill of Rights in most capital cases, particularly those with bad lawyers.

However, there is growing recognition that this is not moral, just or right. Former President Jimmy Carter, who as Governor of Georgia signed into law in March 1973 Georgia's death penalty statute, called on 12 November 2013 for an end to capital punishment, because it is being imposed on the poor, members of racial minorities and people

---

50   *Wood v. Allen*, 542 F.3d 1281, 1324 (11th Cir. 2008) (Barkett, J., dissenting) (quoting testimony
       of teachers), denial of relief affirmed, 558 U.S. 290 (2010).
51   Ibid. (Barkett, J., dissenting) (quoting the testimony of a psychologist of evaluated Wood.
52   Arthur Goldberg, letter to the editor, *Boston Globe, 16 August 1976.*

with diminished mental capacity.[53] Supreme Court Justice John Paul Stevens, who voted to uphold the death penalty in 1976, observed before leaving the Court that there are fewer procedural protections for those facing death, a strong probability that race influences who is sentenced to death, and a "real risk of error" with irrevocable consequences. He concluded that "the imposition of the death penalty represents 'the pointless and needless extinction of life with only marginal contributions to any discernible social or public purposes.'"[54] The death penalty has recently been abandoned by Connecticut, Illinois, Maryland, New Jersey, New Mexico and New York, and governors have declared moratoriums on the death penalty in Colorado, Oregon and Washington.[55] Perhaps there will be a re-examination of the death penalty before too much more damage is done.

---

53 "Remarks by former U.S. President Jimmy Carter at the National Symposium on the Modern Death Penalty in America", 12 November 2013, available from www.cartercenter.org/news/editorials_speeches/death-penalty-speech-111213.html; American Bar Association, *National Symposium on the Modern Death Penalty*, available from www.americanbar.org/groups/individual_rights/projects/death_penalty_due_process_review_project/national_syposium_death_penalty_carter_center.html (including videos of presentations by President Carter and others).

54 *Baze v. Rees*, 553 U.S. 35, 83 (2008) (Stevens, J., concurring), quoting Justice White's concurring opinion in *Furman v. Georgia*, 408 U.S. 238, 312 (1972) (White, J., concurring).

55 John W. Hickenlooper, Governor, State of Colorado, "Executive order: death sentence reprieve", 22 May 2013, available from www.deathpenaltyinfo.org/documents/COexecutiveorder.pdf; "Gov. John Kitzhaber of Oregon declares a moratorium on all executions", available from www.deathpenaltyinfo.org/gov-john-kitzhaber-oregon-declares-moratorium-all-executions; Governor Jay Inslee of Washington, "Governor Inslee's remarks announcing a capital punishment moratorium", available from www.deathpenaltyinfo.org/documents/InsleeMoratorium-Remarks.pdf.

THE DEATH PENALTY IN THE COMMONWEALTH CARIBBEAN: JUSTICE OUT OF REACH?

Arif Bulkan[1]

The Commonwealth Caribbean is made up of 12 independent nations, all former colonies of Great Britain: Antigua and Barbuda, the Bahamas, Barbados, Belize, Dominica, Grenada, Guyana, Jamaica, Saint Kitts and Nevis, Saint Lucia, Saint Vincent and the Grenadines and Trinidad and Tobago. In the remaining countries of the English-speaking Caribbean, namely the dependent territories of Anguilla, Bermuda, British Virgin Islands, Cayman Islands, Montserrat and the Turks and Caicos, the death penalty was abolished in 1999.[2]

The legal systems in these countries remain largely based on the common law system they inherited from Great Britain. They diverged during and after colonisation, but their structure and systems share the same foundation, and substantive laws are similar in many respects. All but three of the countries of the Commonwealth Caribbean have retained the Privy Council based in London as their final appellate court—one residual element of colonialism that has proven significant in death penalty issues. Barbados, Belize and Guyana were the first countries to accept the appellate jurisdiction of the Caribbean Court of Justice, which was established by treaty in 2001 and came into operation in 2005 with its headquarters in Port of Spain, Trinidad and Tobago.[3]

CURRENT STATUS OF THE DEATH PENALTY

In all the colonial possessions of Britain in the Caribbean, the death sentence was mandatory for a number of offences including murder and treason. After independence, although it was increasingly viewed

---

1   Arif Bulkan is a member of the Faculty of Law at the University of the West Indies.
2   Roger Hood and Carolyn Hoyle, *The Death Penalty: A Worldwide Perspective*, 4th ed. (Oxford, Oxford University Press, 2008), p. 104.
3   *Agreement Establishing the Caribbean Court of Justice* (14 February 2001), available from www.caribbeancourtofjustice.org/court-instruments/the-agreement-establishing-the-ccj.

as incompatible with evolving human rights standards and ineffective as a tool of law enforcement, it survived constitutionally across the Commonwealth Caribbean through one principal mechanism. This was the constitutional savings clause, of which there are two types in Caribbean constitutions:

- A "special savings" clause preserves punishments predating independence from challenge based on the prohibition, in the constitution's bill of rights, of torture and inhuman and degrading treatment. It can be found in the bill of rights of all of the constitutions.[4]

- A "general savings" clause preserves laws predating independence from challenge based on any provision of the bill of rights. This far more sweeping provision was only inserted in the constitutions of the first five territories to achieve independence.[5]

Theoretically, these provisions would protect the death penalty in the Commonwealth Caribbean from challenge on human rights grounds, since it predated the independence-era constitutions both as a punishment and as a law. However, over a decade beginning in the early 1990s, the Privy Council restricted the imposition of the death penalty across most of the Commonwealth Caribbean. They did so incrementally, principally by focusing on how the penalty was imposed and carried out. Key issues addressed during this period are described below.

Delays in carrying out sentences

In 1993, in a case from Jamaica in which two convicted murderers had been on death row for more than 12 years, the Privy Council held that the delay constituted cruel and unusual punishment, and as a remedy they commuted the sentences of both to life imprisonment.[6]

---

4   A standard formulation is that contained in s 7(2) of the Constitution of Antigua and Barbuda: "Nothing contained in or done under the authority of any law shall be held to be inconsistent with or in contravention of this section to the extent that the law in question authorises the infliction of any description of punishment that was lawful in Antigua on 31st October 1981."

5   Jamaica, s 26(8) of the 1962 Constitution, replaced by section 13(12) in the amended 2011 version; Trinidad and Tobago, s 6; Guyana, article 152; Barbados, s 26; and the Bahamas, article 30.

6   *Pratt and Morgan v. AG of Jamaica* (1993) 43 WIR 340.

In addition, they held that to keep any condemned prisoner on death row for more than five years would violate the constitutional prohibition against inhuman or degrading punishment, and that the special savings clause did not apply because the delay would not have been lawful prior to independence. The punishment per se was not invalidated but rather its manner of implementation.

This was a fine distinction that some found unsupportable,[7] but the impact was immediate and dramatic. In territories all across the Caribbean, scores of condemned prisoners awaiting execution for more than five years became the beneficiaries of the ban on excessive delay, leading to the observation by two senior Caribbean judges that the five-year rule came to be applied with "guillotine-like finality."[8] The ruling meant that Caribbean countries opting to retain the death penalty had to ensure that their justice systems operated more efficiently. The position of the Privy Council on this was uncompromising: "a State that wishes to retain capital punishment must accept the responsibility of ensuring that execution follows as swiftly as practicable after sentence, allowing a reasonable time for appeal and consideration of reprieve. . . . Appellate procedures that echo down the years are not compatible with capital punishment. The death row phenomenon must not become established as a part of our jurisprudence."[9]

Pardons

Next to be addressed were the procedures around the granting of pardons, also referred to as the exercise of the prerogative of mercy, during which the totality of a condemned person's case is considered by a committee that advises the head of state whether the death sentence deserves to be commuted.[10] Historically, the condemned person had no right to see the material being put before the Mercy Committee or to make representations before it.[11] That position was

---

7   Berthan Macaulay, "The Jamaica Constitution: conflict of powers—the Pratt and Morgan case" (1993) 18 WILJ 45.

8   *Joseph and Boyce v. AG of Barbados* (2006) 69 WIR 104, per de la Bastide P and Saunders J at [49].

9   Macaulay, "The Jamaica Constitution", p. 359.

10 See, for example, Jamaica Constitution, ss. 90 and 91.

11 *De Freitas v. Benny* (1975) 27 WIR 318; *Reckley v. Minister for Public Safety (No. 2)* (1996) 47 WIR 9.

based on the view that mercy is not a legal right but an act of grace. However, the Privy Council reconsidered this position, eventually holding that the prerogative of mercy should be exercised by procedures that are fair and proper and amenable to judicial review.[12] In the case that resulted in this ruling, this meant that condemned prisoners were held to be entitled to sufficient notice of the date on which their case would be considered so that they or their advisers could prepare representations, which the committee would be bound to consider.

This Privy Council decision was foreshadowed by the Court of Appeal of Guyana, which had ruled shortly before that the exercise of the prerogative of mercy operates more as a safety net for those wrongly convicted than as an act of grace.[13] In that case, the court reasoned that, as a constitutional republic, Guyana should not have the same reverence for the prerogative, which is founded on the arbitrary will of kings. In the case of the prerogative of mercy, this meant scrutinising, not the decision itself, but the manner in which it was reached.

These decisions, too, affected many prisoners on death row, for irregularities in the way their cases had been reviewed potentially meant they needed to be reconsidered. Inevitably, this entailed a further delay, which would trigger the embargo on death-row waits of over five years.

Petitions to international bodies

When a country accedes to certain international treaties, its citizens receive the right to petition the treaty body directly regarding a breach of a right affirmed by the treaty. A possibly unanticipated consequence was that as death row inmates availed themselves of this right, the waiting time post-conviction lengthened. Often, by the time a decision was delivered, the five-year time limit had expired, which meant that the state could no longer execute the convict. In frustration, Caribbean states tried in a number of ways to circumvent this problem. Guyana, Jamaica and Trinidad and Tobago withdrew from Optional Protocol 1, which provides the right of

---

12 *Lewis et al v. AG of Jamaica* [2000] 3 WLR 1785.
13 *Yassin and Thomas v. AG of Guyana* GY 1996 CA 3 (Carilaw).

petition to the Human Rights Committee, and both Trinidad and Guyana re-acceded with a reservation.[14] However, the Committee held this reservation to be invalid, since by its discriminatory purpose it offended basic principles embodied in the Convention,[15] and in response the government of Trinidad and Tobago withdrew from the Protocol again in 2000. Other conflicts involved attempts to carry out executions while petitions were pending, one notorious instance being the execution of Glen Ashby in 1994, just one month before the five-year post-conviction deadline would have expired.[16]

These tensions culminated in fierce legal battles, as condemned prisoners challenged the constitutionality of carrying out executions while petitions were still pending. Eventually, it was held by the Privy Council in relation to Trinidad and Tobago that the due process right entitled condemned prisoners to be allowed to complete any appellate or analogous legal processes that were capable of resulting in a reduction or commutation of their sentences before that process was rendered nugatory by executive action (such as prescribing unrealistic time limits for the petitions or executing prisoners whose petitions were pending).[17] At that time, only the Trinidad and Tobago Constitution used the language of "due process" in its bill of rights, but this decision was shortly thereafter held to be applicable to Jamaica (and by extension all the remaining countries of the Caribbean except Guyana) through the guarantee of protection of the law.[18]

Defying predictions that it was going to reverse the perceived abolitionist tendencies of the Privy Council, the Caribbean Court of Justice in its first major death penalty appeal arrived at a similar result, holding that to execute a prisoner while an international petition is pending would be a violation of the right to protection of the law.[19]

---

14 Hood and Hoyle, *The Death Penalty*, p. 108.
15 *Kennedy v. Trinidad and Tobago* CCPR/C/67/D/845/1999, paragraph 6.7.
16 Report of the Special Rapporteur on Extrajudicial, Summary or Arbitrary Executions, 14 December 1994, E/CN.4/1995/61, paragraph 382.
17 *Thomas and Hilaire v. Baptiste* (1998) 54 WIR 387.
18 *Lewis et al v. AG of Jamaica* [2000] 3 WLR 1785.
19 *Joseph and Boyce v. AG of Barbados* (2006) 69 WIR 104.

Mandatory sentences

The next major development was related to the mandatory nature of the death sentence. Early cases had espoused the view that this aspect saved the death penalty from unconstitutionality since it would be applied without discrimination to all those convicted of murder.[20] By the time this view came to be rejected, the death sentence was nonetheless held to be valid in the Caribbean because of the special savings clause (preserving punishments predating independence)—though not for long.

First, in countries such as Belize where the constitution had no savings clause, the sentence was struck down because of its indiscriminate scope—applying to all convictions for murder despite the potential variations in culpability.[21] It was also struck down in Jamaica, which had amended the substantive law to rationalise the offence of murder.[22] In relation to this rationalisation, the Privy Council held that there could be no category of capital murder for which a conviction automatically resulted in a death sentence, and since the law had been amended to create these offences, it was no longer the protected pre-independence law and thus lost its immunity. Reading amendments to the law in the Bahamas strictly, the Privy Council overturned the mandatory aspect of the death sentence there as well.[23]

A more ingenious (and controversial) interpretation was applied to the countries of the Eastern Caribbean, where, notwithstanding the special savings clause, the mandatory nature of the death penalty was struck down on the ground that this clause only preserved punishments that were "authorised." Since the death penalty was mandated for certain offences, it could not be said to be authorised and was therefore not protected by the clause, and thus it constituted a violation of the prohibition against inhuman and degrading punishments.[24]

---

20 *De Freitas v. Benny* (1975) 27 WIR 318; *Ong ah Chuan v. Public Prosecutor* [1981] AC 648.
21 *Reyes v. the Queen* [2002] UKPC 11.
22 *Watson v. the Queen* [2004] UKPC 34.
23 *Bowe and Davis v. the Queen* (2006) 68 WIR 10.
24 *The Queen v. Hughes* [2002] UKPC 12 (St Lucia); *Fox v. the Queen* [2002] UKPC 13 (St Vincent).

At the end of this unprecedented period of judicial activism, only three countries were left with a mandatory death penalty: Barbados, Guyana (which had abolished appeals to the Privy Council and was thus not bound by any of these developments[25]) and Trinidad and Tobago. Barbados and Trinidad and Tobago were able to retain the death penalty because of the general savings clause,[26] since neither country had made changes to the substantive law. In Guyana, statute has since restricted the death penalty to certain categories of murder and eliminated its mandatory aspect.[27] Thus, while the death penalty still exists across the entire Commonwealth Caribbean, only Barbados and Trinidad and Tobago apply it automatically to every conviction for murder.

APPLICATION OF THE DEATH PENALTY

There have been only a few scholarly analyses of the application of the death penalty in the Caribbean, but even the most cursory examination of decided cases suggests the existence of bias at several stages, produced by factors such as economic status, social class and mental capacity. These biases routinely affect the fairness of trials (and by extension, the safety of convictions), because they inevitably involve or lead to breaches of due process, liberty rights and evidential safeguards. In Trinidad and Tobago in particular, a number of recent studies have revealed fundamental deficiencies in the criminal justice system. These studies have been replicated to a lesser extent in other locations, and considering them along with the case law, it can be credibly argued that there are many concerns with regard to the equitable application of the death penalty in the Commonwealth Caribbean. Specific issues are considered below.

Mental capacity

In common law, the test for insanity is whether, at the time of the act in question, the defendant was labouring under such a defect of reason, due to a disease of the mind, as either not to know the

---

25 This was effected in stages in 1970 by the *Guyana Republic Act* 1970-9, s 8 and *Judicial Committee (Termination of Appeals) Act* 1970-14, and then in 1973 by the *Constitution (Amendment) Act* 1973-19, s 4.

26 *Boyce v. the Queen* [2004] UKPC 32 (PC, Barbados); *Matthew v. the State* [2004] UKPC 33 (PC, T&T).

27 Criminal Law Offences (Amendment) Act 2010, Act 21-2010 [Guy].

nature and quality of his act or, if he did know this, not to know that he was doing wrong.[28] From the time of its formulation in the mid-19th century, this test was heavily criticised,[29] yet it has endured in spite of complications regarding what constitutes a disease of the mind and the potential injustice created by the requirement to prove lack of knowledge of the quality of the act. A cursory check of reported cases suggests that this test seems to be too technical for judges to explain adequately or for jurors to evaluate sensibly, with the result that many convictions are overturned on the basis of incorrect directions.[30] Aside from its technicalities, another problem with the legal test seems to be the archaic understanding of mental illness, and its divergence from what may actually constitute a mental incapacity. This creates doubt as to whether directions in any case are properly understood and acted upon, in addition to the doubts as to whether the law adequately treats those with mental illnesses.

A case that well illustrates these difficulties is *Stephen Robinson a/c Psycho v. the State*.[31] The appellant, a destitute and homeless person, was convicted of the January 2002 murder of a security guard and sentenced to death in 2009. Medical evidence established that he had been diagnosed with schizophrenia since 1984. In the opinion of both examining psychiatrists, he had been suffering from an episode when the murder occurred, based not only on this history but also on his attire and unusual behaviour at the time in question. There was no competing evidence to contradict the medical evidence, but the jury rejected it, presumably on the belief that he was experiencing a lucid interval. Thus, the opinion of two experts (one with considerable experience) was discarded in favour of pure speculation. This is difficult to justify, and it underlines the flaws of the outdated insanity test, which are exacerbated by the rules of criminal procedure under which a determination of insanity is a question of fact for the jury.

---

28 (1843) 10 Cl & Fin 200.

29 John Cyril Smith and Brian Hogan, *Criminal Law*, 7th ed. (London, Butterworths, 1992), p. 207.

30 Amnesty International, *Caribbean: Death Penalty in the English-Speaking Caribbean: A Human Rights Issue* (AMR 05/001/2012, 30 November 2012), available from www.amnesty.org/en/library/info/AMR05/001/2012/en.

31 CATT Crim 12/2009, decision dated 29 July 2010, available from www.ttlawcourts.org.

The Court of Appeal of Trinidad and Tobago dismissed an appeal, even while describing the outcome as unfortunate. Reinforcing the incongruity of the decision was the majority's concluding passage:

> *It is unfortunate that the application of clear legal [principles] should result in the imposition of the death penalty on an individual who, on the evidence, has a long outstanding mental disability. The apparent harshness of the result of our decision might best be ameliorated, not by a distortion of the law, but rather by petitioning the appropriate authorities, that is, the Mercy Committee.*[32]

There is something profoundly amiss with a justice system that regards the outcome in a case as approximating an injustice but shunts the responsibility for addressing that injustice to extralegal means. Part of the reason for this outcome was that the legal principles described as clear by the court are in actuality archaic and repeatedly misapplied and misunderstood, so the matter was more appropriate for resolution by the court rather than the Mercy Committee.

Practical concerns also exist in relation to the institutional capacity in many Caribbean states. A recent report of the World Health Organisation disclosed several deficiencies in mental health systems across the Caribbean, including insufficient facilities, outdated practices and lack of treatment protocols.[33] Some of this could probably be traced to weak legislative frameworks, insofar as the majority of countries have mental health legislation predating independence, as well as to the under-resourcing of this sector, with an average of only 3.8 per cent of health budgets in the region being devoted to mental health.[34] Where mental health facilities are nonexistent or substandard, criminal defendants may go undiagnosed and untreated. Once caught up in criminal proceedings, it is not uncommon for people to undergo trial, conviction and sentencing without any

---

32 Ibid., p. 25.
33 World Health Organization, *WHO-AIMS Report on Mental Health Systems in the Caribbean Region* (2011), available from www.who.int/mental_health/evidence/WHO-AIMS/en.
34 Ibid., p. 13.

recognition that legal liability may be absent due to a lack of mental capacity.[35]

The appellant in *Nigel Brown v. the State*[36] had been convicted of murder and sentenced to death; after conviction, fresh evidence was obtained from a psychiatrist that he was suffering from a mental disorder that called into question his capacity to plead and understand the nature of a trial. In allowing his appeal, the Privy Council criticized the failure of the system to detect this issue earlier:

> *There is no doubt that the appellant's legal advisers should have been alert to the question of his fitness to plead. Yet no medical evidence was adduced on his behalf nor was this issue canvassed either on the trial or before the Court of Appeal. This is a matter of obvious and grave concern. The Board has been greatly exercised by the fact that these reports have been produced ex post facto and without any explanation as to why medical evidence on the issue of fitness to plead has not been produced before now.[37]*

A recent report by the Death Penalty Project concluded that "the death penalty [in the Caribbean] is regularly being imposed on persons with significant mental illness and/or intellectual disability."[38]

Expert evidence

Closely linked to the issue of mental incapacity are concerns about the use and availability of expert evidence generally, in which criminal defendants face a recurring disadvantage. This problem was highlighted in a case from Barbados in which the prosecution relied on the evidence of a forensic odontologist to establish that bite marks

---

35 Several of these cases are mentioned in Amnesty International, *Caribbean: Death Penalty in the English-Speaking Caribbean,* pp. 18-21.

36 [2012] UKPC 2 (PC, T&T).

37 Ibid., paragraph 68.

38 Saul Lehrfreund, "The systemic failure to grant special protection and all guarantees to ensure a fair trial in capital cases in the Caribbean, Africa and Asia", presentation at the Office of the High Commissioner for Human Rights panel Moving Away from the Death Penalty—Wrongful Convictions, United Nations Headquarters, New York, 28 June 2013.

on the arm of the respondent matched the teeth of the deceased. For over three years the respondent tried to obtain an independent assessment of the evidence by an expert of his own choosing, but without success since this required highly specialised and expensive expertise. The State was willing to underwrite only some of the cost of the expert's fees, and the Court of Appeal of Barbados agreed it was under no obligation to do more than that.[39] Although the Court of Appeal conceded that "bite mark analysis is a highly complex and controversial subject and it is sufficient to say for the purpose of this judgment that the respondent may be at a disadvantage if he is unable to obtain expert help in dealing with the evidence of the prosecution,"[40] it nonetheless held that the respondent was not entitled to an expert funded by the State. No such right was established in the Constitution, and in any case, an order to that effect would offend the principle of separation of powers.

This decision was overturned on appeal, on the ground that the respondent would be at such a disadvantage without expert evidence of his own as to affect the fairness of the trial.[41] But the decision of the lower court is instructive, as it reflects the disadvantage suffered by criminal defendants without the resources to mount a proper defence. Judges are not always sympathetic to the plight of low-income defendants or willing to order the state to incur expenses on their behalf. Even when a defendant ultimately succeeds, as in this case, a serious cost of airing these issues is the time that it requires, since delays are unpredictable and have the potential to prejudice the trial. The result is to place poor people in a vulnerable and unequal position, a disparity that takes on heightened significance in death penalty cases.

The poster case for such inequality is *Indravani Ramjattan v. the State*,[42] where disabilities of poverty, class and gender combined to produce an appalling instance of state-perpetrated injustice. Ms. Ramjattan was convicted along with two codefendants of the murder of her husband and sentenced to death, and it was not until her final appeal had been dismissed that she was allowed to present evidence of her mental state

---

39   *AG of Barbados v. Gibson* Civil Appeal No 8 of 2007 (decision dated 15 December 2009).
40   Ibid., paragraph 41.
41   *Gibson v. AG of Barbados* [2010] CCJ 3.
42   *Indravani Ramjattan v. the State* (1999) 54 WIR 383 (PC, T&T).

at the time of the crime. This evidence revealed a life of epic suffering. Regularly beaten as a child, she was taken out of school at age 13 and married by her mother at age 17 to a man 18 years her senior.[43] Over the course of 10 years she bore several children, all the while being subjected to extreme physical and emotional abuse by her husband. He repeatedly accused her of having other sexual relationships, while at the same time boasting of his sexual encounters with other women. Violence was a norm of the relationship, including attempted strangulation, wounding, bruising and rape—summed up by the Court of Appeal of Trinidad and Tobago as a "reign of terror."[44]

Ms. Ramjattan eventually summoned up the courage to leave her husband, escaping to live with her childhood sweetheart, but her husband hunted her down and forcibly recaptured her. By the time they got home, she was covered in blood; he then locked her in a bedroom and told her that he was going to sink her head inside her neck with a piece of wood. He struck her on the head, hands, arms, back and feet until she fell unconscious. During the final week of her husband's life, he tortured her and threatened to kill her and the children. All this was corroborated by her 10-year-old daughter, who testified that her father regularly beat her mother with his fists, belt and pieces of wood and threatened to shoot her. She managed to write a letter to her boyfriend, who came with the third accused to rescue her. The two men beat the deceased and killed him. Although she was not present at the scene and denied asking the men to kill her husband, she was convicted along with the other two of his murder, and all three were sentenced to death.

It was only after Ms. Ramjattan lost her appeal that she was able to secure a retrial. It was then revealed that she had been unable to present evidence on her mental state earlier because she did not have the money or a reasonable opportunity to engage a psychiatrist to examine her and make a report capable of being used in legal proceedings. The Privy Council was informed that it was not routine in Trinidad for the mental health of defendants in murder cases to be assessed at or before arraignment.[45] Her petition was allowed and

---

43   These facts are taken from the decision of the Court of Appeal at the re-hearing: *Indravani Ramjattan v. the State (No 2)* (1999) 57 WIR 501.
44   Ibid., p. 504.
45   (1999) 54 WIR 383 at 385.

her case remitted to the Court of Appeal of Trinidad and Tobago to consider the psychiatric evidence.

A litany of procedural irregularities were uncovered as well: Ms. Ramjattan had no counsel at the time of arrest, during the police interviews, and for more than a year after her arrest. She was tricked into signing a confession. She was pregnant at the time of her arrest, and subsequently had a miscarriage while in custody, but received no medical treatment. At the trial she was poorly represented, and her counsel did not present any evidence of the abuse she had suffered—which meant that the jury was faced with a choice of acquittal or conviction for murder.

The Court of Appeal accepted the evidence of the psychiatrist that Ms. Ramjattan, at the time of the crime, suffered from an abnormality of the mind capable of reducing her responsibility for the crime. It was the doctor's opinion that she had suffered from symptoms of depressive illness and post-traumatic stress disorder for several years leading up to the time of the offence and that her psychological reactions were also characteristic of battered-wife syndrome. For the first time anywhere in the Commonwealth Caribbean, evidence of battered-wife syndrome was accepted to establish a defence of diminished responsibility. The Court of Appeal quashed Ms. Ramjattan's conviction for murder and substituted one of manslaughter. By this time, she had already spent eight years in custody, four and a half on death row. Despite the horrific circumstances of her situation, the Court of Appeal still ordered her to serve an additional five years in prison.

This case demonstrates discrimination on several levels. The institutional and systemic failings were especially acute, occurring at every stage of Ms. Ramjattan's life. The background facts, for example, reveal an absence of state regulation so complete that it rendered girls vulnerable to parental abuse and unable to access an education. Later on, the same failings would enable a decade of spousal abuse without the implementation of laws or the intervention of social services to stem such horrific and sustained violence.[46] When she acted to protect herself, the State responded mechanically and harshly, convicting and sentencing her to the ultimate penalty with no apparent realisation of

---

46   In the Court of Appeal, the Chief Justice described this situation as endemic in Trinidad and Tobago: (1999) 57 WIR 501 at 504.

its own responsibility for the events. There were other failings as well: a legal framework that denied the victim of extreme and sustained physical abuse the defences of provocation and self-defence, exacerbated by an institutional structure that showed no understanding or empathy for her circumstances. Her situation was aggravated by poverty, and the absence of legal representation at crucial stages left her at the mercy of the police, who in their own way continued the abuse by denying her fundamental liberties.

Poverty and neglect were compounded by disabilities of gender and race, the latter on display even at the level of the Court of Appeal. Ms. Ramjattan was a woman of East Indian descent who had formed a relationship with a man of African descent—not a figure of much sympathy, as revealed in her treatment at various levels in the criminal justice system and in the transcript of the Court of Appeal proceedings. In his judgment, the Chief Justice of Trinidad and Tobago commented:

> It is, of course, no part of our duty to attribute or apportion moral blame, particularly to a woman who was subjected to that type of treatment. But we must not lose sight of the fact that at the time of the murder she was carrying the child of another man with whom she obviously, from her evidence, hoped to make a new life. There is nothing wrong with that, albeit that the other man appears to have been married himself.[47]

In other words, she did not fit the stereotype of a victim as chaste and passive—and despite the protestations of being nonjudgmental, by referring to the adultery of both participants, the suggestion that Ms. Ramjattan may have been undeserving of sympathy is a powerful subliminal message of this passage.

There are indications that the inequalities suffered by Ms. Ramjattan exist structurally as well. In 2000 one commentator said that in Trinidad and Tobago, "most of the women on death row are there as

---

47 Ibid.

a result of some form of domestic violence."[48] Whether or not this is still true, the multiple failings that existed in the Ramjattan case indicate that gender bias in the criminal justice system is an overlooked problem. One organisation, Equality Now, has suggested that the discriminatory treatment of women works in the opposite direction as well—that when they are murder victims, their perpetrators are treated far more leniently than Indravani Ramjattan was.[49]

Poverty and due process

In 2012 Amnesty International commented:

> *The criminal justice systems in many ESC countries are struggling with caseloads that far exceed their capacity. This often results in violation of due process and prolonged delays. Factors contributing to delays include inadequate staffing levels, resources and legal representation; insufficient jurors; inadequate witness protection programmes; and high and increasing crime rates. Weaknesses in forensic analysis and delays in processing evidence in crime laboratories also contribute to systemic delays and errors in trial proceedings and scheduling.*[50]

These deficiencies are intensified where defendants are poor and unrepresented, a reality of many capital cases across the Caribbean. Even though legal aid is provided by the state, the quality obtained often reflects the paltry remuneration offered. Moreover, legal aid is activated for the first time only at the preliminary inquiry, and after that may not be consistent or structured. This means that at the crucial pretrial and investigative stage, suspects are at the mercy of the state's powerful machinery. Violations thus flourish during this period when suspects are likely to be held incommunicado, without access even to relatives or friends, much less a lawyer. At this time, when a suspect is

---

48 Leonard Birdsong, "In quest of gender-bias in death penalty cases: analyzing the English speaking Caribbean experience", *Indiana International & Comparative Law Review*, vol. 10, no. 317 (2000), p. 324 ff.

49 See Equality Now, "Trinidad and Tobago: the imminent execution of a battered woman and her defenders" (1 October 1998), available from www.equalitynow.org/node/188.

50 Amnesty International, *Caribbean: Death Penalty in the English-Speaking Caribbean.*

at his or her most vulnerable, it is easier to obtain signed confessions, but the possibility that such confessions might be unreliable or just plain fabricated is suggested by the number of convictions that are challenged, often successfully, on this ground alone.[51]

Even after legal aid is provided, it is by no means assured that criminal defendants will have meaningful access to their advisers, who tend to change multiple times throughout the process. There have been several cases in which counsel was appointed on the day of the trial and either forced to go on immediately or given only a short adjournment[52]—or even for no counsel to be appointed, leaving the defendant unrepresented.[53] It is also not unusual for very junior counsel to be appointed—in one case, a lawyer of three months' standing was appointed for a defendant on the morning of the trial.[54] Predictably, in these situations the quality of representation is far below the standard required for a proper defence in any criminal case, much less one in which the possible outcome is a death sentence.

These failings are powerfully exemplified in *Ann Marie Boodram v. the State*, another case from Trinidad and Tobago.[55] The appellant had been assigned several lawyers before one was finally secured to represent her during her retrial. The court-appointed defence counsel failed to object to deposition evidence of a dead witness, failed to object to a confession despite doubts as to its voluntary nature, including an allegation that the appellant was raped by a senior police officer involved in the investigation, and most astonishing of all, conducted the majority of the defence unaware that it was a retrial. When he became aware of this, he failed to obtain the transcript of the earlier proceedings. In quashing the conviction, the Privy Council concluded that "Mr. Sawh's multiple failures, and in particular his extraordinary failure . . . to enquire into what happened at the first trial, reveal either

---

51 The Ramjattan case is a good example of a common situation, but the findings of the HRC substantiate this failing in many cases. See *Christopher Brown v. Jamaica* (775/97); *Kennedy v. Trinidad and Tobago* CCPR/C/67/D/845/1999; *Errol Johnson v. Jamaica* (588/94); *Pennant v. Jamaica* (647/95); and the cases discussed by the Inter-American Commission on Human Rights in *The Death Penalty in the Inter-American Human Rights System: From Restrictions to Abolition* (OEA/Ser.L/V/II., Doc. 68, 31 December 2011), pp. 130–138.

52 Desmond Allum and Gregory Delzin, *Report on the Criminal Justice System in Trinidad and Tobago* (2003), paragraph 88.

53 *Frank Robinson v. Jamaica*, U.N. Doc. CCPR/C/35/D/223/1987 (1989).

54 *Bernard v. the State* (2007) UKPC 34 (PC, T&T).

55 [2001] UKPC 20 (PC, T&T).

gross incompetence or a cynical dereliction of the most elementary professional duties."[56] That this is not an isolated example is revealed by the number of cases across the Caribbean where appeals have been allowed because of inadequate representation.[57]

Another problem with legal aid in most Caribbean countries is that it is often provided for trials and appeals in capital cases, but only for criminal and not constitutional proceedings,[58] and never for non-trial necessities like preparing and filing documents for an appeal.[59] This results in several injustices. Criminal defendants—often poorly educated and sometimes illiterate— are unable to prepare a Notice of Appeal. When they do, appeals are usually confined to the deficiencies of the first trial, and only rarely is fresh evidence forthcoming. With assignments occurring at the time

> "THE BULK OF KILLINGS GO UNSOLVED, THE MAJORITY OF CONVICTIONS ARE OVERTURNED ON APPEAL..."
>
> —Arif Bulkan

of trial, appellate lawyers frequently have little time to prepare the case.[60] Moreover, the state has no obligation to facilitate appeals to the Privy Council in London, and although a number of English solicitors provide pro bono assistance in death penalty cases, where the paperwork is not done in advance, this can be the end of the line for poor appellants, as happened to the last person to be executed in the Commonwealth Caribbean.

Charles Laplace was executed on 19 December 2008 in Saint Kitts and Nevis, shortly after the Eastern Caribbean Court of Appeal upheld his conviction for the murder of his wife. Laplace would have been entitled to a further appeal to the Privy Council, but no appeal was filed—presumably because he did not have the means or ability to do so. Laplace was executed after four years on death row. It remains unclear whether

---

56   Ibid., paragraph 40.
57   For examples, see *Bethel v. the State* (1998) 55 WIR 394 and *Bernard v. the State* (2007) UKPC 34 (PC, T&T).
58   Inter-American Commission on Human Rights, *The Death Penalty in the Inter-American Human Rights System*, pp. 139-146.
59   Allum and Delzin, *Report on the Criminal Justice System in Trinidad and Tobago,* paragraph 86.
60   Ibid.

the pardon guidelines established by the Privy Council[61] were faithfully followed in his case—such as affording him the opportunity to see the documents being presented to the Mercy Committee or to make representations to it. That he was executed when he had not exhausted all appeals is a graphic illustration of the disadvantages faced by the poor and the inequalities of the system.

This situation is partly attributable to the breakdown in regional policing systems, where inadequate training, unrealistic remuneration, lack of effective oversight and high levels of corruption combine to produce a toxic brew of incompetence and dishonesty.[62] Instead of conducting proper analytical and forensic work, police investigators in the Caribbean often rely solely on confessions, a practice that has long been criticised.[63] Such deficiencies inexorably affect the fairness of trials, as demonstrated by the number of convictions overturned for breaches of rights to due process and fair trial.

Arbitrary application

Recent studies of the death penalty in Trinidad and Tobago reveal not just its utter inefficacy as a deterrent but also the arbitrary nature of its application. An analysis of recorded homicides in Trinidad and Tobago between 1998 and 2002 established that the probability of a killing resulting in a conviction for murder is extremely low, with only 5 per cent of murders recorded by the police over this period resulting in a conviction for murder by the end of 2002.[64] Over the five-year period examined, 633 deaths were recorded by the police as murders, of which 280 (44.2 per cent) remained unsolved.

Of the 353 murders classified as solved by the police during this period, only 33 resulted in a conviction for murder by the end of 2005. Moreover, the clear-up rate varies with the type of murder. The authors adopted the categorisation of murders employed by the police:

---

61 *Lewis et al v. AG of Jamaica* [2000] 3 WLR 1785.

62 Carolyn Gomes, "Police accountability in the Caribbean: where are the people?", paper presented at a Workshop on Police Accountability at the Civicus World Assembly, 23-27 May 2007, Glasgow, Scotland.

63 Allum and Delzin, *Report on the Criminal Justice System in Trinidad and Tobago,* paragraph 36.

64 Roger Hood and Florence Seemungal, *A Rare and Arbitrary Fate: Conviction for Murder, the Mandatory Death Penalty and the Reality of Homicide in Trinidad and Tobago,* report to the Death Penalty Project (Oxford, Centre for Criminology, University of Oxford, 2006).

gang- and drug-related killings, killing in the course of a robbery or other crime, killing in the course of a domestic dispute (where the parties are related), killing in the course of an altercation not involving a domestic setting, and those with an unknown motive, also called "body dumped" by the police. Of the 208 killings that were classified as gang- or drug-related or involving body-dumping—just under a third of the total—there were only two convictions for murder and another two for manslaughter by the end of 2005. In contrast, killings in the course of domestic violence, which represented 17 per cent of recorded homicides, accounted for 52 per cent of the murders solved. Thus, the proportion of murders that the police recorded as solved was lowest for the category that has been increasing the most: gang- and drug-related murders, and particularly those where the victim's body was dumped. Clear-up rates were most successful for the crimes least likely to be the subject of a carefully planned act.

Review of the trials of all people charged with murder over the same five-year period revealed that, for the tiny proportion who were convicted of murder, only 8 per cent of their convictions stood after appeal. The low conviction rate was most pronounced in gang- and drug-related cases. Convictions were more likely to be for manslaughter than for murder.

Thus, the death penalty is infrequently applied in Trinidad and Tobago. Paradoxically, the type of murder that is least likely to be planned in advance and most likely to be committed in the heat of emotion, without consideration of the threat of later punishment, is the type most likely to end up with a conviction for murder. Even in this category, as much as 60 per cent of killings do not result in a murder conviction. Studies in other parts of the Caribbean also indicate a low percentage of murder convictions. In the Bahamas, for instance, while 333 murders were recorded between 2005 and 2009, only 10 cases resulted in murder convictions.[65]

International law calls for the death penalty, if it is retained, to be used only in the worst cases.[66] But this is certainly not the case in the

---

65   Amnesty International, *Caribbean: Death Penalty in the English-Speaking Caribbean*, p. 27.

66   The International Covenant on Civil and Political Rights, Article 6(2), states: "In countries which have not abolished the death penalty, sentence of death may be imposed only for the most serious crimes."

Caribbean, where all available studies indicate that it is both infrequently and arbitrarily applied. The study summarized above likened the possibility of receiving the death penalty in Trinidad and Tobago to that of being struck by lightning.[67] This underlines the vagaries and weaknesses of the criminal justice system and its profound unfairness in capital cases.

CONCLUSION

Across much of the Commonwealth Caribbean, the bulk of killings go unsolved, the majority of convictions are overturned on appeal, the administration of justice is slow, and low-income suspects face severe barriers to their ability to present an effective defence. There is strong evidence that the death penalty disproportionately affects the weak, poor and vulnerable. Caribbean states need to strengthen their criminal justice systems at both the investigative and trial levels; retaining the death penalty is unlikely to help them address their rising crime rates.

---

67   Hood and Seemungal, *A Rare and Arbitrary Fate*, paragraph 98.

THE DEATH PENALTY IN INDIA: DOWN A SLIPPERY SLOPE

Usha Ramanathan[1]

The death sentence has generated a great deal of agonized deliberation over the decades. It has been in the Indian Penal Code since 1860 and the Criminal Procedure Code since 1898. India's Constitution, promulgated in 1950, provided for the continuance of "all the law in force in the territory of India immediately before the commencement of this Constitution … until altered or repealed or amended" and "subject to the other provisions of this Constitution" (Article 372). Article 21 of the Constitution reads: "No person shall be deprived of his life or personal liberty except according to procedure established by law."

This has been understood to mean that not only personal liberty, but life itself, may be taken so long as it is "according to procedure established by law." This article in the Constitution does not establish the limits within which this power over life and death is to be exercised; the challenge to it has thus focused on judicial discretion, arbitrariness, delay, the method of execution and how the president is to exercise clemency powers.

From 1950 to the early 1970s, Parliament concerned itself with taming the death penalty. In the early 1960s, abolition of the death sentence was raised in Parliament and sent to the Law Commission to be deliberated upon. Since then, the Supreme Court has addressed it, in part because of abolitionist judges on the bench who argued that the death sentence was unconstitutional, and partly because of the vagaries that judicial discretion in sentencing brought with it.[2] And since the 1980s, Parliament has altered its position, introducing the death sentence in the Terrorism and Disruptive Activities (Prevention) Act 1985, the Narcotics and Psychotropic Substances Act 1985 and its amendment in 1988, section 364-A of the Indian Penal Code, which made kidnapping for

---

1   Usha Ramanathan is an independent law researcher working on the jurisprudence of law, poverty and rights.

2   *Jagmohan Singh v. State of Uttar Pradesh judgment dated 3 October 1972,* reported in AIR 1973 SC 947, which was a decision of a bench of five judges, Rajendra Prasad v. State of Uttar Pradesh judgment dated 9 February 1979, reported in AIR 1979 SC 916, and Dalbir Singh v. State of Punjab, with differing opinions by two judges on the death sentence in judgment dated 4 May 1979, reported in AIR 1979 SC 1384, illustrate the turmoil in the court on the issue of the death penalty.

ransom punishable by death by amendment in 1993, the Prevention of Terrorism Act 2002, and the Unlawful Activities (Prevention) Act 1967 as amended in 2004 for "commission of a terrorist act . . . if such act has resulted in the death of any person."[3] State legislatures have passed laws, such as the Maharashtra Control of Organised Crime Act 1999, that prescribe the death penalty where death results during the commission of organized crime.[4]

Until 1955, where an offence in the Penal Code was punishable by either death or life imprisonment, the death sentence was the rule, and a court imposing the lesser sentence was required, under Section 367 of the Criminal Procedure Code 1898, to set out "special reasons" for that sentence. That requirement was repealed by Parliament in 1955.

A debate in Parliament in 1962 on abolition of the death sentence led to the question being referred to the Law Commission for consideration. The Law Commission concluded in 1967 that India was not ready for abolition.[5] Addressing the question of whether a court should be required to explain its choice between the death penalty and any alternate punishment, the Commission said: "The adoption of either alternative would mean, or be construed as meaning, a legislative determination that the sentence for which reasons are to be given is to be the exception, and the other sentence is to be the rule," and that the court should be required "to state its reasons, wherever it awards either of the two sentences in a capital case." A later report on

---

3   The Terrorism and Disruptive Activities (Prevention) Act lapsed in 1995, but cases registered under the Act continued to trial and judgment and sentence. There are still prisoners on death row under sentence of death convicted under this Act. The kidnapping provision was challenged in the Supreme Court and referred to a larger bench of three judges in *Vikram Singh v. Union of India in judgment dated 2 July 2013, available from http://judis.nic.in/supremecourt/imgs1.aspx?filename=40503.* The matter is pending in the Supreme Court. Section 364A prescribes that the court may impose the death penalty on a convict even where no death or hurt was caused. Allegations of abuse of the provisions of Prevention of Terrorism Act resulted in the law falling into political disrepute and being repealed by Parliament in 2004.

4   Section 3, Maharashtra Control of Organised Crime Act 1999. See also, section 3 of the Andhra Pradesh Control of Organised Crime Act, 2001, and section 3 of the Arunachal Pradesh Control of Organised Crime Act, 2002.

5   The Law Commission of India has periodically revisited the death sentence, in 1967 in its 35th Report (Capital Punishment), available from http://lawcommissionofindia.nic.in/1-50/Report35Vol1and3.pdf; in 1997 in its 156th Report on the Indian Penal Code, volume I, chapter III, "Death penalty", pp. 42-61, available from http://lawcommissionofindia.nic.in/101-169/Report156Vol1.pdf; in 2003 in its 187th Report on Mode of Execution of Death Sentence and Incidental Matters, available from http://lawcommissionofindia.nic.in/reports/187th%20report.pdf. In May 2014, the Law Commission issued a Consultation Paper on Capital Punishment as a prelude to a research project on the death penalty.

recommendations for revising the Code of Criminal Procedure 1898 reiterated this point.[6]

Parliament was more categorical. The revamped Code of Criminal Procedure 1973 read: "When the conviction is for an offence punishable with death or, in the alternative, with imprisonment for life or imprisonment for a term of years, the judgment shall state the reasons for the sentence awarded, and, in the case of sentence of death, the special reasons for such sentence" (Section 354). Parliament had decided that the death sentence would be the exception. A requirement was introduced at the same time that an accused, upon conviction, must be heard before sentencing (Section 235).

CHALLENGES TO THE DEATH PENALTY

The court has been confronted with questions about the constitutionality of the death penalty since the early 1970s. In 1972, when the death penalty was challenged as unconstitutional, the court responded with caution about its role in deciding these matters, and about the sentence itself. It held that the Code of Criminal Procedure 1898 prescribed the procedures to be followed in trial and punishment, that so long as these had not been shown to be invalid, they were valid.[7]

This formalistic approach to the death sentence changed in the late 1970s. The weight of imposing a sentence of death rests on courts, and the deep discomfort with the existence and exercise of judicial discretion in matters of life and death has found expression in the judgments of courts through the years.[8]

---

6   Law Commission of India, *35th Report (Capital Punishment), pp. 254-255, paragraphs 821 and 822; Law Commission of India, 41st Report (The Code of Criminal Procedure, 1898) (1969) volume I, p. 232, paragraph 26.10, available from http://lawcommissionofindia.nic.in/1-50/Report41.pdf.*

7   *Jagmohan Singh v. State of Uttar Pradesh in judgment dated 3 October 1972, reported in AIR 1973 SC 947.*

8   See, for instance, *Rajendra Prasad v. State of Uttar Pradesh judgment dated 9 February 1979, reported in (1979) 3 SCC 646; Ediga Anamma v. State of Andhra Pradesh in judgment dated 11 February 1974, reported in (1974) 4 SCC 443; Dalbir Singh v. State of Punjab judgment dated 4 May 1979, reported in (1977) 3 SCC 745, where the majority of two judges expressed their opposition to the death penalty while the dissenting judge said that abolition was the task of Parliament and not of the courts. Bachan Singh v. State of Punjab, reported in (1980) 1 SCC 754, was referred on the same day, 4 May 1979, to a larger bench prompted by differences between two judges on the bench (which was of three judges) on whether Rajendra Prasad v. State of Uttar Pradesh, which held that "special reasons" for imposing the death sentence must relate not only to the crime but also to the criminal, was good law.*

In 1980, a Constitution Bench of five judges of the Supreme Court debated the constitutionality of the death penalty.[9] Their decision constitutes a landmark in the development of the law on the death penalty in India. Four of the five judges were unwilling to hold that the death penalty was unconstitutional. But at the same time, they adopted the "rarest of rare" standard. "A real and abiding concern for the dignity of human life postulates resistance to taking a life through law's instrumentality," the court said. "That ought not to be done save in the rarest of rare cases when the alternative option is unquestionably foreclosed." The court was open to applying the test of "aggravating" and "mitigating" circumstances when deciding on a sentence, so far as that did not become a fetter on judicial discretion. It also ruled that in "making the choice of punishment or for ascertaining the existence or absence of 'special reasons' in that context, the Court must pay due regard both to the crime and the criminal."[10]

The dissenting judge, Justice Bhagwati, held that "insofar as [the law] provides for imposition of death penalty as an alternative to life sentence it is ultra vires and void as being violative of Articles 14 and 21 of the Constitution since it does not provide any legislative guidelines as to when life should be permitted to be extinguished by imposition of death sentence."[11]

Since then, issues such as what constitutes aggravating and mitigating circumstances, that the crime and the criminal ought both to be considered in deciding the sentence, that hanging is a cruel and unusual punishment, that it is not about a balance between mitigating and aggravating circumstances but that there must be no mitigating circumstances to explain sentencing a person to death, that the possibility of reform must be considered, and the widely varying consequences of judicial discretion that make it a "lottery" have challenged judicial thought.[12] Recent years, especially since 2009, have witnessed renewed concern about the death penalty, especially regarding judicial discretion in imposing it.

9   *Bachan Singh v. State of Punjab, judgment dated 9 May 1980, reported in (1980) 2 SCC 684.*
10   Ibid., paragraphs 132, 207, 201 and 199.
11   Ibid., paragraph 210.
12   Amnesty International, *Lethal Lottery: The Death Penalty in India—A Study of Supreme Court Judgments in Death Penalty Cases 1950-2006 (London, 2008), available from www.amnesty. org/en/library/info/ASA20/007/2008.*

The "rarest of rare" standard, and the consideration of aggravating and mitigating circumstances, have been integral parts of the law since the pronouncement of the Constitution Bench in 1980 in the Bachan Singh case. In 1996, in a decision of the Supreme Court in *Ravji v. State of Rajasthan*,[13] the Bachan Singh dictum was ignored and it was held that it was "the nature and gravity of the crime but not the criminal, which are germane for consideration of appropriate punishment in a criminal trial." Two accused were given the death sentence based on this reasoning. Seven cases that followed relied on Ravji, leading to 13 convicts being sent to death row without applying the Bachan Singh procedure for determining the sentence. In 2009, the court found that the Ravji court had been in contravention of the law.[14]

This meant that there were people on death row who had not been sentenced "according to procedure established by law." In 2012, 14 former judges of the Supreme Court and the High Courts wrote to the President of India drawing his attention to the error in the judgments of the court that had sent 13 convicts to death row—including two, Ravji Ram and Surja Ram, who had already been executed, which the 14 former judges called the gravest miscarriage of justice in the history of crime and punishment in independent India.[15]

In 2004, Dhananjoy Chatterjee, a security guard at an apartment block, was executed after having been convicted of the rape and murder of a 14-year-old schoolgirl. This was believed to have brought to an end a virtual moratorium with no executions in almost 10 years. That is now known not to have been the case, but at the time, the Ravji Ram and Surja Ram executions (which

---

13 *Ravji v. State of Rajasthan, decided on 5 December 1996, reported in (1996) 2 SCC 175.*

14 *Santosh Kumar Satishbhushan Bariyar v. State of Maharashtra* judgment dated 13 May 2009, reported in (2009) 6 SCC 498. Two further decisions of the court—*Dilip Tiwari v. State of Maharashtra*, decided on 10 December 2009, reported in (2010) 1 SCC 775, and *Rajesh Kumar v. State*, decided on 28 September 2011, reported in (2011) 13 SCC 706—made the same finding.

15 V. Venkatesan, "A case against the death penalty", Frontline, 25 August–7 September 2012, available from www.frontline.in/navigation/?type=static&page=archive. Since the letter from the former judges, the President has commuted the sentence of three of the 13, and the Governor of Orissa has done the same in a fourth instance; the mercy petition of six convicts has been rejected by the Governor, and the matter is now pending in the Supreme Court in three of the cases; Saibanna's mercy petition was rejected, and his case is now pending in a writ in the Karnataka High Court; Mohan Anna Chavan has had his mercy petition rejected by the Governor, and the matter is now in the Ministry of Home Affairs. Information from the files of Yug Chaudhry, lawyer, and Anup Surendranath, law teacher and researcher, personal communication, 28 July 2014.

occurred in 1996 and 1997) were not public knowledge. In the eight years following Dhananjoy Chatterjee's execution, there were no further executions, at least in part because of the President not agreeing to reject mercy petitions. Beginning in 2012, with the hanging of Ajmal Kasab for his role in the attack in Mumbai in November 2008, there has been a revival of executive sanction for carrying out the death sentence. Afzal Guru, an accused in the attack on Parliament in December 2001, was executed in February 2013. There followed a spate of rejections of mercy petitions by the President which, but for the intervention of lawyers and civil liberties organisations, who took the matter to the Supreme Court, may have resulted in a steep climb in executions.[16] A decision of the Supreme Court first stayed the executions and then, essentially on the ground of delay in carrying out the sentence, reduced the death sentences to life imprisonment.[17] This has provided a much-needed respite for those questioning the validity and fairness of this sentence, but it is still some way from taking the death penalty out of routine application, and further from doing away with it altogether.

"THERE IS, IN THE RESURGENCE OF THE DEATH PENALTY, A LACK OF RESPECT FOR LIFE, FOR THE LAW AND FOR PROCEDURE ESTABLISHED BY LAW."
—Usha Ramanathan

Outside the courtroom, there has been public outrage over crime, especially the frequency and brutality of crimes against women, particularly rape.[18] This has spilt into the courtroom, as when judges on

---

16 See, for instance, Mayura Janwalkar, "Dead against it", *Indian Express, 1 March 2014, available from http://indianexpress.com/article/india/india-others/dead-against-it/. The Peoples Union for Democratic Rights was among the petitioners who went to court to stop the executions; Shatrughan Chauhan v. Union of India in judgment dated 21 January 2014, paragraph 2, available from http://indiankanoon.org/doc/59968841/.*

17 *Shatrughan Chauhan v. Union of India in judgment dated 21 January 2014, paragraph 2, available from http://indiankanoon.org/doc/59968841/.*

18 See, for example, Jiby Kattakayam, "Two admit to gang rape; anger spills over Delhi streets", The Hindu, 19 December 2012, available from www.thehindu.com/news/national/two-admit-to-gangrape-anger-spills-over-delhi-streets/article4217180.ece?ref=relatedNews; "India Gate, Raisina Hills closed for public, security beefed up", The Hindu, 29 December 2012, available from www.thehindu.com/news/cities/Delhi/india-gate-raisina-hills-closed-for-public-security-beefed-up/article4252191.ece?ref=relatedNews; Betwa Sharma, "Photos: Indian court echoes populist outcry, gives 4 rapists death sentence", Vocativ, 11 September 2013, available from www.vocativ.com/world/india/photos-india-demands-death-for-gang-rape-killers/; Priyanka Kakodkar and Alok Deshpande, "Outrage in Mumbai over gang rape", The Hindu, 20 March 2014, available from www.thehindu.com/news/national/other-states/outrage-in-mumbai-over-gang-rape/article5050225.ece.

the Nagpur bench of the Bombay High Court stated, while imposing the death sentence on a defendant convicted of rape and 30 years without remission on a co-defendant:

> *We also cannot ignore the recent amendments brought to the Indian Penal Code on account of huge public hue and cry that arose on account of dastardly act in the heinous and gruesome rape and murder of Nirbhaya. The amendment as a matter of fact echoes the sentiments of the society at large. The sentiment of the society is glaring (sic), that such heinous crime on hapless women are required to be dealt with an iron hand. We have, therefore, no hesitation to hold that, in the perception of the society it would surely be a "rarest of rare" case wherein the death sentence is required to be imposed. . . . As such, while deciding the present case, we will have to keep ourselves aloof from our personal opinion as regarding the desirability or otherwise of retaining death penalty. What is required by us, is to decide as to whether in the perception of the society at large, the present case is a case which can be considered as rarest of rare case warranting death sentence.[19]*

Yet, there is a growing concern among judges about the use of judicial discretion in deciding matters of life and death.[20]

The resumption of executions in 2004 provoked much debate about the death penalty. In June 2004, when it appeared that the date for the execution of Dhananjoy Chatterjee might be fixed, civil liberties activists launched a series of initiatives to stop the execution, including appealing to the President to exercise his power to commute the sentence to life in prison, and going to court to halt the execution. These efforts did not succeed, and Dhananjoy Chatterjee was hanged on 14 August 2004. Newspapers announced on 15 August, Independence

---

19 *State of Maharashtra v. Rakesh Manohar Kamble in judgment dated 20 March 2014, pp. 109-110 and 105, Nagpur Bench of the Bombay High Court at http://bombayhighcourt.nic.in/generatenewauth.php?auth=cGF0aD0uL2RhdGEvbmFnanVkZ2V1tZW50cy8yMDE0LyZmbm-FtZT1DUkNPTkYzMTMucGRmJnNtZZmxhZz1O.*

20 *See, for instance, Santosh Kumar Satishbhushan Bariyar v. State of Maharashtra in judgment dated 13 May 2009, reported in (2009) 6 SCC 498; Sangeet v. State of Haryana in judgment dated 20 November 2012, reported in (2013) 2 SCC 452; Gurvail Singh v. State of Punjab in judgment dated 7 February 2013, available from http://indiankanoon.org/doc/32917452/.*

Day, that a virtual moratorium on the death penalty had been broken. From June to August, there had been a flurry of media reports on the crime, the victim's background, and the hangman.[21] Public opinion was aroused to the point that the President, who would not sign the death warrant for any other prisoner, signed this one.

Years later, the then President, Abdul Kalam, wrote about his surprise that almost all cases of clemency "had a social and economic bias" and that deciding the matter of clemency was one of the more difficult tasks that he had to undertake as President. About the only case in which he refused clemency, he said: "Of course there was one case where I found that the lift operator (Dhananjoy Chatterjee) had in fact committed the crime of raping and killing the girl without doubt. In that case I affirmed the sentence."[22] Nothing in the President's statement explained why he made an exception of Dhananjoy Chatterjee, whose case was based on circumstantial evidence. He was from an impoverished background in rural West Bengal.[23] He had been on death row for 10 years and there was nothing to indicate that he had been any trouble while in prison that would warrant anxious concern.. The public sentiment whipped up by the media, and the call for the execution that it engendered, could offer an explanation.

RAPE AND THE DEATH PENALTY

In this period, members of the women's movement met to discuss how we should respond. The Indian women's movement has had violence against women on its agenda, and rape in particular, since

---

21   "Dhananjoy's death", *Hindustan Times, 27 December 2004 at http://www.hindustantimes.com/ news-feed/nm3/dhananjoy-s-death/article1-26259.aspx; Sujoy Dhar, "Death penalty: an Indian hangman speaks", National Confederation of Human Rights Organizations, India, available from http://nchro.org/index.php?option=com_content&view=article&id=5267:death-penalty--an-in- dian-hangman-speaks&catid=2:capital-punishment&Itemid=10; Dipannita Ghosh Biswas, "Hangman's tale", India Today, 27 June 2005, available from http://indiatoday.intoday.in/story/ documentary-on-hangman-nata-mullick/1/194691.html; "Hang him and save our daughters", Rediff.com, 30 June 2004, available from www.rediff.com/news/2004/jun/30hang.htm.*

22   "APJ Abdul Kalam: Pendency of death cases had social, economic bias", *Times of India, 2 July 2012, available from http://timesofindia.indiatimes.com/india/APJ-Abdul-Kalam-Pen- dency-of-death-penalty-cases-had-social-economic-bias/articleshow/14590447.cms; A.P.J. Abdul Kalam, Turning Points: A Journey through Challenges (New Delhi, HarperCollins Publishers India with The India Today Group, 2012). The Supreme Court judgment, Dhananjoy Chatterjee v. State of West Bengal in judgment dated 11 January 1994, reported in (1994) 2 SCC 220, records him as having been a security guard.*

23   Suhrid Sankar Chattopadhyay, "The case of death sentence" *Frontline, 14-27 August 2004, available from www.frontline.in/static/html/fl2117/stories/20040827004602100.htm.*

at least 1979[24]. The law on rape, and on other forms of violence, had been amended to reflect the growing concern about tolerance of crimes such as rape—where the process re-victimised the victim, and all too often let the perpetrator off with a light sentence. In 2002, the Home Minister said in Parliament that he would introduce the sentence of death for rape. This set off much discussion among women's groups, which rejected this penalty.[25] As a practical issue, feminists like Vina Mazumdar expressed alarm that the possibility of a death sentence was more likely to result in the victim of rape also being murdered so as to remove the witness. This was not protection for women. As a political issue, the women's movement and the human rights movement, which overlapped significantly, agreed that the work of the state was to protect life and liberty, and it would be unwise to hand over the power to kill to the state—and that the death penalty was a diversion from the real issue, safety of women and the working of the criminal justice system in a way that stigma and disbelief would be displaced by a process that led to a fair trial and conviction of the offender.

This was not an isolated resort to paternalism and patriarchy to address the issue of rape. In the latest amendment to the Indian Penal Code in 2013, Parliament again acted to prescribe the death penalty in the name of women. Until then, where the death sentence had been imposed for rape, it has been because the rape was accompanied by murder. Without murder, there could be no sentence of death. The 2013 amendment introduced the death sentence in cases in which a person who has been previously convicted for rape, or inflicts "an injury which causes the death of the person or causes the person to be in a persistent vegetative state," is subsequently convicted of as a repeat offence.

---

24 Upendra Baxi, Vasudha Dhagamwar, Raghunath Kelkar and Lotika Sarkar,`An Open Letter to the Chief Justice of India' published in (1979) 4 SCC (Journal) 17; the case that prompted the Open Letter was Tukaram v. State of Maharashtra in judgment dated September 15, 1978 reported in (1979) 2 SCC 143.

25 "Advani favours death sentence for rapists", *Times of India, 26 November 2002, available from http://timesofindia.indiatimes.com/india/Advani-favours-death-sentence-for-rapists/article-show/29451444.cms; Laxmi Murthy, "Why L.K. Advani is wrong", Boloji, 12 January 2003, available from www.boloji.com/index.cfm?md=Content&sd=Articles&ArticleID=6324; "Advani remarks, a political grandstand play", The Hindu, 29 November 2002, available from http://hindu.com/2002/11/29/stories/2002112905720900.htm; "Death penalty for rapists", news24 archives, 27 November 2002, available from www.news24.com/World/Death-penalty-for-rapists-20021127.*

There is a significant prelude to this amendment. In December 2012, a young woman accompanied by a friend boarded a bus after watching a film and was brutally raped; she died of her injuries less than two weeks later. There was an outpouring of anger against a government that had paid little or no attention to the lack of safe spaces for women in the city. The incident revealed the inadequate approach to crime prevention, and it was suggested that the crime could have been prevented if the police had acted when alerted. In a bid to contain the reaction, the central government set up a committee of three people— Justice J.S. Verma, former Chief Justice of India, Justice Leila Seth, former Chief Justice of the Himachal Pradesh High Court, and Gopal Subramanium, a senior counsel in the Supreme Court Bar—to report on how the law should be changed to deal with the escalating violence against women. The committee heard women's groups expressly reject the introduction of the death penalty in the name of protecting women. Its report included the following:

> *Taking into account the views expressed on the subject by an overwhelming majority of scholars, leaders of women's organisations, and other stakeholders, there is a strong submission that the seeking of death penalty would be a regressive step in the field of sentencing and reformation.* [26]

The law was amended to include the death penalty despite this advice. In April 2014 it produced the first conviction and sentence of death, leading a legal scholar and women's rights activist to lament that:

> *The verdict, though expected, has left us with a bitter taste and a sense of betrayal. Not only is the sentence meted out to the young boys from impoverished background too harsh, but our fear is that it will set a bad precedent and serve to dilute the "rarest of rare" premise upon which a verdict of death penalty must hinge as per our criminal jurisprudence.*

---

26 Justice J.S.Verma (Chairperson), *Report of the Committee on Amendments to Criminal Law (2013), p. 245, paragraph 24.*

While most countries are moving towards abolition of death penalty, this is a move in the reverse direction.[27]

One of those implicated in the December 2012 rape and murder was a juvenile. The clamour to have the law amended so that a juvenile could stand trial as an adult because of the heinous nature of the crime also saw a case being filed in the Supreme Court asking that the age at which a person may stand trial be reduced from 18 to 16. The Supreme Court turned down the petition, citing, among other things, developments in international law.[28]

This case is symptomatic of expressions of public ire that have now become common. Who was this boy? A national daily newspaper who visited his village quoted his mother as saying "I thought he was dead":

> *Ever since she was told that her son had been arrested in a gang rape case—police claim he was the most brutal of the six—the woman has not stirred out of her home. It's a hut with no roof, only a plastic sheet as cover. Residents of the village say the family of the juvenile is the poorest among them. When The Sunday Express met the juvenile's mother, she said her son used to send them Rs 600, twice a year. But that stopped five years ago. Neighbours told her he had been spotted at a hotel in East Delhi where he worked as a waiter. Later, they told her they couldn't find him. She said he left the village eleven years ago. "His father is mentally ill. He was the eldest, so he went to Delhi to work at a hotel with some people from the village. Rs 600, twice a year, was a big help," she said.*[29]

27 Flavia Agnes, "Opinion: Why I oppose death for rapists", *Mumbai Mirror, 5 April 2014*, available from *www.mumbaimirror.com/mumbai/cover-story/Opinion-Why-I-oppose-death-for-rapists/articleshow/33250078.cms.*

28 *Subramanian Swamy v. Raju thru Member, Juvenile Justice Board, judgment dated 28 March 2014*, available from *http://judis.nic.in/supremecourt/imgs1.aspx?filename=41356.*

29 Prawesh Lama, "I thought he was dead, says mother of juvenile accused", *The Sunday Express, 6 January 2013*, available from *http://archive.indianexpress.com/news/i-thought-he-was-dead-says-mother-of-juvenile-accused/1055151/;* Matthias Williams and Arup Roychudhury, "Delhi rape accused lived on margins of India's boom" *Reuters, 12 January 2013*, available from *http://in.reuters.com/article/2013/01/12/india-rape-delhi-accused-juvenile-ram-sin-idINDEE90B01S20130112.*

It is one of the tragedies reflected in this episode that the police visited the village twice after the crime: once to inform the parents about the arrest, and a second time as part of their inquiries into his age. In the years between his leaving home and the crime, the state seems not to have been there. The public outcry after the crime was directed as much at the failures of the state, but the trial and conviction of the four accused and the focus on the juvenile defendant deflected attention and anger to the accused and the crime.

Poverty is invariably accompanied by powerlessness in the making of criminal law policy. The idea of post-conviction investigation is nonexistent. Far too often the criminal justice system has failed to produce convincing convictions. A well-respected public intellectual, Gopalkrishna Gandhi, who has also served in the bureaucracy and been a governor, said recently:

> *There has been a steady, and now a steep, decline in the ability of the system to deal with crime. The machinery grows, crime grows. But the latter, remaining one step ahead. Attempts to preserve the legitimacy of the system, however, have produced ironic phenomena such as scapegoating, which amounts to saying "Go find someone, anyone, but there needs to be a conviction."[30]*

TERRORISM AND THE DEATH PENALTY

In 1985, the Terrorism and Disruptive Activities (Prevention) Act started a dilution of procedure and process in the conduct of criminal trials. It survived till 1995, when it lost political support. In 2002, following an attack on Parliament in December 2001, the Prevention of Terrorism Act was enacted; it survived until 2004. The trials under these laws have, however, been taken to judgment. There are features of trial under these extraordinary laws that hold them apart from regular law. For instance, they create special tribunals to deal with terrorist offences. The Evidence Act 1872 makes confession to

---

30 Gopalkrishna Gandhi, "Eclipse at noon: shadows over India's conscience", D.P. Kohli Memorial Lecture delivered on 15 April 2014 in New Delhi.

a police officer inadmissible[31]—an implicit acknowledgment of the prevalence of torture and coercion during investigation. But anti-terror laws make confessions to a police officer admissible, so long as the police officer is of a certain rank, the presumption being that high-ranking officials will not be complicit in torture.[32]

Disturbing decisions may result from the process. Illustratively, Devinder Pal Singh Bhullar's petition for clemency was rejected by the President on 8 May 2011.[33] Bhullar's wife then moved the Supreme Court seeking commutation on the ground of delay and because, while in prison, he had become mentally ill, and in keeping with human rights norms, a person with mental illness should not be executed. On 12 April 2013, a bench of the Supreme Court refused relief, holding that the factor of delay in execution was inapplicable in situations where the conviction was under the terrorism law or similar statutes.[34] The court refused to accept the document on his mental health condition, saying that it did not convince the court that the convict was of unsound mind sufficiently to halt execution. On 31 March 2014, this decision was categorically set aside by a larger bench of the Supreme Court,[35] but not before the vagueness in the application of the law was revealed.

It seems clear that anti-terror laws are made in political contexts that are invariably weighted against a distinctive community of people. In 1985, militancy in Punjab led Parliament to enact the anti-terrorism law. People tried under this law were almost invariably Sikhs. And the carrying out of the sentence of death could be understood to serve the symbolic purpose of establishing that the state was dealing with

---

31 See *Arup Bhuyan v. State of Assam judgment dated 3 February 2011, available from www. indiankanoon.org/doc/792920/*.

32 This provision, Section 15 of the Terrorist and Disruptive Activities (Prevention) Act, which makes admissible confessions made to a police officer, was upheld by the Supreme Court in *Kartar Singh v. State of Punjab in judgment dated 11 March 1994, reported in (1994) 3 SCC 569 even as, p. 687, paragraph 250*.

33 For a brief setting out of the circumstances of Bhullar's case, see Usha Ramanathan, "Futile penalty", *Frontline, 25 August-7 September 2012, available from www.frontline.in/navigation/?-type=static&page=archive*.

34 *Devinder Pal Singh Bhullar v. State of NCT of Delhi in judgment dated 12 April 2013, available from http://judis.nic.in/supremecourt/imgst.aspx?filename=40266*.

35 *Navneet Kaur v. State of NCT of Delhi in judgment dated 31 March 2014, available from http://judis.nic.in/supremecourt/imgst.aspx?filename=41363, exercising its "inherent jurisdiction." This is in the nature of a power given to the Supreme Court in the Constitution, Article 142, for "doing complete justice."*

terror. Jinda and Sukha, who were tried and executed for the murder of General Vaidya, were convicted on the basis of their alleged confessions.[36] They refused to appeal the decision, seeing their executions as their martyrdom. Rajoana, convicted of the assassination of the ex-Chief Minister of Punjab, has refused to appeal or claim clemency, writing to the Chief Justice of the High Court that "the legal system, judicial system of this Country and the rulers of this Country have been discriminating" and that "slavery of such system is not acceptable to me."[37] That the death penalty has been counterproductive in dealing with terrorist crimes is evident. Years after militancy in Punjab had reached a quietus, the death sentences given to these prisoners only served to reopen wounds.

The 1985 anti-terrorism law was applied in dealing with the aftermath of the assassination of former Prime Minister Rajiv Gandhi in May 1991. A total of 26 people were tried for the crime in a special court; all 26 were convicted and sentenced to death. The Supreme Court later acquitted 19 of the 26 of the capital offence. One person was acquitted altogether, and 18 others were convicted of lesser offences and released soon after the case concluded. The sentence of death was confirmed for four of the prisoners.[38] None of the accused who stood trial were at the core of the conspiracy. Till 17 May 1991, the court observed in its judgment, only three people—Sivarasan, Subha and Dhanu—knew the object of the conspiracy, which was to kill Rajiv Gandhi. One of them was the suicide bomber, who died on the spot; all three were dead before they could be sent to trial. The four people, one woman and three men, who were given the death sentence, were peripheral participants at best. Perarivalan, for instance, was convicted of having purchased a 9-volt battery used in the explosive device that killed Rajiv Gandhi. His knowledge, according to the court, was that a 9-volt battery can be used to detonate an explosive device; and, although the court did not attribute knowledge of the crime to any of the accused before 17 May 1991 (the assassination

---

36   *State of Maharashtra v. Sukhdeo Singh judgment dated 15 July 1992, available from* http://indiankanoon.org/doc/1824507/.

37   Ruchi Gupta, "Why Balwant Singh Rajoana never appealed his death sentence", *Times of India,* 29 March 2012, *available from* http://timesofindia.indiatimes.com/india/Why-Balwant-Singh-Rajoana-never-appealed-against-his-death-sentence/articleshow/12458451.cms.

38   *State through Superintendent of Police, CBI/SIT v. Nalini judgment dated 11 May 1999, reported in (1999) 5 SCC 253.*

was on 21 May), it declared that he was "in the thick of conspiracy."[39] The leadership in this conspiracy was seen as leading up to Sri Lankan separatist leader Prabhakaran, but he could not be reached by the law. The people who could be found, it appears, received the penalty that could not be imposed on those who were truly responsible for the assassination.

Perarivalan (Arivu) has asserted his innocence through the years. In 2006, his protestation of innocence was published as a book, An Appeal from the Death Row: Rajiv Murder Case—The Truth Speaks, with a series of forewords written by retired judges, senior journalists and human rights activists. In November 2013, newspapers carried a startling statement: A retired police officer who had recorded Perarivalan's confession had said, in a documentary, that he had not recorded it verbatim. V. Thiagarajan IPS (retired), who was the then CBI SP of the Kerala Branch, said he had been assigned the task of recording the statement of accused persons in 1991. "Arivu told me that he did not know why they asked him to buy that [the battery]. But I did not record that in the confessional statement. Then the investigation was in progress, so that particular statement I did not record. Strictly speaking, law expects you to record a statement verbatim. . . . we don't do that in practice," The Hindu reported him as saying.

> Mr. Thiagarajan went on to explain that though he felt this before, he could not do anything at that stage. With regard to Arivu in particular, he always felt "a little uneasy" that the confessional statement was not appreciated the way it should have been. "Superficially they took it and jumped to the conclusion. . . . they took a strong view that Arivu knew of the killing and he bought the battery. That is not the truth. We cannot speculate, it is very dangerous to speculate." And that "there was subsequent internal evidence to clearly say that Arivu had no prior knowledge that Gandhi was going to be killed."[40]

39 Judgment of Justice D.P. Wadhwa in State through Superintendent of Police, CBI/SIT v. Nalini judgment dated 11 May 1999, reported in (1999) 5 SCC 253.
40 S. Vijay Kumar, "Former CBI official says he did not record Perarivalan's confession verbatim", The Hindu, 24 November 2013, available from www.thehindu.com/news/national/tamil-nadu/former-cbi-official-says-he-did-not-record-perarivalans-confession-verbatim/article5384370.ece.

On 18 February 2014, the Supreme Court commuted the sentences of the three people still under a sentence of death in connection with the Rajiv Gandhi assassination to life imprisonment on the ground of delay.[41]

In an attack on Parliament in December 2001, though all five intruders were shot dead, four others were charged and tried for having conspired in the attack. All four were convicted, and three were given the death sentence. By the time the case had run its course through the High Court and the Supreme Court,[42] two had been acquitted, including Gilani, who had been given the death sentence by the trial court. Shaukat had the death sentence reduced to 10 years in prison, and Afzal Guru was given the death sentence. Afzal Guru was hanged in February 2013, in circumstances that have raised serious questions about violations of procedure and about the ethics of executions carried out by the court in secrecy and announced after their occurrence.[43] Nothing more is known about who the five intruders were. The Home Minster said from the floor of the Assembly that they were Pakistani terrorists, because "the dead men looked like Pakistanis," and no further information has emerged since then. But this resulted in troops being massed along the border in an eyeball-to-eyeball confrontation; and the High Court increased the sentence from life imprisonment to death for the offence of waging war, as conspirators, because "the clouds of war with our neighbour loomed large for a long period of time" and "the nation suffered not only an economic strain but even the trauma of an inhuman war."[44]

---

41   *T. Suthendra Raja @ Santhan v. Union of India judgment dated 18 February 2014, available from http://judis.nic.in/supremecourt/imgst.aspx?filename=41228. This followed a ruling earlier in the year in the landmark case of Shatrughan Chauhan v. Union of India judgment dated 21 January 2014, reported in (2014) 3 SCC 1). The death sentence of the fourth person who had been handed the death penalty by the courts, Nalini, was commuted to life in prison on 24 April 2000 after Sonia Gandhi, wife of the slain former Prime Minister, petitioned for clemency. Nalini had by then had a child while in prison.*

42   *State v. Mohd Afzal judgment dated 29 October 2003, reported in (2003) 107 Delhi Law Times 385, available from http://indiankanoon.org/doc/1031426/; State (NCT of Delhi) v. Navjot Sandhu judgment dated 4 August 2005, available from http://indiankanoon.org/doc/1769219/.*

43   *See also Nirmala George, "India's secret executions cause concern in the wake of Mohammad Afzal Guru hanging", Huffington Post, 23 February 2013, available from www.huffingtonpost. com/2013/02/23/indias-secret-executions-mohammad-afzal-guru-_n_2749329.html; Usha Ramanathan, "The disturbing truth about an execution", The Hindu, 13 March 2013, available from www.thehindu.com/opinion/lead/the-disturbing-truth-about-an-execution/article4501567. ece.*

44   *Nirmalangshu Mukherji (2005), December 13, available from http://books.google.co.in/ books?id=PeVW26gYhsYC&printsec=frontcover&source=gbs_ge_summary_r&cad=0#v=onepage&q&f=false; see also, Usha Ramanathan, "A case for a public inquiry", Frontline, 23 April–6 May 2005, available from www.frontline.in/navigation/?type=static&page=archive.*

There are questions about what the death penalty has achieved in cases such as these. Considering the role attributed to those given the death sentence, the potential for defence seems small. There may be an element of retribution which answers the call of the "collective conscience" of the people—a reason that the court has used to explain why it affirms the death sentence.[45] Women's rights and human rights activists and others have distanced themselves from this imagined collective,[46] even as the death penalty has indeed become a rallying cry for those angry and rendered insecure by a state that seems unable to ensure safety. The death penalty has intensified controversy generated by the failures of the criminal justice system.[47]

The trial, conviction and execution of Ajmal Kasab, the sole surviving member of the attack on Bombay in November 2008, raises some of the same concerns as the anti-terror cases described above, but there is more.

Ajmal Kasab was a Pakistani national who, along with nine others, entered Bombay illegally and attacked and killed 164 people, injuring many others. He was charged with killing seven people as well as other offences. How is a fair trial to be ensured in an environment that is (with reason) hostile to an accused foreigner whose country does not extend any support—in law, language or any other way—and whose understanding is limited by his experience and education and by the isolation of prison life?

---

45 *Machhi Singh v. State of Punjab judgment dated 20 July 1983, reported in (1983) 3 SCR 413,* p. 431.

46 See, for instance, Justice JS Verma (Chairperson), *Report of the Committee on Amendments to Criminal Law (2013), p. 245, paragraph 24; Flavia Agnes, "Opinion: Why I oppose death for rapists", Mumbai Mirror, 5 April 2014, available from www.mumbaimirror.com/mumbai/cover-story/ Opinion-Why-I-oppose-death-for-rapists/articleshow/33250078.cms.*

47 Voices were raised against the death sentence given to Devinder Pal Singh Bhullar in Punjab (for example, www.siasat.pk/forum/showthread.php?175761-Bhullar-case-Akali-Dal-seeks-PM-s-intervention-Sikh-s-Upset-in-India), Afzal Guru in Kashmir (for example, www.bbc. com/news/world-asia-india-21406874), the Tamilnadu government's decision to remit the sentences of those incarcerated in connection with the Rajiv Gandhi assassination (Arundhati Ramanathan, "Tamil Nadu decides to free Rajiv Gandhi case convicts", *Livemint, 19 February 2014*), which the Centre protested the state government did not have the authority to do, and which *has now been referred to a five-judge bench of the Supreme Court for a decision ("SC refers case of Rajiv Gandhi's killers to Constitution Bench", Tehelka, 25 April 2014, available from www.tehel-ka.com/sc-refers-case-of-rajiv-gandhis-killers-to-constitution-bench/), Rajoana in Punjab ("India puts Sikh radical Rajoana's execution on hold", BBC News, 28 March 2012, available from www. bbc.com/news/world-asia-india-17532832).*

This problem is not unique to Kasab; it is uncomfortably common, but only the politically explosive cases seem to reach the public eye, and this needs the attention of the international community.

That Kasab was put through the "ossification test" to establish whether or not he was a juvenile should worry those watching the use of the death penalty. The effects on the trial of the publicity surrounding the case—the crime occurred in public, and parts of his involvement were aired in the media, which raised the pitch of public disapprobation—have yet to be fully understood. The case presents a range of traditional fair-trial concerns, including legal assistance and representation, defence access to documents, and language barriers.[48]

Clemency jurisdiction

The Indian Constitution gives the executive, acting through the President (Article 72) or the governor of a state (Article 161), the power to commute the death sentence. The power has in recent times been used to reject mercy petitions, clearing the way for executions.[49] The Supreme Court has stepped in and, essentially accepting the ground of delay, reduced the sentences from death to life.[50] In the meantime, the record raises questions about how clemency is exercised. Bandu Baburao Tidake's death sentence was commuted by the President on 2 June 2012—but he had been dead since 18 October 2007; "the report about his death apparently did not reach the Home Ministry when it recommended his commutation."[51] No guidelines apply to

---

48 Mohammed Ajmal Kasab v. State of Maharashtra in judgment dated 29 August 2012, available from http://supremecourtofindia.nic.in/outtoday/39511.pdf. See also Ritesh K. Srivastava, "Legal aid for Kasab?", Zee News, available from http://zeenews.india.com/MumbaiTerror/story.aspx-?aid=498251; V. Venkatesan, "Gaps in Kasab case", Frontline, 3-16 November 2012, available from www.frontline.in/static/html/fl2922/stories/20121116292203700.htm.

49 Bharti Jain, "President rejects mercy pleas of Nithari killer, 5 others", Times of India, 19 July 2014.

50 Shatrughan Chauhan v. Union of India judgment dated 21 January 2014, reported in (2014) 3 SCC 1; T. Suthendra Raja @ Santhan v. Union of India in judgment dated 18 February 2014 at http://judis.nic.in/supremecourt/imgst.aspx?filename=41228; Navneet Kaur v. State of NCT of Delhi in judgment dated 31 March 2014, available from http://judis.nic.in/supremecourt/imgst.aspx?filename=41363.

51 Manoj Mitta, "After six years on death row, spared for being a juvenile", Times of India, 21 August 2012, available from http://timesofindia.indiatimes.com/india/After-six-years-on-death-row-spared-for-being-a-juvenile/articleshow/15577973.cms; V. Venkatesan, "A case against the death penalty", Frontline, 25 August-7 September 2012, available from www.frontline.in/static/html/fl2917/stories/20120907291700400.htm.

executive clemency, and no reasons are required to be given. While the death penalty is still on the statute book, the mercy jurisdiction has to be re-imagined as a state responsibility. Ravji Ram and Surja Ram were executed in 1996 and 1997 after an erroneous judgment was reached without following the procedure established by law—a constitutional prerequisite to depriving life. Ankush Maruti Shinde, a convict on death row, was declared a juvenile and removed from death row;[52] there is nothing to indicate an enquiry into why a juvenile was made to stand trial in a capital case.

CONCLUSION

In recent years, India has seen a number of troubling events related to the death penalty. Two people have been executed under an order arrived at without following the procedure established by law. An amendment to the criminal law provides for the imposition of the death sentence where hurt or death is threatened, even where it may not have been caused. A law made under the pretext of protecting women prescribes an alternative sentence of death for a repeat offender who has been convicted of rape. The threat of execution of people convicted in anti-terror cases has given rise to a politics that exacerbates regional and community passions. A juvenile has been made to stand trial, convicted and sent to death row, from where he was removed only after a human rights lawyer took his matter to a sessions court, and where the judge was willing to entertain a petition in a matter that had already been decided by the Supreme Court.[53] The reaction to the involvement of young persons in violent crime, including rape, has generated a clamour for reducing the age of the juvenile from 18 to 16. A President has written, in an autobiographical account of his years in office, that in his experience, almost all pending cases "had a social and economic bias." Secret executions have been carried out. The judiciary has expressed concern about the injustices that the criminal justice system has been seen to produce, including delay and error, while the executive has set the clock back on executions. The Law Commission has found that there has been no research on the death penalty, and so we know very little about its efficacy or its absence. And a number of other ills beset the criminal

---

52 Venkatesan, "A case against the death penalty".
53 Mitta, "After six years on death row, spared for being a juvenile".

justice system, including torture in custody, poor investigative skills, severe deficiencies in legal aid and legal representation, overcrowded dockets, delays and lack of witness protection.

At this point, the reasonableness of the death penalty is questionable. There is no evidence that it has any deterrent effect. Whether executions happen in secret or in public, are barely noticed or treated as spectacles, the logic of the sentence is not evident. "Collective conscience" seems to have substituted for all other understandings of punishment, along with a return of retribution. The recent spate of rejections of clemency applications threatens to lead to a spate of executions. There is, in the resurgence of the death penalty, a lack of respect for life, for the law and for procedure established by law.

THE DEATH PENALTY IN BOTSWANA: BARRIERS TO EQUAL JUSTICE

Alice Mogwe[1]

Discrimination is treating people differently based on their actual or perceived membership in a certain group or category, "especially in a worse way from the way in which you treat other people."[2] Exclusion forms the basis of discrimination. In addressing the topic of discrimination and the death penalty, I would like to take you on a journey through my country, Botswana, a country that has retained the death penalty. We have a population of about 2 million. Our most recent execution was in 2013, when Orelesitse Thokamolelo was hanged on 27 May.

Opponents of the death penalty believe that its arbitrariness and the influence of socio-political and economic conditions on its implementation mean that it must be abolished. Studies have found that the effect of race and class on human rights have serious implications for defendants' ability to obtain a fair trial and equal access to justice.[3] The permanence of the death penalty makes its use particularly dire when there is any question about the fairness of the trial.

THE AFRICAN HUMAN RIGHTS CONTEXT

Botswana is a member of the African Union and the African Commission on Human and People's Rights. The right to life is protected in the following documents:

- The African Charter on Human and Peoples' Rights, Article 4, states, "Human beings are inviolable. Every human being

---

1 Alice Mogwe is director of DITSHWANELO, the Botswana Centre for Human Rights.

2 *Cambridge Dictionaries Online*, "Discrimination", available from http://dictionary.cambridge.org/us/dictionary/british/.

3 Amnesty International, *United States of America: Death by Discrimination: The Continuing Role of Race in Capital Cases* (2003); International Federation for Human Rights and Center for Constitutional Rights, *Discrimination, Torture, and Execution: A Human Rights Analysis of the Death Penalty in California and Louisiana* (2013).

shall be entitled to respect for his life and the integrity of his person. No one may be arbitrarily deprived of this right."

- The African Charter on the Rights and Welfare of the Child, Article 5, states, "Every child has an inherent right to life. This right shall be protected by law. . . . [the] death sentence shall not be pronounced for crimes committed by children."

- The Protocol to the African Charter on Human and People's Rights on the Rights of Women in Africa, Article 4, states, "Every woman shall be entitled to respect for her life and the integrity and security of her person."

In 1999, the African Commission adopted a resolution at its 26th ordinary session in Kigali, Rwanda, urging States parties to the African Charter to consider the possibility of a death penalty moratorium and eventual abolition. In 2006 the Working Group on the Death Penalty was established. In October 2012, its mandate was renewed and expanded and it was renamed the Working Group on Death Penalty and Extrajudicial, Summary or Arbitrary Killings in Africa. It reports twice a year to the African Commission.

The Working Group's *Study on the Question of the Death Penalty in Africa* was adopted by the African Commission at its 50th ordinary session in 2011. The study was officially launched in April 2012, in collaboration with the partners of the Working Group, namely, the International Federation for Human Rights, FIACAT and World Coalition against the Death Penalty. One of the key strategies recommended in the study is that the ACHPR should continue working closely with United Nations organs, in particular the Office of the High Commissioner for Human Rights, as well as with national human rights institutions and civil society organisations, to mobilise action towards the abolition of the death penalty.[4] Another key strategy recommended in the study is the production of a protocol to the African Charter on Human and Peoples' Rights on the abolition of the death penalty in Africa.[5]

---

4   Part VII, Strategies, p. vi.
5   Ibid., p. vii.

As at January 2014, the status of the death penalty in Africa could be summed up as follows:[6]

- **17 formally abolitionist countries**: Angola, Benin, Burundi, Cabo Verde, Côte d'Ivoire, Djibouti, Gabon, Guinea-Bissau, Mauritius, Mozambique, Namibia, Rwanda, Sao Tome and Principe, Senegal, Seychelles, South Africa and Togo.

- **24 de facto abolitionist countries** (no executions for at least 10 years—the year of the last execution is given in parentheses): Burkina Faso (1988), Cameroon (1988), Central African Republic (1981), Chad (2003), Comoros (1997), Republic of the Congo (1982), Democratic Republic of the Congo (2003), Eritrea (before independence in 1993), Ghana (1993), Guinea (2001), Kenya (1987), Lesotho (1995), Liberia (2000), Madagascar (1958), Malawi (1992), Mauritania (1987), Morocco (1993), Niger (1976), Sierra Leone (1998), Swaziland (1982), Tanzania (1994), Tunisia (1991), Zambia (1997) and Zimbabwe (2003).

- **2 retentionist countries observing a moratorium on executions**: Algeria and Mali.

- **11 retentionist countries**: Botswana, Egypt, Equatorial Guinea, Ethiopia, Gambia, Libya, Nigeria, Somalia, South Sudan, Sudan and Uganda.

In Botswana, the most recent execution was in 2013. As at 13 June 2013, Botswana had executed 47 people since independence in 1966.[7]

THE BOTSWANA HUMAN RIGHTS CONTEXT

Botswana is a signatory to the International Covenant on Civil and Political Rights, which refers to the death penalty in Article 6: "Anyone sentenced to death shall have the right to seek pardon or commutation of the sentence. . . . Sentence of death shall not be

---

6   *Hands Off Cain* (2014).

7   T. Kgalemang, "Botswana hangs 47 since independence", *Botswana Gazette*, 13 June 2013, available from www.gazettebw.com/?p=3350.

imposed for crimes committed by persons below 18 years of age and shall not be carried out on pregnant women." Botswana is a State party to the African Charter on Human and Peoples' Rights and the African Charter on the Rights and Welfare of the Child, but not to the African Charter on Human and People's Rights' Protocol on the Rights of Women in Africa.

The Botswana Constitution (Section 3) recognises the right to life, liberty and security of the person and protection of the law. However, the Penal Code provides for the death penalty for murder, treason, instigating a foreigner to invade Botswana and committing assault with intent to murder in the course of piracy. The Botswana Defence Force Act also contains capital offences: aiding the enemy, cowardly behaviour and mutiny.

The Penal Code provides that any person convicted of murder shall be sentenced to death unless the court believes that there are extenuating circumstances. To determine the extenuating circumstances, the court shall take into consideration the "standards of behaviour of an ordinary person of the class of the community to which the convicted person belongs" (Section 203). The Penal Code further states that the death sentence shall not be pronounced against any person who is under the age of 18 or pregnant women under any circumstances (Section 26). When a woman facing a death sentence can prove that she is pregnant, her sentence will be reduced to life imprisonment.

BARRIERS TO EQUAL JUSTICE

DITSHWANELO, the Botswana Centre for Human Rights, worked on a death penalty case (*DITSHWANELO v. Attorney General of Botswana*[8])—that exemplifies some key barriers to equal justice for poor people and ethnic minorities in Botswana. Tlhabologang Maauwe and Gwara Brown Motswetla, two indigenous men of the Basarwa/San ethnic group, were found guilty of the murder of a herdsman whose ox they had killed. The Basarwa/San are generally poor and have few economic and educational opportunities. They tend to depend for survival on employment by wealthier cattle owners and on government

---

8   MISCRA Case No. 2 of 1999.

assistance programmes. At the time of the murder, Botswana was experiencing the severe drought of 1994-1995. The crops had failed, and
the families of the defendants had little to eat. The only animals in the
area which the families were legally allowed to hunt were squirrels,
but they had not been successful in finding any. Mr. Maauwe and Mr.
Motswetla killed a stray ox, and when the herdsman came across them
with the remains of the ox, a fight ensued and the herdsman was killed.
They were arrested for the murder.

During the original trial, some of the defendants' court-appointed
lawyers never consulted them, a clear case of inadequate representation. The prison log books did not contain any evidence of the
lawyers visiting their clients in prison. One of the pro deo lawyers
fled Botswana amid allegations of fraud. The other initially resisted
handing over his file to DITSHWANELO, until he was informed
that a court order would be sought. The file contained no consultation or trial notes. Mr. Maauwe and Mr. Motswetla had not
been informed by their legal representatives about their options
under Botswana law—an accused can choose to remain silent or
give sworn testimony subject to cross-examination or an unsworn
statement not subject to cross-examination. While the latter can be
persuasive to the court, it has less evidentiary weight than sworn
testimony. Both men had given unsworn statements without being
informed of the implications. No substantive extenuating circumstances were presented to the court following the handing down of
the death sentence.[9]

In January 1999, DITSHWANELO intervened in the case upon
reading in the media about their impending execution. The judge
recognised that lack of resources and remoteness from centres of
development and communication can militate against an individual's
access to human rights. He also recognised that certain "organisations
may have the ability to motivate the protection of individuals, who
may not be able to act for themselves in any meaningful way." He
consequently recognised that DITSHWANELO had legal standing
in the case.[10]

---

9   Elizabeth Maxwell and Alice Mogwe, *In the Shadow of the Noose* (Gaborone, DITSHWANE-
     LO, 2006), pp. 30 and 40.
10   Ibid., p. 42.

The two men were ultimately released in 2006, following the Court of Appeal decision to grant a permanent stay, prohibiting the carrying out of both men's death sentences as well as any further criminal proceedings against them in relation to the death of the herdsman. Arrested in 1995, they were released seven years after coming to within hours of their execution in 1999.

This case illustrates a number of the problems defendants can have in accessing equal justice; these will be discussed further in the sections below.

Access to representation

The Constitution guarantees the right to legal representation in criminal cases at the accused's own expense (Section 10). State-funded (pro deo) counsel is available for defendants charged with a capital offence. The Government recognises that the fees paid to counsel are not attractive compared with those that obtain in private practice. The Registrar of the High Court has reportedly tried to address the problem by instructing every law firm to take up one pro deo case a year, but this has not resolved the problem of the quality of representation for the indigent.[11] The University of Botswana runs a legal clinic staffed by law students and supervised by a law lecturer in an attempt to fill the void, but it is poorly resourced. A few NGOs provide extremely limited legal aid for the indigent. In 2011, a State-funded Legal Aid Project was established. It is, however, limited to civil matters.

The indigent experience discrimination as they are forced to rely on a legal system to which their access is limited because of their poverty and poor education. They are dependent on the pro deo system, which tends not to attract skilled, experienced and committed lawyers. Senior lawyers tend to refer pro deo cases to their junior partners. The role of non-governmental organisations is critical in facilitating access to justice for the poor.

---

11 *Botswana Initial Report to the United Nations Committee on Civil and Political Rights*, 12 September 2005, Article 6 (Right to Life), p. 42.

Transparency of clemency proceedings

The Constitution (Sections 53 and 54) provides for appeal to the President for the commutation of the death sentence on the advice of the Advisory Committee on the Prerogative of Mercy. Neither the appellant nor his or her legal representative have the right to appear before the Committee. The lawyers and families of the appellant learn of the outcome of an unsuccessful appeal through the announcement of the execution after it has been conducted.

"DISCRIMINATION IS A PROBLEM IN THE APPLICATION OF THE DEATH PENALTY AROUND THE WORLD."

—Alice Mogwe

In 1998, DITSHWANELO wrote to the Commissioner of Prisons to enquire about the outcome of the clemency process of Mr. Maauwe and Mr. Motswetla. The response from the Commissioner of Prisons was that such information was classified.[12] The secrecy surrounding the clemency process renders it a ritualistic process with little substantive significance for those seeking mercy. There has been only one reported case of a commutation of a death sentence to a life sentence since independence in 1966; this occurred in 1975.[13]

In the case of *Lehlohonolo Bernard Kobedi v. the State Court of Appeal*,[14] Mr. Kobedi's new legal representative presented new ballistic evidence that proved that he could not have committed the murder. However, according to the rules of the court, that evidence ought to have been presented to the lower court, and it was not admissible. The Court declared itself "functus officio," or unable to act further in the case, and advised that the appellant seek mercy from the President. The request for mercy was not successful, and Mr. Kobedi was executed.

Defendants represented by inexperienced counsel, who lack the resources and commitment to adequately prepare for capital cases, experience discrimination as they have less chance of receiving a fair trial. Even an

---

12 Ibid., p. 32.
13 *Botswana Initial Report to the United Nations Committee on Civil and Political Rights*, p. 43.
14 Criminal Appeal No. 25 of 2001, High Court Criminal Trial No. F.29 of 1997.

ideal judicial system is run by human beings, and all humans are fallible. A clemency process provides an essential "fail-safe."[15] But in Botswana, the exercise of the prerogative of mercy (clemency) is not guided by any publicly accessible procedures or restricted by rules of evidence.

Language barriers

Botswana is home to more than 30 ethnic groups. Its official language is English and its national language is Setswana, the language of eight of the ethnic groups. Language barriers can seriously hinder the judicial process, from investigation to interrogation and appearance in court. In the case of *DITSHWANELO v. Attorney General of Botswana*,[16] the prisoners, Mr. Maauwe and Mr. Motswetla, were illiterate and did not know their exact dates of birth. They could understand some words of the national language, Setswana, but spoke neither Setswana nor the other commonly spoken language of their area, iKalanga. They spoke Secherechere, a dialect of Sesarwa.

They argued that they had not understood the confession documents on which they had affixed their thumbprints, had not been able to communicate with the authorising officer when their statements were taken in Setswana, and had complied when asked for their thumbprints because they feared the police. The three-way communication in the High Court—Sesarwa to Setswana to English—used a dialect of Sesarwa unknown to them. They had a letter written on their behalf stating, "We are Basarwa and we do not understand Setswana well. Therefore we had difficulties in communication at the High Court." The Registrar of the High Court received the letter, but neither assigned them a new lawyer nor placed the letter in their file for the Court of Appeal. It was during the case that the issue of poor interpretation, inability to communicate and the letter that had been written about it were discovered and raised.

Members of ethnic minorities who cannot communicate in the language(s) of the court depend on the help of skilled translators. Often these are not provided. Their combination of poverty and illiteracy

---

15   *Herrera v. Collins,* 506 US 390 (1993), quoted in Amnesty International, *United States of America: Death by Discrimination.*

16   MISCRA Case No. 2 of 1999.

made it impossible for Mr. Maauwe and Mr. Motswetla to meaningfully engage the legal system and receive a fair trial.

Race

Race has not been a striking factor in most capital cases in Botswana courts. There has, however, tended to be a noticeably different reaction when a white person is involved in a case, whether as a victim or a perpetrator. In 2001, South African Mariette Bosch was executed after being found guilty of murdering the wife of a man with whom she was engaged in a romantic affair. They married three months after the murder. Ms. Bosch was the first white person to be executed in Botswana. Local lawyer Themba Joina, whose black male client Lehlohonolo Kobedi (also a non-national, from Lesotho), was on death row at the time, said, "The foreign media were only concerned about Bosch because she is white. Since she was hanged, we don't see cameras in Botswana anymore."[17] There was a marked difference in international reaction to the execution of Ms. Bosch, including from international human rights organisations, compared with other executions before and since.

Secrecy of executions

Those on death row in Botswana suffer due to the secrecy with which the death penalty is carried out. The accused is entitled to a minimum of 24 hours notice. In many cases, legal representatives and family members are not notified prior to the execution. In one case, while the legal representatives were preparing a request for clemency, the accused were executed. Lehlohonolo Kobedi, whose case was discussed above, had written asking DITSHWANELO to visit him on death row. The Commissioner of Prisons refused to grant permission for this visit, and Mr. Kobedi was executed soon thereafter.

Other challenges to fair and equal access

Additional concerns include delays in processing of cases and physical distance from urban areas where most legal services are located.

---

17 *Executed Today*, "2003: Lehlohonolo Bernard Kobedi", archive for 18 July 2013, available from www.ExecutedToday.com. Mr. Joina's client was Lehlohonolo Kobedi, whose case was discussed above.

Families of victims of murder and families of the executed are excluded from the judicial process. Various groups working with families of victims have raised concerns about the death penalty and its inability to bring them closure. Others have expressed serious discomfort at not being kept informed about the progress of the cases of their family members. Within a retributive justice system, there is little room for restoration or restitution.

CONCLUSION

Discrimination is a problem in the application of the death penalty around the world. It remains an open question whether it will be possible to end discrimination without systemic change concerning the fundamental issue of access to justice for all.

The call by the African Commission on Human and People's Rights for a moratorium on the death penalty appears to be bearing fruit in Africa. With only 11 of the continent's 54 states actively retaining the death penalty, there is hope that the message will be heard that it violates the most fundamental of all human rights. Commitment to sustainable people-centred development, based on promotion, protection and respect for human rights, is key to ensuring that the full range of rights—civil, political, socio-economic and cultural, including the right to life—are enjoyed by all citizens. As United Nations Secretary-General Ban Ki-moon has said, "The right to life is the most fundamental of all human rights."[18]

---

18 Ban Ki-moon, "Secretary-General's message to the International Commission against the Death Penalty", delivered by Ms. Kyung-wha Kang, Deputy High Commissioner for Human Rights, Geneva, Switzerland, 25 February 2013.

THE DEATH PENALTY IN ZIMBABWE: LEGAL AMBIGUITIES

Innocent Maja[1]

On 20 December 2012, the United Nations General Assembly passed Resolution 67/176, Moratorium on the Use of the Death Penalty. It recommended among other things reduction of the number of offences punishable by death, restrictions on who can be sentenced to death and a moratorium on executions. This paper analyses the extent to which Zimbabwe, which retains the death penalty,[2] has heeded these recommendations.

REDUCTION OF THE NUMBER OF OFFENCES PUNISHABLE BY DEATH

Since independence, the list of crimes punishable by death has changed several times. The 1979 Constitution applied the death penalty to nine offences (including attempted murder, rape and political violence). This list was limited to murder, treason and mutiny in the 1990s.[3] In the year 2000, the Genocide Act extended the imposition of the death penalty to genocide crimes that result in death. In 2004 the Criminal Law (Codification and Reform) Act expanded the application of the death penalty to attempted murder, incitement or conspiracy to commit murder and terrorism-related crimes that result in death.

However, Section 48(1) of the 2013 Constitution establishes a right to life limited only by Section 48(2), which provides that a "law may permit the death penalty to be imposed only on a person convicted of murder committed in aggravating circumstances." Under Section 48(2), there is still no mandatory death penalty. The death penalty could be established if a law were passed imposing it for murder in

---

1 Innocent Maja is a senior partner in Maja & Associates and a lecturer at the University of Zimbabwe.

2 From 1980 to 2004, when the last executions were carried out, 78 people were executed.

3 Sections 20(1) and 47(2-3) of the Criminal Law (Codification and Reform) Act [Chapter 9:23] and Section 75(1-2) of the Defence Act [Chapter 11:02].

aggravating circumstances, but passage of such a law is discretionary, as shown by the use of the word "may."[4]

> "PEOPLE CONVICTED OF MURDER ARE
> USUALLY REPRESENTED ON A PRO BONO
> BASIS BY JUNIOR LAWYERS." —Innocent Maja

At the time of this writing, no law had been passed imposing the death penalty. Thus, technically a person convicted of murder committed in aggravating circumstances cannot be sentenced to death. To formally abolish the death penalty, Zimbabwe could take the step, in realigning the laws—especially the Criminal Law (Codification and Reform) Act, the Criminal Procedure and Evidence Act and the Defence Act—of removing all provisions relating to the death penalty from the statute books.

RESTRICTIONS ON WHO CAN BE SENTENCED TO DEATH

Resolution 67/176 encourages the progressive restriction of the use of death penalty on children below age 18 and pregnant women. Section 48(2)(c) of the Zimbabwean Constitution provides that the death penalty must not be imposed on people who were less than 21 years old when the offense was committed, people more than 70 years old and women. Thus the potential imposition of the death penalty is restricted to men aged between 21 and 70 who commit murder in aggravating circumstances.

The Zimbabwean government is urged to totally abolish the death penalty for a number of reasons:

---

4   This is radically different from the pre-2013 Constitution, under which the death penalty was mandatory unless extenuating circumstances were proved. For instance, section 47(2) and (3) of the Criminal Law (Codification and Reform) Act [Chapter 9:23] states that "a person convicted of murder shall be sentenced to death unless (a) the convicted person is under the age of eighteen years at the time of the commission of the crime; or (b) the court is of the opinion that there are extenuating circumstances; in which event the convicted person shall be liable to imprisonment for life or any shorter period. (3) A person convicted of attempted murder or of incitement or conspiracy to commit murder shall be liable to be sentenced to death or to imprisonment for life or any shorter period." Section 337 of the Criminal Procedure and Evidence Act [Chapter 9:07] empowers the High Court to sentence to death any person who commits murder unless there are extenuating circumstances. The lacuna that currently exists is that these laws have not yet been revised to align with the new Constitution.

1. People convicted of murder are usually represented on a pro bono basis by junior lawyers inexperienced in trial work. Legal representation is also limited to the trial stage. This essentially means that people convicted of murder who cannot pay for legal representation go through the appeal process without it.

2. Even though Section 112 of the Constitution empowers the President to commute a sentence of death upon submission of a mercy petition, presidential discretion in this matter is broad. There is no right for the petitioner to be heard. Neither is the court permitted to inquire into the manner in which the President exercises this discretion.

3. Inmates sentenced to death are kept in cells that are small and dirty and have little ventilation and no sanitary facilities. They use a 20-litre bucket to relieve themselves. They are kept in solitary confinement for 23 hours a day with very limited access to the outside world. This section of the prison is referred to as the condemned section.[5] The trauma that death penalty inmates experience is further worsened by the delay in executions.

4. The method of killing by hanging[6] is horrendous, inhuman, brutal and uncivilised.[7]

MORATORIUM ON EXECUTIONS

There are currently 90 male inmates on death row. The last execution was carried out in 2004 when Stephen Chidumo and others were executed for murder. The current Minister of Justice, Emerson Mnangagwa, is on record as opposing the death penalty and saying that he would rather resign than sign an execution warrant. However, there is no official moratorium on executions.

---

5   See *Catholic Commission for Justice and Peace v. Attorney General and Others, 1 Zimbabwe Law Reports 242 (1993), Supreme Court, Harare, Zimbabwe.*

6   Section 339(2) of the Criminal Procedure and Evidence Act. Section 75(1) and (2) of the Defence Act [Chapter 11:02] provides that a sentence of death passed by a court martial shall be executed in private by a firing squad.

7   See the Tanzanian High Court decision of *R v. Mbushuu, Tanzania Law Report 146 [1994], High Court, Dodoma, Tanzania.*

Even though Zimbabwe can be deemed a de facto abolitionist country, its refusal to adopt an official moratorium on executions,

coupled with the employment of an executioner in 2011, raises the question of whether Zimbabwe intends to resume executions.[8]

It is recommended that the Zimbabwean government maintain the status quo of not executing those on death row and go a step further to commute death sentences to either life imprisonment or a lesser penalty.

---

8   This fear is not misplaced. In 1995, Zimbabwe resumed executions after seven years of not
     executing. It will be sad if history repeats itself.

"The way to restore a wrong is not through another wrong. Rather, a counterweight is needed, so that the more evil there is on the one side, the more good there is on the other side."

—*Mario Marazziti*

CHAPTER 4

VALUES

This chapter, which focuses on values, contains articles by a Catholic nun who works with prisoners on death row, two authors active in both civil society and politics and two experts in human rights. Sister Helen demonstrates the fruitlessness of the death penalty from the perspective of the healing process for family members of the victims. Marazziti finds arguments against the death penalty in the world's religions, while Bhatti warns of its social and political dangers. Rodley describes the evolution of Human Rights Committee's jurisprudence on the death penalty, while Heyns focuses on the right to life and the way that the UN and regional bodies increasingly interpret it to reduce the scope of the death penalty.

Helen Prejean, a Catholic nun, has for over three decades engaged in accompanying the condemned on death row and through this experience, has also come to know many murder victims' families. From her experience, wounded and grieving families—even after many years of waiting—can never be healed by watching the Government kill the perpetrators. What they need instead are compassionate people who will accompany them on the long road to healing, as well as counselling and sometimes financial help.

Mario Marazziti, an Italian parliamentarian and affiliate of the Community of Sant'Egidio, a Christian lay association, examines the doctrines of Buddhism, Hinduism, Judaism, Islam and Christianity as they apply to the death penalty, looking for arguments against it. Each of these large, complex communities of believers has an ancient tradition that has inspired both reverence for life and, sometimes, support for the taking of life. But while individual believers have sometimes chosen death, he argues, these religions' core teachings emphasize the sacredness of life.

For Dr. Paul Bhatti, civil society activist and former Minister for National Harmony and Minorities Affairs in Pakistan, giving or taking a human life is a divine prerogative. However, there are social and political arguments against the death penalty as well. National criminal justice systems are less than perfect, and the death penalty can be misused against political opponents. He argues that imposing the death penalty on terrorists is dangerous, as it may transform criminals into martyrs, justify the taking of life, and aid future recruitment.

Nigel Rodley, member and a long time Chair of Human Rights Committee, describes the process of broadening and deepening of the human rights consciousness that has led to the death penalty to be discussed in human rights terms. If the state is the principal guarantor of human rights, why would the state then deprive anyone from the inherent right to life?

Christof Heyns, the UN Special Rapporteur on extrajudicial, summary and arbitrary executions, and Thomas Probert, his colleague from the University of Pretoria, point to an emerging consensus that at least the practice of executions is no longer acceptable for the UN human rights mechanisms, leaving states to determine the best manner in which to achieve a moratorium. Regional organizations can act as important fora for discussion of trends towards abolition that are more regionally, and perhaps culturally, sensitive.

DEATH PENALTY: VICTIMS' PERSPECTIVE

Sister Helen Prejean[1]

Over the three decades I have been engaged in accompanying the condemned on death row and seeking every means I know to save their lives, I have also come to know many murder victims' families. At first, I was so intimidated by the enormity of their loss and sorrow that I avoided them. I wondered why they would want to have anything to do with me, working passionately to abolish the very penalty they were seeking. Staying away from them was a very big mistake. I've learned a lot since, and I wish to share some of what I've learned with you, whom I regard as our most representative global forum to achieve peace.

I'm pleased that you're hosting a forum to explore the plight of murder victims' families vis a vis the death penalty. In my experience I've seen over and over the tragic effects that government's imposition of death to the offenders wreaks on these families, despite the popular perception (or, perhaps, at root, the *political* assumption) that only the execution of the perpetrator is capable of rendering "justice" to those harmed by their crimes.

We couldn't have a more direct view into the tragic dynamic that occurs between victims' families and the death penalty than what happened in Boston on June 24, 2015: the day of Dzhokhar Tsarnaev's formal sentencing to death for his participation in the Boston Marathon bombing in 2013. As part of this proceeding, victims' families are allowed to present Victim Impact statements about how the crime has affected their lives, which is unspeakably horrible. As they testify about their loss, grief, and traumatized lives, most believe the death penalty is justified, and some express their defiance by refusing to call themselves "victims," determined to carry on with their lives. Not all, however, seek death. Some want to see Mr. Tsarnaev live

---

1 Sister Helen is a Roman Catholic nun, a member of the Congregation of St. Joseph and a leading American advocate for the abolition of the death penalty.

in prison for the rest of his life because they consider that a greater punishment, others, so that over time he can come to grips with and take responsibility for his horrendous crime. I have witnessed this tragic scene many times: victims' families in the public spotlight, laying bare their pain, reliving their unspeakable trauma – all because their testimony is a necessary part of prosecution's decision to seek a sentence of death.

Descending now into the complexity of the legal machinery of death - if Mr. Tsarnaev's fate had been left to a Massachusetts's jury, no death penalty would have been sought. That's because, since the late 60s, Massachusetts has not had the death penalty. But in this case the federal government, designating the bombings as a "terrorist" attack, trumped state law and sought the death penalty. Consequently, during the trial traumatized victims' families have had to recount and re-live

> ## "THERE'S NOTHING HONOURABLE IN KILLING FELLOW HUMAN BEINGS WHO ARE DEFENCELESS."
> —Sister Helen Prejean

their horror over and over: once during the guilt phase, again during the sentencing phase, and now again, at the formal sentencing. If government prosecutors had chosen, they could have accepted the defendant's admission of guilt and apology and sentenced him to life imprisonment, where he would have disappeared behind prison walls, and victims' families would seldom if ever hear his name again. But now on the news they will hear his name again and again as the years of appeals drag on, which capital cases inevitably bring in their wake. In an effort to avoid this very situation, after Mr. Tsarnaev was found guilty, the Richard family, whose young son, Martin, was killed in the bombing, made a public plea on the front page of the Boston Globe begging prosecutors, not to seek the death penalty. To no avail.

My state, Louisiana, was the first state to offer victims' families the option to witness the execution of the perpetrator convicted of killing their loved one. The rationale was straightforward: who better than these families deserve to be official witnesses for the state? In my book, *Dead Man Walking*, I tell of one such victim's family, the Harveys, for whom the execution of Robert Lee Willie, the killer of their daughter could not happen quickly enough. A week before Willie's execution in the electric chair, Vernon Harvey held his own press conference, urging the authorities to "bring it on" and he wished he could be the one to "pull the switch." What I'll always remember (as spiritual advisor to the condemned, I was also present at the execution) is that immediately after the execution, members of the media asked Mr. Harvey if witnessing the execution had satisfied him, and he said, "Anybody got any whiskey? Anybody want to dance? We killed that SOB tonight, and I got to watch him die! Then he added: "But you know what? The SOB died too quick. I hope he burns in hell." And as he said this he jerked his thumb downward over and over. As I heard him that night, I remember thinking to myself that this poor, distraught man could have watched his daughter's murderer die a thousand times, and it would never be enough. And now that the object of his hatred was dead, where could all that pent-up rage of his go? My image of him that night is of a very thirsty man who had just drunk a long drink of salt water.

I've been studying the death penalty in the U.S. for a very long time. I keep learning about it, and one of the key things I've learned about its application is that very few death sentences are actually handed down, and then, how exceptionally few murder victims' families ever get to witness the execution of their loved one's killer. And then it is almost exclusively reserved for those who kill people of European descent, almost never those who murder people of color. Evidently their lives, their deaths don't seem to matter in the same way, no outrage is felt at their passing, and, often enough no serious investigation of their murders is pursued.

When we do abolish the death penalty in the U.S. and we are now on our way toward that day as public support plummets and executions become more and more rare, a significant part of our enlightenment, I believe, will be the recognition that wounded, grieving families, after long years of waiting, can never be healed by watching as the government kills the perpetrator. If anything, witnessing such violence only serves to re-traumatize them. Such was the testimony of many murder victims' families to the legislature in New Jersey as the state set about to repeal the death penalty in 2007, the first state to legislatively do so in the modern era. "Don't kill for me" they said.

In my journey on this death penalty road, I have seen how the violent process of government killings produces its own collateral victims: among them, guards in execution squads whose job demands that they must seize from their cells prisoners, rendered defenseless, and forcibly strap them down onto gurneys to be killed. In my book, *Dead Man Walking*, I tell the story of Major Kendall Coody in Louisiana, who assisted in five executions. One day he called me into his office and confided that he was going to quit his job, that he couldn't be part of executions anymore, that he knew the crimes of the men and how ghastly their murders were, but he said that when you're up close to it, when you're the one to take an alive human being out to kill them, and knowing that they're defenseless and can't fight back, and how afterwards you come home and you can't sleep and you can't eat and you know you just can't do it anymore.

Prison wardens, whose job it is to signal the executioner to begin the killing, are also emerging as victims of the death penalty process. Former Florida Warden Ron McAndrew presided at three executions, and that was more than enough for him. He now speaks publicly, testifying openly that he is still in therapy, trying to heal from his participation in executions and how the memory of them haunts him still. He tells how he had taken on the job as prison warden, believing it was an honorable profession to protect the citizens and possibly help to restore the fractured lives of the prisoners. But presiding at executions had undone him. There's nothing honorable in killing fellow human beings who are defenseless, he says.

What murder victims' families really need, I've found out, are compassionate people to talk to, who will accompany them on the long road to healing. They need counseling and sometimes financial help when they lose their jobs because the trauma and grief causes them to lose focus or even the energy to get out of bed to go to work. Parents who lose a child often also lose their marriage. Seventy percent of them divorce. They need counseling and encouragement and community support. And the siblings of murdered children all too often slip through the cracks and are in need of attention and help. In one grieving family I knew, the parents became so fixated on the court proceedings and getting the perpetrator executed that their younger daughter became invisible to them. She told me that all they cared about, all they ever talked about was getting justice for her dead sister, and she didn't matter anymore, and how they would always remember the anniversary date of her sister's death, but when her birthday came, they never even noticed. Sometimes families even need financial help with funeral expenses. Most States have Victim Compensation Funds, but they're often meager and difficult for families to access. And now most District Attorneys' offices have victims' assistance staff, whose job it is to reach out in a supportive way to families traumatized by murder. But murders are many and the sheer numbers of hurting families are overwhelming. And when DAs are more bent on chalking up capital convictions than on real justice, the only murder victims' families that matter to them are the ones who agree to testify in support of the death penalty. Meanwhile, the enormously inflated cost of seeking the death penalty sucks the coffers dry, pre-empting real and effective efforts toward actual crime prevention. Which, as I see it, is at the heart of the heart of the matter. The most genuine help we can ever give victims' families, the best would be to prevent the violence and crime that makes them victims' families in the first place.

WORLD RELIGIONS AND THE DEATH PENALTY

Mario Marazziti[1]

After the Dalai Lama finished speaking at an event on the Capitoline Hill in Rome, I asked him to be one of the first signatories of the Community of Sant'Egidio's Appeal for a Moratorium on the Death Penalty. He accepted immediately—he signed in green ink—and frankly, it was no surprise. Who more than the Dalai Lama is identified with unconditional respect for life?

Buddhism, however, exists in many forms, so it is hard to say that it has one clear message on the death penalty. And so it is with all world religions. On the one hand, their core teachings seem to argue strongly against taking life; on the other, religious bodies have often vigorously supported the death penalty.

BUDDHISM

All schools of Buddhism emphasize compassion, nonviolence and respect for human life, and they encourage their adherents to abstain from killing or injuring any living creature. But the Buddha, while against physical punishment in general, left no clear statement about capital punishment.

The way to restore a wrong is not through another wrong. Rather, a counterweight is needed, so that the more evil there is on the one side, the more good there is on the other side. Buddhists believe in the cycle of birth and rebirth, Samsara, and that the death penalty will negatively affect both souls, the one who is punished and the one who punishes. Trying to gain recompense for evil, even violent death, by inflicting further death will simply cause a greater imbalance in the world; only rehabilitation has a chance to restore the harmony in life.

---

1   Mario Marazziti, spokesperson for the Community of Sant'Egidio and currently a member of the Italian legislature.

The cruel ultimate punishment has little chance of healing society and re-establishing the law, because excessive cruelty injures the mind of the offender and of those who administer death, whatever the reason. Compassion cannot cope with capital punishment; if a crime is horrible, as a last resort, the offender should be banished from the community so as not to do any further harm.

But in many countries where Buddhism is influential, such as Myanmar and Thailand, the death penalty is still legal and executions are still carried out; the practical needs of the society have prevailed. It seems that capital punishment and Buddhism are on two opposite sides philosophically but not historically.

> *Buddhist doctrines hold nonviolence and compassion for all life in high regard. The First Precept of Buddhism requires individuals to abstain from injuring or killing all living creatures and Buddha's teaching restricts Buddhist monks from any political involvement. Using historical documents and interviews with contemporary authorities on Buddhist doctrine, our research uncovered a long history of political involvement by Buddhist monks and Buddhist support of violence. Yet, there seems to be limited Buddhist involvement in Southeast Asian countries in death penalty issues.*
> . . .
>
> *The death penalty is inconsistent with Buddhist teachings. . . . Yet, evidence suggests that most Southeast Asian countries practiced capital punishment long before the Buddhist influence emerged in India in 400 to 500 B.C.[2]*

Tomoko Sasaki, a former member of the Japanese parliament, evoked retribution: "A basic teaching [in Japanese Buddhism] is retribution. If someone evil does something bad, he has to atone with his own life. If you take a life, you have to give your own."[3] The concept of retribution could be seen as consistent with the central concept of karma in Buddhism, the way in which the Buddha explained inequality and

---

2   Leanne Fiftal Alarid and Hsiao-Ming Wang, "Mercy and punishment: Buddhism and the death penalty", *Social Justice*, vol. 28 (2001), pp. 231-247.

3   Charles Lane, "Why Japan still has the death penalty", *Washington Post,* 16 January 2005.

contradictions in the world. But capital punishment can be a deadly interruption of the possibility of balancing the different karmas and improving the world, favouring a higher level of mercy and life: a death sentence would be a powerful obstacle to communication between the reproductive karma, the supportive karma, the obstructive karma and the destructive karma.

When the Dalai Lama subscribed to the appeal I submitted on behalf of the Community of Sant'Egidio in Rome, he also submitted this message, read at an event organized by Peace Center on April 9, 1999:

> *The death penalty fulfills a preventive function, but it is also very clearly a form of revenge. It is an especially severe form of punishment because it is so final. The human life is ended and the executed person is deprived of the opportunity to change, to restore the harm done or compensate for it. Before advocating execution we should consider whether criminals are intrinsically negative and harmful people or whether they will remain perpetually in the same state of mind in which they committed their crime or not. The answer, I believe, is definitely not. However horrible the act they have committed, I believe that everyone has the potential to improve and correct themselves. Therefore, I am optimistic that it remains possible to deter criminal activity, and prevent such harmful consequences of such acts in society, without having to resort to the death penalty.*

HINDUISM

"An eye for an eye makes the whole world blind." This adage of Mahatma Gandhi, who is regarded as a sage by many Hindus and others, is often quoted by opponents of the death penalty. India, while home to diverse religions, is heavily influenced by Hinduism. The country recently restarted executions after an almost decade-long de facto moratorium. But given the small number of executions, the death penalty is almost non-existent.

Those who do support the death penalty give reasons that are different from those most often heard in the West. The founder of the Hare Krishna movement, Srila Prabhupada, said that the reason a murderer should be condemned to death is so that "in his next life he will not have to suffer for the great sin he has committed."[4] Another Hindu thinker has argued that

> *Hinduism is full of compassion and forgiveness. Leave aside human beings; we are supposed to be kind even to insects and animals. We are not supposed to kill a small insect. Therefore, taking the life of a human being is a very big issue for us. Our Hindu dharma is very clear that use of violence against anyone is not allowed. Any other type of punishment may be given, but we should not take anyone's life. Our scriptures and Vedas do not favor capital punishment. They advocate the principle of non-violence.*[5]

That is akin to the teachings that Mahatma Gandhi made well known, rooted in Ahimsa, a Hindu form of thinking based on non-violence: "By birth I am a Vaishanavite, and was taught Ahimsa in my childhood. . . . In its negative form, it means not injuring any living being, whether by body or mind. I may not therefore hurt the person of any wrong-doer, or bear any ill will to him and so cause mental suffering."

This attitude is very nearly inscribed in the Indian Constitution, where the death penalty is reserved for "the rarest of the rarest cases." On the one hand, this means that the framers of the Constitution must have approved of capital punishment; on the other hand, it suggests that disagreement among them was strong enough that they sought to strictly limit its use. Babasaheb Ambedkar, a primary architect of the Indian Constitution, wanted to keep capital punishment out of it. He said that while many people who believe in nonviolence may not follow it in practice, "they certainly adhere to the principle of non-violence as a moral mandate which they ought to observe as far

---

4   Srila Prabhupada, *Bhagavad-Gita as It Is* (New York, Macmillan, 1968).
5   Samvidananda Saraswati, the head of Kailam Ashram, in *Hinduism Today* (October-December 2006).

as they possibly can" and therefore "the proper thing for this country to do is to abolish the death sentence altogether."

JUDAISM

The Bible and the Talmud contain passages treating the death penalty as legitimate and widespread: 36 crimes in the Bible are punished by death, among them idol worship, profanation of the Sabbath, adultery, incest and public incitement to apostasy. The Mishnah (Sanhedrin 7:1) lists the methods of execution as slaying by the sword, stoning, burning and strangling. But it also says that a death sentence can only be imposed after a trial before 23 judges. Other Talmudic texts contain discussions that lead towards a denial of the right to execute, requiring at least two witnesses to testify to something that is unlikely in practice: both that they witnessed the brutal crime for which the defendant is on trial, and that they had warned the defendant in advance so that he or she had full awareness that it would incur the death penalty. In this perspective, not even the defendant's own confession was accepted as evidence.

The Mishnah Makkot (1:10) says: "A Sanhedrin that puts a man to death once in seven years is called destructive. Rabbi Eliezer ben Azariah says: even once in seventy years. Rabbi Akiba and Rabbi Tarfon say: had we been in the Sanhedrin none would ever have been put to death. Rabbi Simeon ben Gamaliel says: they would have multiplied shedders of blood in Israel."

Like Hinduism, Judaism seems to have developed a gap between theory and practice on capital punishment. Scriptural passages favouring the death penalty are set against the respect for human life and the uniqueness of each life, created in the divine image and with the sacred right to life:

> One of the most striking expressions of this in Jewish Jurisprudence is the text of the admonition recorded in the Mishnah (Sanhedrin 4:5) given by the court to witnesses in capital cases. "Know you," the judges would say to the witnesses "that capital cases are not like civil cases . . . for

in civil cases (if false testimony is given intentionally or unintentionally and the defendant is unjustly convicted) he may make financial restitution and thus atone (for his sin or error). While in capital cases, his blood and that of his descendants through all eternity are upon him. For that reason the human being was (originally) created singly; to teach you that he who destroys one person's life, it is considered as if he destroyed a whole world, and he who preserves one person's life, it is as if he has preserved a whole world. . . . And to declare the greatness of the Holy One Blessed be He, for when a human person mints coins from the one mold they all appear identical, but the Holy One Blessed be He "minted" every person from the mold of the first human being, but not one is identical to another, therefore a person should say, the world was created for me.[6]

In Orthodox Judaism, it is held that in theory the death penalty is a just punishment for some crimes.[7] However, in practice the application of such a punishment can only be carried out by humans whose system of justice is nearly perfect.

When the State of Israel was founded, the Knesset ruled as a secular body. And the Knesset decided to abolish the death penalty completely except as a punishment for genocide or treason committed in time of war. Israel has administered capital punishment only once, to Adolf Eichmann, a principal organizer of the Holocaust.

In the United States, the Central Conference of American Rabbis and the Union for Reform Judaism have publicly opposed the death penalty since 1959. The Union for Reform Judaism has stated: "We believe that there is no crime for which the taking of human life by society is justified, and that it is the obligation of society to evolve other methods in dealing with crime." This practical approach is echoed, but strengthened by a refusal "both in concept and in practice" —formally stated by the Central Conference of American Rabbis in 1979.

---

6   David Rosen, *Judaism and Human Rights*.
7   "Orthodox Judaism", *Wikipedia*, available from http://en.wikipedia.org/wiki/Orthodox_Judaism.

The Union for Reform Judaism has appealed "to our congregants and to our co-religionists and to all who cherish God's mercy and love to join in efforts to eliminate this practice [capital punishment] which lies as a stain upon civilization and our religious conscience."

ISLAM

The mercy of God is at the centre of Islam's vision about the death penalty. But of Arab and Islamic countries, only Albania has repealed capital punishment. Several countries with a large Muslim population, such as Algeria, Bosnia, Morocco, and even Pakistan, with the largest death row in the world, have a de facto moratorium. Thus, there is no automatic relationship between being strongly rooted in Islam and using capital punishment.

Forgiveness is in principle always preferable to retribution, since forgiveness and peace are crucial Koranic themes. The mainstream of Islam prefers forgiveness and peace; the *umma* or Muslim community is spread across a huge variety of nations, uniting more than one billion people with many diverse traits. In 2005, Muslim scholar Tariq Ramadan called in Geneva for a global moratorium of executions in the Islamic world.

The Koran (6:151) says: "Take not life, which God has made sacred, except by way of justice and law." Some Islamic countries have established sharia (Islamic law), while others follow secular law. The 2011 Moroccan Constitution says that Islam is the religion of the State, but not that Morocco is an Islamic State. Article 20 says: "The right to life is every human being's right." In February 2013, the group Moroccan Parliamentarians against the Death Penalty was organized, a few months before the Fifth World Congress against the Death Penalty took place in June 2013 in Madrid, where the process of creating an international network of World Parliamentarians against the Death Penalty was begun.

In Islamic law the death penalty is related to two types of crime. One is intentional murder. In these cases, the families of the victims are given the option to insist on the death penalty, ask for compensation instead, or simply forgive. Their decision is binding on the state.

The second type of death-penalty-eligible crime, according to the Koran, includes *fasad fil-ardh*—spreading mischief in the community or in the land. This can have a broad meaning or a strict one, but it includes acts thought to undermine the authority of the state or destabilize the community. This can be a way for authoritarian regimes to control opposition, spread terror or eliminate political opponents. Treason, but also apostasy, terrorism, rape, piracy, adultery and homosexual activity may fall in this group of capital crimes.

The Koran (5:32) says: "Whoever slays a soul, unless it be for manslaughter or for mischief in the land, it is as though he slew all men; and whoever keeps it alive, it is as though he kept alive all men."

"THE CRUEL ULTIMATE PUNISHMENT HAS LITTLE CHANCE OF HEALING SOCIETY." —Mario Marazziti

Imad-ad-Dean Ahmad, the President of the Minaret of Freedom Institute, said:

> *The views of American Muslims on the death penalty vary somewhat, but the range is narrow compared to the enormous disagreements among Christians. All Muslims accept the permissibility of the death penalty because it is addressed in the Qur'an. However, our views range from those who would apply it for a moderately short list of crimes (short compared to the enormous list of capital crimes in the Old Testament) to those who would apply it to a somewhat shorter list still, and finally, to those who would call for a moratorium on the death penalty in America altogether.*

In fact, those references in the Koran may be read as narrowing dramatically the circumstances in which a murderer's life can be taken, and as well as providing an exemption from the general prohibition on killing a human being.

Many majority-Muslim countries are considering official steps towards a legal moratorium, and many are already applying a de facto moratorium. But it remains an open question whether capital punishment is structurally related to Islam. Theoretically, there is some limited acceptance of the death penalty in the Koran. But opposition to capital punishment is a giant leap forward compared to the habits of the people to whom the Koran was first addressed. Most Koranic commentators would have difficulty in accepting that the interpretation of the text may have evolved over time. But some hold that it can and must be interpreted and that, to be faithful to the deep meaning, an evolving interpretation is necessary.

Siti Musdah Mulia, a professor of Islamic theology and Islamic law at the University of Jakarta, is fighting for an end to the use of the death penalty in Indonesia, the most populous Muslim country in the world. Indian Muslim scholar Wahiduddin Khan, a peace activist and author of a commentary on the Koran, explained to me that if among God's creations, human beings are the most perfect (Koran, Sura al-Isra', 17:70), they must be respected without prejudice to race, ethnicity, religion, colour, language or gender. One form of respect for human beings is not to take their lives (Koran, 27:33; 5:32) or cause them to suffer physical or psychological pain (5:45).

Iman al-Ghazali, who died in AD 1111, said that the core objective of Islam is to protect five basic human rights: the rights to life, free expression of opinions, religious freedom, reproductive health and property, which later became known as *al-kulliyah alkhamsah*. In these, Siti Musdah Mulia found a basis for acceptance of something like a declaration of human rights and said that "the Islamic teaching is not compatible with the death penalty."

CHRISTIANITY

From its beginning, the Christian church was marked by a strong rejection of the death penalty and of violence. Nonviolence was part of the moral framework of the first generations of Christians. This included refusal to serve in the army and was connected to refusal to honour the Emperor as a divinity.

The Bible contains many references to killing and to crimes punishable by death. But even the famous eye-for-an-eye code was a way of reducing revenge and punishment from "seventy times seven" to a more proportionate measure. And the seal on Cain's forehead to protect him from physical vengeance, after he killed his brother, showed a second line of teaching that culminated in the Book of Job, where life and the soul are in the hands of God and no one else can have power over them. Thus, no state has the authority to take life away.

Finally, the commandment to love one's neighbour and the Gospels' call to break down walls between the enemy and the brother, as in the parable of the Good Samaritan, and the invitation to forgive and not even to say a bad word to the one who offends us, are just some of the many reasons that the taking of human life has been considered incompatible with Christianity.

In the fourth century AD, Roman Emperor Constantine legalized Christianity and established a special link between religion and politics. Beginning with the Council of Arles, military service was no longer banned; rather, to refuse to serve in the army caused exclusion from the sacraments. Not long afterwards, St. Augustine introduced the concept of just war. The legitimization of the death penalty continued in the Middle Ages. St. Thomas Aquinas argued for it, introducing the concept of a higher good for society, which may require the acceptance of a lesser good or an evil. Centuries later, Martin Luther argued that the power of life and death that is in God's hands had been delegated to the political authorities. He opposed the use of the death penalty for ecclesial crimes, so as not to mingle the gospel and human rules, in which regard he differed from other Protestant thinkers such as Calvin and Zwingli, who considered heresy a crime with political consequences and as such punished by ordinary laws.

With the Second Vatican Council, the Catholic Church came closer to the original spirit of Christianity and contributed to Europe's process of relinquishing the death penalty. Paul VI abolished the death penalty in the Vatican State in 1967. Its full elimination from the Penal Law was carried out by John Paul II in 2001.

On Christmas day 1998, during the Urbi et Orbi blessing, John Paul II called for a ban on the death penalty. On 23 January 1999, in Nuestra Senora de Guadalupe basilica in Mexico City, while reaffirming the need to fight for a "culture of life . . . from conception to natural death," he launched the appeal: "Never again terrorism and narco-trafficking, never again torture and the death penalty." In St. Louis four days later, he said "I renew the appeal . . . to end the death penalty, which is both cruel and unnecessary."

With John Paul II there was an acceleration away from the death penalty. While the new catechism of the Catholic Church still acknowledges the death penalty as an option, it speaks to its practical inutility in the presence of alternative means to guarantee security and effective, rehabilitative punishment. Thus, the first step has been a practical and partial repudiation of the death penalty.

Cardinal Ratzinger, later Pope Benedict XVI, established a difference in moral gravity between the violation of life through euthanasia and abortion (exclusion from the sacraments) and the violation of life through participation in a war or in carrying out the death penalty. John Paul II had already asked the Governor of Missouri to save the life of a prisoner sentenced to death during his visit to the state and inaugurated the regular intervention of the Holy See to try to stop individual executions in the United States and elsewhere.

Nowadays the Christian churches are among the organizations with the longest and most continuous advocacy against the death penalty.

In 2007, the Primate of the Church of England, Rowan Williams, said:

> *People will sometimes still speak as if the only way of honouring the value of human life, let's say in the case of murder, were to take a life as a punishment. And I think there is a contradiction in there somewhere. The culture of life means a culture of profound respect for every life, however much we may disapprove of actions or wish to condemn them. The culture of life is one which is essentially a culture of hope. And the death penalty is one of those things which always speaks against hope.*

In so many countries where the death penalty exists, it is not the death penalty alone, it is the whole environment that grows up around it: the environment of the condemned cell, of the long periods where many people wait for execution.

I have been in countries where people . . . have been on death row for 20 years. That is an inhumanity. I've also been in countries where it's quite clear that certain races, certain classes, certain sections of the population are much more likely to receive the death penalty than others. So we need to remember: it's not only the infliction of death itself, it is everything that goes with it that dehumanizes.

Pope Francis reminded us in 2014 that our world still asks for "human sacrifices" and "laws allow to do so." He could not be clearer.

THE DEATH PENALTY AS A HUMAN RIGHTS ISSUE

Nigel S. Rodley[1]

For the first 70 years of the 20th century, law students examined the question of the death penalty, if their curriculum touched on it at all, either as an ordinary criminal-justice policy issue or in the context of theoretical conceptions of legal justice. When discussed in Parliament in the United Kingdom, the discourse fell largely within the same paradigms: Did the ultimate penalty deter and so prevent capital crime, and did it offer an appropriate form of justice for the grave crimes (in practice, murder) for which it was meted out? Another key element was public opinion: Was the public ready for abolition? The answer to the last question was invariably negative; in fact, although the death penalty was effectively abolished in Britain as long ago as 1965, it was not until 2015—50 years later—that public support for the death penalty dropped below 50 per cent.[2]

It seems that in any national debate on the death penalty similar notions are in play. But a new, potent dimension has been added: the human rights perspective. In line with a broadening and deepening human rights consciousness that moved from marginality onto the centre stage of international politics in the last quarter of the 20th century, the death penalty, too, came to be analysed and discussed in human rights terms. After all, if human rights values proclaim that every human being has the inherent right to life, by what logic could the state, the principal guarantor of human rights, deprive someone of life? In the naïve words of a lapel badge of that decade: "Why do we kill people to show that killing people is wrong?" Moreover, if Article 5 of the Universal Declaration of Human Rights (UDHR) ordained that "no-one shall be subjected to torture or to cruel, inhuman or degrading treatment or punishment," by what mental gymnastics could deliberately and cold-bloodedly putting someone to death be exempted from categorization as cruel, inhuman and degrading?

---

1   Sir Nigel Rodley is Professor of Law and Chair of the Human Rights Centre, University of Essex, and a Member and former Chairperson of the United Nations Human Rights Committee.

2   NatCen Social Research, British Social Attitudes, "Support for the death penalty falls below 50% for the first time," 26 March 2015, available from www.bsa.natcen.ac.uk/media-centre/latest-press-releases/bsa-32-support-for-death-penalty.aspx?_ga=1.76012437.189869271.1430156008.

THE UNITED NATIONS AND THE DEATH PENALTY

It was no accident that many of the early discussions on the death penalty at the United Nations took place from a crime prevention rather than a human rights perspective. The first product of that approach was Marc Ancel's seminal 1962 study *Capital Punishment*, the first of several periodic studies of the practice. There is only one explicit reference to human rights in this 68-page study:

> *At the end of the second world war, there was a renewed upsurge of those humanitarian tendencies which, like the desire to safeguard human rights and human dignity, had been the mainspring of the movement for the abolition of the death penalty.[3]*

The issue of the death penalty, then, may have been *like* human rights issues, in the sense of reflecting analogous humanitarian tendencies, but it was not itself a human rights problem. Even in the section of the study dealing with the "present state of the controversy," Ancel only mentioned that capital punishment was "a form of cruelty and inhumanity unworthy of a civilization which claims to be humane."[4] This is at least resonant with the prohibition in Article 5 of the UDHR.

The United Nations has dealt with the death penalty in theory and as applied in practice. The human rights implications of the (mis-)application of the death penalty have always been easy to recognize. This has not been so true of the death penalty as an institution. If the death penalty were acknowledged as inherently violating human rights, then the conclusion would have to be that it is unlawful under international law, since there is no doubt that the human rights that are principally at issue (right to life, prohibition of cruel punishment) are solidly grounded in international law. Yet, for virtually all of the last century, a majority of states were retentionist in law and a majority of these in practice. So, since states are

---

3   Marc Ancel, *Capital Punishment* (New York, United Nations Department of Economic and Social Affairs, 1962), paragraph 1.

4   Marc Ancel, *Capital Punishment,* paragraph 227.

the framers as well as the subjects of international law, it was clear that states were not prepared to recognize the death penalty as being incompatible with that law.[5] From this it followed that they could not accept an interpretation of the human rights in question that would acknowledge that the death penalty transgressed them. This reflected a political stand-off that had first appeared at the time of the drafting of the UDHR itself. Article 3 of the UDHR declares, "Everyone has the right to life, liberty and the security of person." That is all that is said of the right to life. Voices had been raised to bring the death penalty within its remit, but the matter was left for further consideration in the context of drafting the International Covenant on Civil and Political Rights (ICCPR).[6]

In fact, the human rights dimension of the death penalty issue was referred to as early as the first General Assembly resolution contemplating abolition. This was Resolution 2857 (XXVI) in 1971, in which the Assembly modestly affirmed (in operative paragraph 3) that "the main objective to be pursued is that of progressively restricting the number of offences for which capital punishment may be imposed, with a view to the desirability of abolishing this punishment in all countries." The purpose was stated as "fully to guarantee the right to life, provided for in article 3 of the Universal Declaration of Human Rights." This elegant language managed to invoke the values underlying the right to life without requiring acceptance that its current interpretation prohibited the death penalty. At the time, there was no consensus that the UDHR was legally binding.

The resolution was far from uncontroversial. It was adopted by a vote of 59 in favour and 1 against, with 54 abstentions. Thus, the affirmative votes barely exceeded the rest. Moreover, it remained the high point for the next quarter of a century in United Nations action promoting the normative proscription of the death penalty. In 1977, General Assembly Resolution 32/61, this time accepted by consensus, picked up the same language but dropped the phrase "in all countries." The human rights language was moved from an operative paragraph to the preamble; but this time, by referring not only

5   See William A. Schabas, *The Abolition of the Death Penalty in International Law,* 3rd edition (Cambridge, Cambridge University Press, 2002).
6   Lilly E. Landerer, "Capital punishment as a human rights issue before the United Nations," *Revue des droits de l'homme – Human Rights Journal,* vol. 4 (1974), 511, 517-518.

to Article 3 of the UDHR but also to Article 6 of the ICCPR, the Assembly invoked the notion of legal obligation, though evidently a limited obligation (as discussed below), and only applicable to the states parties to the ICCPR.

For some two decades after 1977, attempts failed even to reaffirm the limited normative proscription of the death penalty achieved in 1971. A number of retentionist countries mobilized against abolition with some success. Thus, at the Sixth United Nations Congress on the Prevention of Crime and the Treatment of Offenders in Caracas in 1980, a vigorous attempt by Austria and Sweden to promote abolition in a full-throated human rights framework was beaten back and the sponsors had to withdraw the text to avoid defeat. The text would have called for "the total abolition of capital punishment throughout the world." The human rights perspective was framed as follows:

> *Capital punishment raises serious questions in relation to respect for the dignity of all human beings and for human rights, in particular, the right to life, which is the most fundamental of all human rights, and the right not to be subjected to cruel, inhuman or degrading punishment.*[7]

The scene had been set by the Secretary-General himself, who opened the Congress by stating that "the taking of life of human beings violates respect for the dignity of every person and the right to life, as declared in the basic postulates of the United Nations."[8]

Effectively the last attempt in that United Nations venue to address the issue took place at the Eighth United Nations Crime Congress in Havana in 1990. All that would have been sought was a reaffirmation of the language of the General Assembly resolutions of the 1970s, together with a recommendation that states consider imposing a moratorium of at least three years. The draft resolution was approved by a majority, but not the two-thirds majority needed for adoption. By then, action on the issue had moved to the human rights sector. The 1970s resolutions were the main abolitionist legacy,

---

7   UN Doc. A/CONF.87/C.1/L.1. On these and subsequent proceedings in the crime congresses and the General Assembly, see Nigel S. Rodley and Matt Pollard, *The Treatment of Prisoners under International Law,* 3rd edition (Oxford, Oxford University Press, 2009), pp. 284-286.

8   UN Doc. A/CONF.87/9, paragraph 98.

with their invocation of the right to life but not the prohibition of cruel punishment. The crime prevention part of the Secretariat (now the United Nations Office on Drugs and Crime) is still responsible for commissioning the (now quinquennial) United Nations studies on the death penalty.

After the disappointment at the 1980 Caracas Crime Congress, the governments traditionally most active on the issue (Austria, Costa Rica, Italy, Portugal and Sweden, joined by the Federal Republic of Germany) introduced a draft optional protocol to the ICCPR, whereby states becoming parties would commit themselves to abolition. The ICCPR had not required states parties to abolish the death penalty. Its Article 6(6) stated that nothing in it should be invoked to justify non-abolition, but it did allow retentionist states to become parties, while subjecting them to certain restrictions. The Human Rights Committee, the expert body established to monitor implementation of the Covenant, stated that Article 6 "refers generally to abolition in terms which strongly suggest . . . that abolition is desirable."[9] It also asserted that "all measures of abolition should be considered as progress in the enjoyment of the right to life." Thus the 1980 draft was aimed at translating desirability into legal obligation.

In 1982, the Assembly referred the matter to the Commission on Human Rights, which two years later passed the buck further down to its expert sub-body, the Sub-Commission on Prevention of Discrimination and Protection of Minorities. Despite not having a specific mandate to adopt a text (as opposed to studying the idea), the Sub-Commission decided to adopt an amended draft text on the recommendation of Special Rapporteur Marc Bossuyt. The Sub-Commission forwarded the text to the Commission, which referred it on, through the Economic and Social Council to the General Assembly. The Assembly, by a majority vote (59 votes for, 26 against and 48 abstentions), adopted the text of

> "WHY DO WE KILL PEOPLE TO SHOW THAT KILLING PEOPLE IS WRONG?"
> —Nigel S. Rodley

9   "General comment no. 6: the right to life" (1982), reproduced in UN Doc. HRI/GEN/1/ Rev.9 (Vol. I) (2008), paragraph 6.

what is now the Second Optional Protocol [to the ICCPR] Aiming at the Abolition of the Death Penalty.

The preamble to the Protocol refers to the right to life in language borrowed from the Human Rights Committee's general comment on ICCPR Article 6; it also directly cites UDHR Article 3 and ICCPR Article 6. It does not explicitly invoke the prohibition of cruel punishment, though it expresses the belief that abolition "contributes to the enhancement of human rights and progressive development of human rights." Presumably, the drafters preferred to avoid the use of language like "cruel, inhuman or degrading" to characterize the penal practices of states that may not yet be ready to ratify but would be willing to abstain from voting on adoption of the text, as long as they did not feel insulted. Meanwhile, by 1994, the Human Rights Committee was making clear that, had Article 6 of the ICCPR not provided for retention, Article 7's prohibition of cruel punishments would have been applicable.[10]

Also in 1994, Italy tried unsuccessfully to get another weak abolitionist resolution through the General Assembly.[11] In 1997, Italy decided to centre its efforts on the United Nations Commission on Human Rights, where it successfully proposed a stronger text. This repeated the earlier General Assembly call for the progressive restriction of capitally punishable offences and establishment of a moratorium "with a view to completely abolishing the death penalty."[12] After a number of resolutions reiterating this language, by 2003 the Commission was able to make the stronger direct call, in its Resolution 2003/67, "to abolish the death penalty completely and, in the meantime, to establish a moratorium on executions." It repeated the approach in its final substantive session in 2005 (Resolution 2005/59). Like earlier initiatives, it referred to UDHR Article 3 and ICCPR Article 6.

---

10 *Ng v. Canada*, UN Doc. CCPR/C/49/D/469/1991 (1994), paragraph 16.2; see William A. Schabas, *The Death Penalty as Cruel Treatment and Torture* (Boston, Northeastern University Press, 1996).

11 States would merely have been invited to "consider" progressive restriction of the number of capitally punishable offences and the "opportunity" of instituting a moratorium, albeit with the ambitious goal of abolition by the year 2000; UN Doc. A/C.3/49/L.32 (1994).

12 Commission on Human Rights Resolution 1997/12—27 for, 11 against and 14 abstentions; see Nigel S. Rodley and Matt Pollard, *The Treatment of Prisoners under International Law*, 286-287.

The successor Human Rights Council has not so far addressed the issue. Nor has it needed to, for the issue has now returned to the General Assembly. In 2007, Italy successfully proposed General Assembly Resolution 62/149, calling for "a moratorium on executions with a view to abolishing the death penalty." The resolution's preamble acknowledged the important role of the Commission on Human Rights. While the softening of the language on abolition to a tone reminiscent of earlier formulations is notable, the General Assembly's support for a moratorium is an important step. It was controversial, but an absolute majority voted for it (104 for, 54 against and 29 abstentions). Since then, several similar resolutions have been adopted, with a larger adopting majority each time. The latest was General Assembly Resolution 69/186 in 2014, with 117 votes in favour, 37 against and 34 abstentions.

One other development in these resolutions has been the invocation of human rights in general terms, without reference to any specific right, even the right to life. The UDHR and ICCPR are invoked in the preamble without reference to specific articles, with the statements that "the use of the death penalty undermines human dignity" and a moratorium "contributes to the enhancement and progressive development of human rights." It is hard to evaluate the significance of this. On the one hand, no right is identified as being (potentially) violated by the death penalty. On the other, the language implies that, in addition to the right to life, other rights relating to human dignity may be at stake. The most prominent of these would be the right not to be subjected to torture or cruel, inhuman or degrading treatment or punishment, which has traditionally been depicted as at the core of the notion of human dignity. For instance, according to Article 2 of General Assembly Resolution 3452 (XXX) of 1975, "Any act of torture or cruel, inhuman or degrading treatment or punishment is an offence to human dignity."

THE ROLE OF CIVIL SOCIETY

If substantial majorities of United Nations member states are now willing to express themselves repeatedly in favour of abolition of the death penalty, this must be primarily attributable to the fact that a clear majority (105) of the world's 198 states are now abolitionist for all crimes (98) or for "ordinary crimes" (crimes not imperilling state security, such as treason or other serious crimes committed in wartime) (7). In comparison, in 1973, only 25 states were abolitionist. That was the year that Amnesty International adopted a policy supporting abolition of the death penalty, not only in political cases but also for ordinary crimes.

In 1977, Amnesty International convened a major international conference on abolition of the death penalty that took place in Stockholm. It was accompanied by a book-length report on the death penalty worldwide, and it met while representatives of the organization were receiving the Nobel Peace Prize in Oslo. This confluence of events led to substantial media coverage of the issue. After that, the organization intensified its existing collaboration with other non-governmental organisations (NGOs) in the human rights field to promote abolition and, particularly important, to intervene to try to save people sentenced to death from execution. Whatever the individual results of such actions were, it was evident that international awareness of the issue was on the rise. This took place within the context of a dominant human rights discourse. NGOs had no hesitation in invoking both the right to life and the prohibition of cruel and inhuman punishment. Human rights discourse was beginning to play an influential role in international politics generally; the death penalty component of it caught this wave.

At the United Nations, NGOs did not play a powerful role in instigating action, and they were unable to prevent the setbacks discussed earlier. However, at the regional level, their role was unmistakable. In 1983, the Council of Europe adopted the Protocol to the European Convention of Human Rights, which pledged states to abolition of the death penalty, at least for ordinary crimes. The initiator of the process leading to this achievement was Austrian Justice Minister Christian Broda, who had attended the Stockholm conference. Four years later, in a speech in Strasbourg accepting the Council of Europe's 1987 Human Rights Prize, he said:

> *We owe to the World Conference against the death penalty, organized in Stockholm by Amnesty International on 10-11 December 1977, the idea . . . that anyone who opposes torture must favour abolition of the death penalty.*[13]

---

13   Council of Europe, press release, 28 January 1987, doc. D (87) 3.

Amnesty International went on to lobby Council of Europe member states in favour of adoption (and later ratification) of the Protocol. It is also likely that its adoption influenced the adoption, six years later, of the Second Optional Protocol to the ICCPR. To this extent at least, it may be inferred that NGOs influenced the adoption of the latter protocol, and from a purely human rights perspective.

HUMAN RIGHTS ISSUES IN THE APPLICATION OF THE DEATH PENALTY

The human rights dimensions of the application of the death penalty have been more evident and less controversial. Thus, General Assembly Resolution 2393 (XXIII) of 1968, invoking Articles 3 and 5 of the Universal Declaration of Human Rights, called on governments of retentionist countries "to ensure the most careful legal procedures and the greatest possible safeguards for the accused in capital cases." In 1980, General Assembly Resolution 35/172 urged states "to respect as a minimum standard the content of the provisions of articles 6, 14 and 15 of the International Covenant on Civil and Political Rights." The formula was followed in several subsequent resolutions.

The significance of this was that states were being asked to respect treaty-based standards, regardless of whether they were parties to the treaty. Those standards involved substance as well as procedure. Article 6 requires that the death penalty be reserved for only the most serious crimes and crimes not contrary to other provisions of the Covenant (evidently implying those involving the exercise of the other human rights, such as the freedoms of speech, assembly and association). Articles 6 and 15 both prohibit retroactive punishments of any sort, particularly in capital cases. Article 14 lays down the basic elements of a fair trial and requires the possibility of review by a higher tribunal. Article 6 also demands the possibility of seeking pardon or commutation of sentence. And it insulates from the death penalty people who committed crimes when they were under 18 years old, as well as pregnant women. These standards were resumed and given some limited elaboration in Economic and Social Council Resolution 1989/64 on Safeguards Guaranteeing Protection of the Rights of Those Facing the Death Penalty.

The case law of the Human Rights Committee is also relevant to interpretation of the ICCPR provisions. Each of the standards lends itself to extensive commentary, but this is not the place for that. Rather, the message is that, to the limited extent that the death penalty may still be permitted, human rights are centrally relevant to the legitimacy of its application in practice.

Furthermore, one only has to read the other chapters of this book to see how human rights principles are offended by the inherently and inescapably arbitrary and discriminatory application of the death penalty. The maintenance of the death penalty and respect for human rights must surely soon come to be seen universally as mutually incompatible goals.

THE RIGHT TO LIFE AND THE PROGRESSIVE ABOLITION OF THE DEATH PENALTY

Christof Heyns and Thomas Probert[1]

By a number of measures, support for the death penalty is diminishing worldwide. There has been a slow but steady decline in the number of states that legally recognise it.[2] The number of states that actually practise the death penalty also continues to drop.[3] Moreover, while the death penalty used to be a global practice, of all executions known to have been conducted in 2014 outside of China, nearly three-quarters took place in just three countries: Iran, Iraq and Saudi Arabia.[4] If unconfirmed reports of a drastic reduction in executions in China over the last decade are accurate,[5] then the absolute number of people being executed per year is also going down. If represented as executions per capita, the trend is even more striking.

It would appear, therefore, that the death penalty is in gradual—quite possibly terminal—decline worldwide. This chapter places this observation in the context of the treatment of the right to life in international law, which is evolving towards the idea that life may as a general rule not be taken intentionally except if there is no other

---

1   Christof Heyns is the United Nations Special Rapporteur on extrajudicial, summary or arbitrary executions and professor of human rights law at the University of Pretoria, where he co-directs the Institute for International and Comparative Law in Africa. Thomas Probert is the senior researcher of the Unlawful Killings Unit of the Centre for Human Rights at the University of Pretoria and a research associate at the Centre of Governance and Human Rights at the University of Cambridge.

2   According to the classification of abolition used by Amnesty International, Fiji became the 99th abolitionist state in early 2015.

3   According to Amnesty International, at least 22 countries were known to have carried out executions in 2014. Though this number is the same as in 2013, and a slight increase from 21 in 2012, the trend over the last two decades has been one of decline from a high of 41 in 1995. See Amnesty International, *Death Sentences and Executions in 2014* (London, Amnesty International, 2015), p. 5.

4   Amnesty International do not attempt to estimate the number of people executed in China, where the extent of the practice remains a state secret, but is thought to extend to thousands of executions each year. Of the remaining States, Iran executed at least 289 people, Iraq at least 61, and Saudi Arabia at least 90, out of at least 607 executions worldwide. Next in number of executions was the United States (35), followed by Sudan (at least 23) and Yemen (at least 22). See Amnesty International, *Death Sentences and Executions in 2014*, p. 5.

5   Dui Ha, "China executed 2,400 people in 2013, Dui Hua", 20 October 2014, available from http://duihua.org/wp/?page_id=9270.

way to preserve another person's life. This evolution is taking place in the context of an international legal framework that imposes an obligation on states at least progressively to work towards abolishing the death penalty. In the context of that framework, there is a trend among a range of international actors explicitly to turn away from capital punishment.

In the gradual transition away from the death penalty, many have worked in a way that was in practice abolitionist, while taking care to note that international law was not inherently abolitionist.[6] An understanding of the international law surrounding the right to life (such as the International Covenant on Civil and Political Rights, Article 6) as being at least "progressively abolitionist" could allow an approach that is more in line with current state practice. It thus seems fair to say that international law is abolitionist in the sense that it requires the abolition of the death penalty, either immediately, or through the taking of steps in that direction. States that expand the scope of the death penalty are not acting in conformity with their international obligations, but so are states that maintain the status quo and do not take measures to reduce the scope and application of this form of punishment. This normative position has been reinforced by important initiatives taken by regional mechanisms, which can play a significant role in the promotion and protection of the right to life around the world.

THE "PROTECT LIFE" PRINCIPLE

If one proceeds from the starting point that each life is of immeasurable value and each unwarranted loss of life is a tragedy, then it is clear that there is no room for complacency as long as there is deadly violence anywhere. Yet encouragement can be taken from the general trend worldwide towards the realisation of what might be termed the "protect life" principle, which underlies the understanding of the right to life in international law. This principle requires that, as a

---

6   The mandate of the United Nations Special Rapporteur on extrajudicial, summary or arbitrary executions (most recently stated in July 2014 by Human Rights Council Resolution 26/12) includes a responsibility "to monitor the implementation of existing international standards on safeguards and restrictions relating to the imposition of capital punishment." For an example of an interpretation of the mandate as at least formally non-abolitionist, see Philip Alston, *Report of the Special Rapporteur on Extrajudicial, Summary or Arbitrary Executions on Mission to the United States* (28 May 2009) [A/HRC/11/2/Add.5], paragraph 3.

general rule, for one human being to take the life of another, the act must as a minimum be necessary in order to save another life.[7] The "protect life" principle is the standard posed in law enforcement and in personal self-defence and the defence of others.[8] It is increasingly seen as the global norm, and there is arguably increasing compliance in practice as well.

There has thus been a gradual movement away from the historical notion that the state could use force against its population to protect law and order (or the sovereign power of the ruler) or to impose other abstract values and towards the notion that it may use force only to protect life and limb.[9]

It is also possible to discern the impact of the "protect life" principle on the application of the death penalty. Not long ago, there were few constraints on using the death penalty to enforce state authority in general or to punish a wide range of offences. Now, if used at all, it is only as a punishment for the "most serious crimes," understood to be crimes involving murder.

The contemporary approach is moving closer to the "protect life" principle, insofar as the intentional taking of life—murder—is usually seen as the only crime that merits the death penalty. However, this approach still falls short of fully honouring the "protect life" principle, because the taking of life by the state comes as a punishment after the act, and its value as a deterrent, once assumed, is now strongly contested.[10] If the death penalty cannot be shown to prevent loss of life, there is little justification for its potential violation of human rights—it does not meet the "protect life" standard.

Regrettably, though the standard of "most serious crimes" is well established in international human rights law, some states that still

---

7   See Principle 9 of the *Basic Principles on the Use of Force and Firearms by Law Enforcement Officials*, adopted by the Eighth United Nations Congress on the Prevention of Crime and the Treatment of Offenders, Havana, Cuba, 27 August to 7 September 1990, available from www.ohchr.org/EN/ProfessionalInterest/Pages/UseOfForceAndFirearms.aspx.

8   Christof Heyns, *Report of the Special Rapporteur on Extrajudicial, Summary or Arbitrary Executions* (1 April 2014) [A/HRC/26/36], paragraphs 70-73.

9   This historical shift has been explored by theorists such as Michel Foucault, among others.

10   J. J. Donohue and J. Wolfers, "Uses and abuses of empirical evidence in the death penalty debate", *Stanford Law Review,* vol. 58 (2006), pp. 791-846.

impose the death penalty do so for lesser crimes, often meeting with strong condemnation from the international community.

THE REQUIREMENT FOR PROGRESSIVE ABOLITION UNDER INTERNATIONAL LAW

The stronger the normative consensus on the "protect life" principle grows, the more apparent it becomes that the death penalty, even if confined to the most serious cases, does not sit easily with human rights norms. While this tension is not new, the increasing willingness of human rights actors to address the question of capital punishment lends support to the contention that there is a logic of progressive realisation (normally associated with social, economic and cultural rights) within international law concerning the death penalty.

During the drafting of the International Covenant on Civil and Political Rights of 1966, the compromise between abolitionist and retentionist states was to prohibit arbitrary deprivation of life (in paragraph 1 of Article 6), while still carving out some space for the death penalty (in paragraph 2) by stating that "in countries which have not abolished the death penalty" it may be imposed only for the "most serious crimes," subject to certain further restrictions. This exception was expected to shrink. According to the chairperson of the drafting group, the wording of Article 6, paragraph 2, was intended to "show the direction" in which it was hoped that practice would move, meaning that a "constant reappraisal" of the scope of the term would be necessary. The wording chosen reflected the expectation that the category of permissible capital offences would narrow over the years as the value attached to life and other human rights increased.[11]

This expectation is underlined in Article 6, paragraph 6, which states that nothing in Article 6 "shall be invoked to delay or to prevent the abolition of capital punishment by any State Party". The fact that the death penalty has a foothold, albeit a shrinking one, in article 6 (2), may thus not serve as an argument against the contention that the modern interpretation of rights such as the right against torture, cruel

---

11 Roger Hood, "The enigma of the 'most serious' offences", Working Paper No. 9 (Center for Human Rights and Global Justice, New York University School of Law, 2006), p. 3. Also see William A. Schabas, *The Abolition of the Death Penalty in International Law*, 3rd ed. (Cambridge, UK, Cambridge University Press, 2002), p. 68

or inhuman dignity or treatment, or the right to dignity, demand an end to this form of punishment.

This approach that article 6 (2) envisages the withering away of the death penalty was affirmed in 1971 by the United Nations General Assembly, which affirmed in Resolution 2857 (XXVI) that "in order fully to guarantee the right to life ... the main objective to be pursued is that of progressively restricting the number of offenses for which capital punishment may be imposed, with a view to the desirability of abolishing this punishment in all countries."

While the debate continues about whether the death penalty conflicts with the right to life, it has meanwhile become widely seen as a violation of the right to be free from torture and cruel, inhuman or degrading treatment or punishment, the right to equality and the right to dignity. The debate has thus taken a practical turn, leaving the question of whether the death penalty per se is a violation of the right to life, and turning to the practical question of whether it can ever be implemented without violating other human rights. Likewise, as discussed above, the mandate of the special rapporteur on extrajudicial, summary or arbitrary executions has in the past been interpreted as not necessarily abolitionist, instead focusing on ensuring that relevant international safeguards are observed.

However, given the shift that has taken place in state practice, it seems accurate to say that the mandate of the special rapporteur is at least progressively abolitionist. For the same reason, it is no longer necessary to state in an unqualified manner that the death penalty per se is not contrary to the requirements of international law. Over the past several years, the perspective has emerged that international law requires the progressive abolition of the death penalty. This is not to say that it requires immediate compliance, as is usually the case with civil and political rights. Instead, the drafting history suggests that international law requires at least the gradual, progressive abolition of the death penalty, as is often the case with socio-economic rights.

The progressive-abolition perspective is further bolstered by the language of the Second Optional Protocol to the International Covenant on Civil and Political Rights of 1989, which observed that the language of Article 6 "refers to abolition of the death penalty in terms that strongly suggest that abolition is desirable" and underlined that "all measures of abolition of the death penalty should be considered as progress in the enjoyment of the right to life."

This would bring the mandate into line with most global human rights organisations, the Secretary-General of the United Nations, and the Office of the High Commissioner for Human Rights, all of which are unambiguous in their calls for the end of at least the practice of the death penalty. In July 2014, stating that the death penalty "has no place in the 21st century," the United Nations Secretary-General called on states to support the biennial General Assembly resolution calling for a global moratorium on its application.[12] The language of these resolutions has been designed to be broad and inclusive, calling not for the abolition of the death penalty but for a moratorium on executions with a view to future abolition. The goal of these General Assembly resolutions thus fits the pattern described above—progressive abolition.

A moratorium does not completely solve the problem of the death penalty. The Special Rapporteur on torture and other forms of cruel, inhuman and degrading treatment or punishment has expressed the view that lengthy detention on death row, even if a moratorium is in place, may constitute cruel and inhuman treatment. However, from the perspective of the right to life, a moratorium is a very helpful step forward; it allows the sometimes lengthy processes of legal and constitutional reform to take place without further loss of life.

Each iteration of the General Assembly resolution has been passed by a wider margin, reflecting the progressive global movement away from the death penalty. In 2014, 117 states voted in favour of the resolution, an increase from 111 in 2012, 109 in 2010, 106 in 2008 and 104 in 2007.[13]

The ways in which states vote on United Nations moratorium resolutions has been taken into account in several instances. For example,

---

12   UN News Service, "Death penalty has no place in 21st century, declares UN chief", 2 July 2014, available from www.un.org/apps/news/story.asp?NewsID=48192#.U_WzhsWSySp.

13   The most recent of these resolutions, General Assembly Resolution 69/186, was adopted in December 2014.

in 2014, the Human Rights Committee, in a decision concerning extradition to Ghana, found that, although there had been no recorded execution for more than 20 years, a de facto moratorium did not ensure that an execution would not be carried out in the future, citing as a consideration the fact that Ghana had not voted for any of the United Nations resolutions calling for a moratorium.[14]

On the other hand, several United Nations special rapporteurs were concerned by executions that took place in Somalia earlier in 2015. A statement issued through the Office of the High Commissioner for Human Rights drew attention to the fact that Somalia had voted *for* the 2012 resolution calling for a global moratorium, and that Somalia was therefore directly contravening its commitments at the international level.[15]

> "TRADITIONALLY, THE DEATH PENALTY WAS THE NORM, NOW ABOLITION IS THE NORM."
> —Christof Heyns and Thomas Probert

The United Nations currently regards 10 years as a suitable threshold for a state to pass without conducting an execution before it might be considered de-facto abolitionist. One could debate which country is more de facto abolitionist—one that has not executed anyone for five years since a change of administration and in that time has voted for three General Assembly resolutions calling for a death-penalty moratorium, or one that has not executed anyone for 10 years but has consistently opposed these resolutions? In either case, the subsequent resumption of executions would be regarded as a step backwards and—depending on the circumstances, especially regarding notice given—possibly an arbitrary killing; but the question remains, in which case would it be the greater surprise?

The trend towards the abolition of the death penalty is not linear, and a number of states have resumed the death penalty or increased its

---

14 Human Rights Committee decision in *Johnson v Ghana* (2014) [CCPR/C/110/D/2177/2012] paragraph 7.2.
15 UN News Centre, "Somalia: UN rights office calls for moratorium after 'hasty' execution of alleged murderer", 4 April 2014, available from www.un.org/apps/news/story.asp?NewsID=47503&Cr=death+penalty&Cr1=#.U_XvE8WSySp

scope. In the past two years, 10 countries have conducted executions after a period of two years or more without any. In some cases—for example, The Gambia, India and Nigeria—the practice of non-execution had been firmly entrenched.[16] Another troubling recent phenomenon has been the sentencing of large groups of individuals in mass trials, which has occurred in several countries including in Viet Nam and Egypt. This has led to serious concerns that such mass trials violate international fair-trial standards and other safeguards. Without a fair trial, the death penalty cannot be applied in a non-arbitrary fashion.

These setbacks notwithstanding, it can still be said that the normative shift of international law away from the death penalty is reflected and reinforced by state practice. Though the number of executions in any given year varies (at least in part because in several jurisdictions around the world the full statistics are not publicly available), the fact that international law explicitly prevents states that have abolished the death penalty from re-introducing it means that the number of abolitionist states should always be increasing.[17]

It seems likely that in the coming years a number of factors will play a role in further reducing the space for the death penalty. Meanwhile, there will be increased pressure on states and corporations that collaborate with states that carry out executions, as well as increased pressure for transparency, since General Assembly Resolution 69/186 has called on states to release information about their use of the death penalty. In an interconnected world there will be less room for states to hide their practices and insulate themselves from scrutiny and pressure. The fact that China has become identified as the only country not publicly revealing its execution figures may exert pressure to change its practice.

The increased availability of DNA testing has the potential of showing that the death penalty has been wrongfully imposed, which undermines its credibility. The global visibility of botched executions and

---

16 See Christof Heyns, *Report of the Special Rapporteur on Extrajudicial, Summary or Arbitrary Executions* (6 August 2014) [A/69/265].

17 See Human Rights Committee decision in *Piandong et al. v Philippines* (no. 869/1999) CCPR/ C/70/D/869/1999 paragraph 7.4.

the resulting embarrassment is also likely to discourage the practice. It will become increasingly difficult to execute someone in a manner agreed to be humane. Hanging, shooting by firing squad, electrocution, asphyxiation and lethal injection have all in one way or another become discredited or at least seriously questioned. But what are the alternatives?

There seems to be a growing disbelief in the myth of deterrence. In spite of all the opposition to the death penalty and the increased availability of crime data, the deterrent effect of capital punishment has not been proven. And the onus is on those who want to limit the right to life to justify that limitation. Those relying on deterrence alone to justify the death penalty need to address the fact that to obtain its maximum possible deterrent effect, it would have to be mandatory, or at least highly probable, and therefore used on a substantial scale across most categories of homicide—which is not an option for democratic states bound by the rule of law and concern for human rights.[18]

There is increasing support for the view that the death penalty violates the prohibition of torture and cruel, inhuman and degrading treatment or punishment. The normative perspective has shifted: While traditionally, the death penalty was the norm, now abolition is the norm. The onus is on those states that want to retain the death penalty to justify their position. The increasing number of states that have either abolished the death penalty, ceased to practice it or revised the law to restrict its scope—often in the context of engagements with international human rights bodies—presents a clear pattern. This trend increases the weight of the claim that international law requires the gradual abolition of the death penalty.

THE IMPORTANCE OF REGIONAL INITIATIVES

Regional human rights systems play an important role in the protection of the right to life, including with respect to the death penalty. The system is a holistic unit, with each component playing a vital role. Regional systems are in many cases closer to the people concerned

---

18   For a general discussion of deterrence, see Roger Hood and Carolyn Hoyle, *The Death Penalty: A Worldwide Perspective,* 5th ed. (New York, Oxford University Press, 2015), chapter 9.

than the global system and, as such, are able to facilitate greater participation in the international system and to foster its legitimacy.[19]

The Council of Europe is the only regional human rights mechanism to have achieved universal abolition in practice, through its Protocol 6 (1983) and Protocol 13 (2002). Three Council of Europe member states, (Armenia, Azerbaijan and Poland) have abolished the death penalty but not ratified Protocol 13. Russia has not abolished the death penalty in law, but it has not applied it since 1999 following a moratorium decision by its Constitutional Court.[20] In continuing this moratorium and trying to move towards abolition, the Court has highlighted that invitation into the Council of Europe occurred in part because of its expressed intention to establish a moratorium and take steps towards abolition.[21]

Significantly, from the perspective of the progressive-abolition argument advanced above, the European Court of Human Rights argued in 2010 that the protocols, combined with state practice across the region, "are strongly indicative that article 2 has been amended so as to prohibit the death penalty in all circumstances."[22] In July 2014, the Court held that "the fact that imposition and use of the death penalty negates fundamental human rights has been recognised by the member States of the Council of Europe."[23] This represents the moment of realisation for a process of progressive abolition, whereby the death penalty is declared to be a violation of the European Convention despite the explicit wording adopted 60 years earlier.

Article 2(1) of the European Union Fundamental Rights Charter, which is part of the European Union Treaty, states that "everyone has the right to life." According to Article 2(2), the death penalty may not be imposed or executed. Formal abolition of the death penalty is a condition of entry into the European Union. It is also a central plank of the human rights component of its foreign and security policy.

---

19 See Christof Heyns, *Report of the Special Rapporteur on Extrajudicial, Summary or Arbitrary Executions* (6 August 2014) [A/69/265].

20 Constitutional Court of the Russian Federation, Decision No. 3-P/1999 (2 February 1999).

21 Constitutional Court of the Russian Federation, Decision No. 1344-O-R/2009 (19 November 2009).

22 European Court of Human Rights, *Al-Sadoon and Mufdhi v. UK*, [no. 61498/08], 2 March 2010, paragraph 120.

23 European Court of Human Rights, *Al Nashiri v. Poland*, [no. 28761/11], 24 July 2014, paragraph 577.

The Organization for Security and Co-operation in Europe also has an admirable record: Of its 57 participating states, all but six have abolished the death penalty, and only two—the United States and Belarus—still carry out executions. It does not explicitly require the abolition of the death penalty, but participating states have committed to limiting its use to the most serious crimes and in a manner not contrary to their international commitments, and to keeping the question of eliminating capital punishment under consideration (agreed, respectively, in Vienna in 1989 and Copenhagen in 1990). In addition, participating states that retain the death penalty have pledged to ensure transparency regarding its application by making relevant information available to the public and to other participating states (agreed at Copenhagen in 1990). The Organization's Office for Democratic Institutions and Human Rights monitors the situation regarding the death penalty in member states and produces an annual report.[24]

In Africa, 43 states have abolished the death penalty either in law or in practice, with only 11 having conducted executions in the last 10 years. An Additional Protocol to the African Charter on Human and Peoples' Rights on the death penalty has been developed and is in the process of being adopted.[25] The African Commission on Human and Peoples' Rights is also developing a general comment on the right to life.

There has also been a role for sub-regional mechanisms in Africa with respect to the death penalty. In 2014, the Community Court of Justice of the Economic Community of West African States ruled against Nigeria to uphold the rights of a juvenile defendant, affirming that execution of a minor and execution while an appeals process is on-going are violations of international human rights protections.[26] In order to become a member the Community of Portuguese Language Countries, it is necessary at least to have a moratorium on

---

24 Organization for Security and Cooperation in Europe, Office for Democratic Institutions and Human Rights, *The Death Penalty in the OSCE Area: Background Paper 2014* (Warsaw, 2014), available from www.osce.org/odihr/124105.

25 Declaration of the Continental Conference on the Abolition of the Death Penalty in Africa (the Cotonou Declaration), available from www.achpr.org/news/2014/07/d150.

26 Avocats Sans Frontières France, "West African court finds against Nigeria in abusive capital cases", 3 July 2014, available from www.worldcoalition.org/nigeria-ecowas-court-death-penalty-human-rights-minor-appeal.html.

executions. It has been suggested that this may account for the moratorium announced in Equatorial Guinea in 2014. Unfortunately, two weeks before the announcement, the government had executed at least four people, its first executions since 2010.[27]

In the Americas, the death penalty is still legal in several countries. However, with the exception of the United States, the region has been execution free for several years.[28] The Protocol to the American Convention on Human Rights to Abolish the Death Penalty has been ratified by 13 states. The Inter-American Court of Human Rights observed in 1983 that the imposition of the death penalty in states which have not abolished it must strictly meet international procedural standards; its application must be restricted to the most serious crimes; and the personal circumstances of the defendant must be taken into account.[29] Several rulings have held that the death penalty may only be imposed for the most serious crimes resulting in the loss of life.[30]

The Association of Southeast Asian Nations Inter-governmental Commission on Human Rights is developing a thematic study of the right to life, with a particular focus on the question of a moratorium on the death penalty. This is an important development with much potential.

The Arab Charter on Human Rights (Articles 6 and 7) established safeguards regarding the application of the death penalty—that it be imposed only for the most serious crimes, and always with the right to seek pardon or commutation, that under no circumstances could it be applied for political offenses, and that it could not be inflicted on those under 18 or pregnant or nursing mothers.

---

27 Amnesty International, "Equatorial Guinea: executions just weeks before announcement of a 'temporary moratorium' on the death penalty raise serious questions", 26 March 2014, available from www.amnesty.org/en/documents/document/?indexNumber=A-FR24%2F001%2F2014&language=en.

28 The United States ranks fifth in the world in terms of number of executions, but within the country, there is significant variation. In 2015 Nebraska became the 19th state (in addition to the District of Columbia) to abolish the death penalty. Governors in Colorado, Oregon, Pennsylvania and Washington have also established moratoria. Another five states, in addition to the federal government and the US military, have not conducted an execution for 10 years and by some measures might be considered abolitionist in practice.

29 Inter-American Court of Human Rights, *Advisory Opinion OC-3/83* (1983)paragraph 55.

30 Inter-American Court of Human Rights, *Hilaire, Constantine and Benjamin et al. v Trinidad and Tobago*, 21 June 2002, IACHR Series C No 94; *Dacosta Cadogan v Barbados*, Case 1460-01, Report No. 7/08, IACHR Series L/V/II.130 Doc. 22, rev. 1 (2008); *Raxcacó-Reyes v Guatemala*, 6 February 2006, IACHR Series C No 143.

Of the 53 members of the Commonwealth, 35 still have the death penalty on their statute books, and some (five in 2013) conduct executions. The Privy Council's jurisprudence has played a role in the demise of the mandatory death penalty in the Commonwealth Caribbean, but its legitimacy as standard bearer for the constitutional principles of the Commonwealth could be challenged.[31]

CONCLUSION

It is time for the world community to close the chapter on the death penalty, not only because of its effects on those directly and indirectly involved, but also because it distracts attention from the other human rights challenges that lie ahead. The international community has placed violence reduction on the post-2015 development agenda. If this leads to evidence-based evaluations of the drivers of violence and best mechanisms for its reduction, then it seems likely that the anachronistic nature of the death penalty will become increasingly clear. Ending the death penalty could serve as an inspiration about the possibility of the greater realisation of the right to life in general.

Public calls for a moratorium from high-profile figures—ranging from the Secretary-General of the United Nations to the High Commissioner for Human Rights—speak to an emerging consensus that the practice of executions is no longer beyond the scope of human rights mechanisms. International law makes clear the desirability of abolition but leaves states to determine the best manner in which to achieve it. In the 50 years since the pronouncement of the International Covenant on Civil and Political Rights, some 160 countries have abolished the death penalty either in law or practice. While waiting for the remaining states to find the appropriate vehicle for abolition, it is important that international actors, including regional organisations, continue to insist that, when the death penalty is imposed, it is within the very narrow scope allowed by law.

Regional organisations can also act as important forums for discussion of trends toward abolition that are more regionally, and perhaps

---

31 For a critical appraisal, see Quincy Whitaker, "Challenging the death penalty in the Caribbean: litigation at the Privy Council", in *Against the Death Penalty: International Initiatives and Implications,* Jon Yorke, ed. (Farnham, UK, Ashgate, 2008), pp. 101-124.

culturally, sensitive. They are forums in which individual member states often feel more prominently represented. European and American human rights mechanisms have shown how emerging regional consensus (in advance of global consensus) can be employed to achieve traction for regional agreements or standards on the issue of the death penalty. Efforts along similar lines are under way in the African Commission on Human and Peoples' Rights and the Association of Southeast Asian Nations. These efforts are encouraging for those working more broadly on the right to life, and should be supported.

TOWARDS A MORATORIUM ON THE DEATH PENALTY

Paul Jacob Bhatti [1]

Life is a precious gift from Almighty God, and only God has the right to give it or take it away. There is no justice without life, and you can't appreciate life if you don't reject death.

Some people believe that the death penalty is warranted under limited circumstances and with the strictest procedural safeguards. But even in the best jurisdictions, mistakes happen, evidence is incomplete, and innocent people are erroneously executed.

In the worst jurisdictions, and there are many, the death penalty is used by fanatics and fascists to purge innocent religious and political minorities in the name of extremist ideologies and agendas. Due to political strife, war, poverty and famine, the best jurisdictions can and do devolve into the worst, making even well-reasoned death penalty schemes a moral landmine.

For these reasons, I see no viable moral basis for capital punishment to remain a sentencing option in any criminal justice system. The risk and the injustice of losing innocent human life is too great.

I realize that implementing a moratorium on the death penalty is no trivial matter. This is a complex question with no simple solutions. Providentially, such a moratorium is now vigorously supported by a wide and growing array of influential religious scholars, human rights activists and political and social leaders. In the 1970s, some 20 countries had abolished capital punishment. Today about 160 countries have stopped using it, either by law or on a de facto basis. The momentum is palpable and energizing.

There is growing agreement that the essential objectives the death penalty is meant to serve—crime control, deterrence and

---

1   Paul Jacob Bhatti is a surgeon and former Pakistani Minister for National Harmony and Minority Affairs.

retribution—can be achieved without it, and are often not achieved with it. And it is necessary to understand that the death penalty causes loss of innocent human life in two ways: through mistakes and through deliberate misuse.

First, our criminal justice systems are less than perfect. In many jurisdictions, money and greed drive biased and corrupt tribunals or kangaroo courts to adjudicate unjust convictions, resulting in the imprisonment and execution of the innocent while the guilty rich and powerful walk free.

Erroneous convictions also occur when poor and poorly educated defendants cannot afford competent legal counsel, witnesses make honest mistakes about identities and other facts of the case, evidence is fabricated or suppressed, and juries are prejudiced or incompetent. Convictions in these instances can result in the shedding of innocent blood, an intolerable cost.

The United States is a country with a vigorous and venerable legal tradition, known for its strong constitutional procedural safeguards regulating the imposition of capital punishment. But even in this jurisdiction, appellate courts have reversed numerous death sentences based on procedural and evidentiary errors in the trial courts. A staggering study by Columbia Law School reported on the exoneration of many death row convicts using newly available DNA testing technology.[2] The work also underscores the high percentage of reversible errors in death penalty sentences in the United States from 1973 to 1995.

In July 2013, the Washington Post reported that the Department of Justice and Federal Bureau of Investigation had agreed to review thousands of cases in which hair sample analysis methods that modern scientific assessments have deemed deeply flawed may have led to wrongful convictions. More than 120 convictions have already been reported as suspicious, including 27 death penalty convictions.[3] If innocent people are being executed in the United States, a country with vast legal and technical resources, the problem is likely to be

---

2   Jeffrey A. Fagan, *Capital Punishment: Deterrent Effects and Capital Costs* (New York, Columbia University School of Law, 2014).

3   Spencer S. Hsu, "Convicted defendants left uninformed of forensic flaws found by Justice Department", *Washington Post*, 16 April 2012.

much worse in poor and developing countries with limited procedural safeguards and more readily compromised judiciary systems.

Second, there is outright malevolent use of legal systems, and
the death penalty in particular, to purge, control, intimidate and
manipulate populations. And herein lies my main argument. It is
no secret that fanatic extremists, often pursuing religious or racial
purity, twist the criminal justice system to their own ends to extir-
pate religious and political minorities. Hitler and Stalin are obvious
examples. Therefore, protecting religious and racial minorities is a
moral cause of the same order as the fight against human trafficking
and child prostitution, or past wars against Nazism and other racist
and fascist tyrannies.

It is a moral cause undergirded by comprehensive and unassailable
arguments. These arguments are self-evident and resonate with fundamental principles concerning the value of human life articulated
in the constitutions of the Member States of the United Nations
and the holy scriptures of the world's great faiths. An international
moratorium on the death penalty is an indispensable component in
our fight to eliminate wrongful executions and the terroristic use of
capital punishment.

State-sanctioned executions of the innocent tend to occur in many
places where the justice system is less than transparent and heavily
influenced or controlled by fanaticism, extremism, terrorism and
racism; my country, Pakistan, is no exception.

My late brother, Shahbaz Clement Bhatti, was a lifelong human rights
activist. He founded a minority rights movement, the All Pakistan
Minorities Alliance, and courageously promoted religious freedom in
Pakistan and advocated for the protection of the basic human rights
of all peoples, especially the poor. He became the first Federal Minister of Minorities in Pakistan in 2008. He opposed the death penalty
and, in 2008, worked within the Government of Pakistan to support
the United Nations General Assembly's proposed moratorium on the
death penalty. He was assassinated in 2011 for his convictions and
faith while driving to work from our mother's home. Today, the All
Pakistan Minorities Alliance continues to aid victims of oppression,

discrimination and violence. Whenever possible, it seeks to identify and assist the falsely accused and imprisoned.

Before I discuss moving forward to change policy, I want to discuss how the death penalty can actually encourage terrorism and perpetuate a culture of death.

A government-sanctioned execution broadcasts an unambiguous message to citizens that punishment by death is justified. But the problem is that terrorists are co-opting the state's prerogative for their own malicious objectives. Death perpetuates death. On the face of it, the death penalty seems an expedient tool in the fight against terrorism, but the opposite is true in many countries like Iran, Iraq and Pakistan. In this environment, the death penalty is not a deterrent but an incentive to high-risk terror.

In many countries it is not uncommon for convicts under a death sentence to escape prison by force or subterfuge. Many instances of these "walking dead" escaped convicts attacking and killing innocent victims plague our headlines. This is an issue stuck in the morass of an underfunded criminal justice and prison system.

Even more disturbing is the morbid and warped interplay between fanatic religious extremism, illiteracy and poverty. The vast majority of suicide bombers and other criminal extremists originate in societies where the illiteracy and poverty rates are high. Entrenched poverty leads to suffering, loss of hope and opportunity and a sense of grievance. In Pakistan, half of all adults, including two out of three women, are illiterate. In 2012, an estimated 20 million children of all school ages, including 7.3 million primary-school-age children, did not attend school. Poor and illiterate people are susceptible to predatory extremist ideologies and agendas. Empty stomachs and empty heads make children especially easy prey for extremists.

In many countries children are actively recruited and brainwashed in extremist ideologies and agendas. They inculcate our children with the conviction that to kill and/or die a martyr in the name of their religion is not only the norm, but also the basis for an eternal reward. The children grow up with no other objective in life than to die for their ideology.

No major religion advocates hatred, violence and discrimination. All condemn killing in the name of religion. In the Holy Koran, killing one human being is considered the equivalent of killing all of humanity. But there are religions in many parts of the world that have been hijacked to attack, divide, control and create hatred and fear among innocent people, including towards different faiths. This misuse of religion is a violation of human rights. It is evil.

> "NO MAJOR RELIGION ADVOCATES HATRED, VIOLENCE AND DISCRIMINATION."
> —Paul Jacob Bhatti

In fanatic and fundamentalist societies, the presence of religious minorities sometimes triggers aggressive reactions from those who view them as a threat. Often, false accusations are made to settle personal scores and to target easy victims, who mostly belong to the oppressed and marginalized sector of the community—and to further extremist agendas, breeding real acts of violence against them, including execution.

My brother, the late Shahbaz Bhatti, was a strong advocate of a moratorium on the death penalty in Pakistan to protect the poor and religious minorities from being executed by fanatic extremists under false charges and lesser forms of overt discrimination and harassment. Although he is no longer with us, his work continues and there is still much hope.

Implementing an international moratorium on the death penalty will reap enormous benefits that will cascade through the generations.

- First, the execution of innocent defendants caused by judicial corruption, jury bias and error, technological malfunctions and defects in procedural safeguards will halt immediately.

- Second, fanatic extremists will lose a powerful tool for controlling and intimidating populations, when religious and racial identity will no longer be crimes subject to capital punishment. This will be a great day indeed.

- Third, religious extremists may be discouraged from committing acts of terror if they face spending the rest of their lives in a jail cell, instead of the delusion of instant glory through martyrdom by state execution.

I propose that we move forward towards implementing a moratorium on the death penalty as a major component in the creation of a peaceful and better world. It is imperative, in these perilous times, that the United Nations act now to overcome evil with good. We seek to promote a fair and just world, where peace, security, welfare and human dignity are the bedrock and baseline of who we are and how we live.

Let us join together to impose a universal moratorium on the death penalty. Let us save all those innocent children who are victims of an imposed ideology that leads them to kill and die for a false reward. Let us work together to educate our children so that they have a true hope of becoming productive and informed citizens. And let us pray together that Almighty God grant us the strength and resources to resist and overcome the spirit of terror with whatever is true, noble, right and pure.

"Our mission is to continue advocating, because the mat
is not just about people whom we need to save from a
barbaric and ineffective punishment, but also about helpi
society advance towards a higher degree of civilization.
— *Moncef Marzouki*

CHAPTER 5
ROLE OF LEADERSHIP

Chapter 5 contains articles dealing with the importance of leadership in moving away from the death penalty.

Federico Mayor, President of the International Commission against the Death Penalty, offers practical examples from a number of countries— such as Haiti, Mexico, Mongolia, Rwanda, Senegal, South Africa and the United States—of the key role of political leadership in the abolition of the death penalty. This includes political and judicial leaders but also lawyers, members of the media, and religious and civil society leaders.

Mai Sato, an academic from Japan working in the UK, demonstrates how offering a life sentence without parole as an alternative to the death penalty decreases popular support for the death penalty.

Contributions of Heads of States or Governments reflect their commitment and contribution to move away from the death penalty globally or nationally. Didier Burkhalter, President of the Swiss Confederation (2014) pledges for a dialogue and experience sharing on the death penalty as the best way in moving away from it. Tsakhiagiin Elbegdorj, President of Mongolia, describes the process how Mongolia under his leadership moved away from the death penalty, motivated by human rights concerns. Laurent Fabius, Foreign Minister of France, explores the long path that France took towards abolition. Moncef Marzouki, President of Tunisia (2011-2014), speaks of his personal commitment and difference it has made in Tunisia. Matteo Renzi, Prime Minister of Italy, describes the relevance of the UN moratorium resolutions in moving away from the death penalty. Boni Yayi, President of Benin, describes the process in his country, calling others to follow their example.

LEADERSHIP AND THE ABOLITION OF THE DEATH PENALTY

Federico Mayor[1]

Principled political leadership, within the domestic realm and internationally, is an essential factor in the momentum that is driving the movement for the abolition of the death penalty. The role played by leaders—such as prime ministers, presidents, ministers, authorities within ministries dealing with domestic and international affairs, national human rights institutions, the judiciary (including judges and magistrates who pass rulings that shape the debate and jurisprudence), lawyers and bar associations, and key figures in the media, religious bodies and civil society organisations—has been and will remain crucial to ensuring progress towards a world free of capital punishment.

Ultimately, it is the state that must decide to abolish the death penalty and protect the fundamental human right to life. Political leadership has been very important in overcoming domestic opposition to abolition in several countries. Political leaders have recognized that while public opinion is relevant, nations face difficulties if popular sentiment, which is difficult to gauge accurately, is allowed to determine penal policy. Experience shows that the majority of the public is willing to accept abolition of capital punishment once it is achieved.

Leaders of several countries have initially granted clemency or imposed moratoriums on executions which, in turn, have paved the way for legislative or constitutional repeal of capital punishment. Many leaders have recognized the ever-present risk of executing innocent people, as well as other powerful arguments for abolition, including the discriminatory and arbitrary nature of judicial processes and the danger of capital punishment being used as a tool of political repression.

---

1   Federico Mayor is President of the International Commission against the Death Penalty.

International leadership is very important and complements domestic political leadership in abolishing capital punishment. Often, it is a response to pressure, support and recommendations from international bodies such as the United Nations General Assembly, the United Nations Secretary General and the Office of the High Commissioner for Human Rights; treaty bodies such as the Human Rights Committee, the Committee against Torture and the Committee on the Rights of the Child; and statements and reports that are drafted by special procedures. The role of regional bodies such as the European Union, Organisation of American States and African Union has been important in ensuring that Europe (barring Belarus), the Americas (with the exception of the United States of America) and Africa (with the exception of five countries) have become execution-free. The majority of the executions take place in regions such as Asia and the Middle East where there are no regional organisations spanning the continent (such as the European Union and organisations mentioned above) and where regional leadership is weak or non-existent.

THE INTERNATIONAL COMMISSION AGAINST THE DEATH PENALTY

The International Commission against the Death Penalty (ICDP), founded in Madrid in October 2010, is currently composed of 14 people of high international standing from all regions of the world who act with independence and neutrality. Its commissioners are leaders, with long and respected experience in public life, who believe in the fundamental right to life and who are using their moral voice, influence and access to advocate with leaders and governments of death-penalty-retentionist countries for abolition of capital punishment. These individuals include former presidents, prime ministers, government ministers and senior United Nations officials, a former US state governor, a former judge and president of the International Court of Justice, a senior judge and a leading academic. Each commissioner has expertise in international law and human rights and has shown leadership in and commitment to the global abolition of capital punishment. Their experience and knowledge enable them to address politically sensitive issues and engage with senior officials from countries where the death penalty is still used. Their knowledge, influence and broad geographical representation provide ICDP with a high profile in the international arena.[2] ICDP opposes the death penalty under any circumstances, believing that it violates the right to life enshrined in the Universal Declaration of Human Rights

ICDP works with the United Nations and other international and regional organizations, governments, parliamentarians, lawyers, media and nongovernmental organizations to further the abolition of the death penalty worldwide. Its work is supported by a diverse group of 18 states from all regions of the world that are committed to abolition. Its secretariat is located in Geneva.

DIFFERENT PATHWAYS TO ABOLITION

Countries have arrived at the same goal—abolishing the death penalty—in different ways. A few examples are described below.

In Haiti, political leaders helped prepare the ground for changing the penal code; the commutation of all death sentences under the 1987 Constitution was a key step in that direction. The penal code of 1953 had established the death penalty for criminal and political offences. During the presidency of Francois Duvalier between 1957 and 1971, numerous death sentences were imposed following summary trials, and executions were frequently carried out in public. A 1985 governmental decree abolished the death penalty for political offences except high treason. Following the collapse in 1986 of the Jean-Claude Duvalier government, which had been responsible for widespread human rights violations, former government officials were sentenced to death for human rights abuses. A new Constitution in 1987, approved in a national referendum under President Henri Namphy, abolished the death penalty. All death sentences were commuted. The 1987 Constitution was temporarily abolished following a military coup in 1988, but President Leslie Manigat issued a decree on 12 July 1988 reaffirming the abolition of the death penalty. Haiti has since supported four resolutions of the United Nations General Assembly calling for a moratorium on the application of the death penalty, most recently in 2012. During its Universal Periodic Review in 2011, Haiti agreed to sign and ratify the Second Optional Protocol to the International Covenant on Civil and Political Rights,

---

2   The ICDP's website can be found at www.icomdp.org/.

which is the only international treaty with global coverage that calls for abolition of the death penalty.

Mexico abolished the death penalty in 2005, first in legislation and then in a constitutional amendment. The last execution, of a soldier under the Code of Military Justice, was carried out in 1961. Most Mexican states had already abolished capital punishment by the end of the 19th century. The Code of Military Justice did, however, retain capital punishment for specific offences, and people were occasionally sentenced to death under its provisions. There was widespread opposition from Catholic bishops, political leaders, senators and prominent lawyers to a suggestion by a presidential candidate in 1988 to hold a referendum on reintroducing the death penalty. In April 2005, the only remaining provision in the Mexican criminal law permitting the death penalty was abolished. The Mexican Chamber of Deputies unanimously voted to reform the Code of Military Justice and replace capital punishment with prison terms of 30 to 60 years for serious offences. To reinforce abolition at the constitutional level, the Mexican House of Representatives approved a constitutional reform bill in June 2005 that explicitly prohibits the death penalty for all crimes. President Vicente Fox signed the bill amending Articles 14 and 22 of the Constitution of the United Mexican States, and it came into force on 9 December 2005.

In Senegal, a predominantly Muslim country, the abolition of the death penalty took place due to a number of factors including a change in the position of President Abdoulaye Wade to support abolition, along with the assertion by then Justice Minister Sergine Diop that crime figures were not lower in retentionist countries than in abolitionist countries, and advocacy by civil society organisations. Since independence in 1960, Senegal had carried out two executions, the last in 1967. The penal code provided for the death penalty for offences including murder and made it mandatory for, among others, espionage and treason. Discussion about constitutional reform in 2001 included the possible abolition of the death penalty, though at that time it was resisted by President Wade, who argued that abolition should be brought about through legislation. Article 7 of the 2001 Constitution stated that "all human life is sacred and inviolable" and that everyone has the right to life. When the courts handed down death sentences in 2003 and 2004, a vigorous debate on the death penalty resumed, especially when a bill to abolish it was presented in parliament in 2004. With the support of Justice Minister Diop, civil society organisations and, most importantly, President Wade, the bill was unanimously approved by the Government in July 2004, and on 10 December 2004, the Senegalese parliament abolished the death penalty by a large majority.

In South Africa, the Constitutional Court played a key role by ruling that the death penalty violated human rights as a form of cruel, inhuman or degrading punishment. During the apartheid era, the death penalty was widely and disproportionately used against the black population.

> "POLITICAL LEADERSHIP IS A KEY FACTOR IN THE ABOLITION OF THE DEATH PENALTY." —Federico Mayor

In 1990, anti-apartheid leader Nelson Mandela, who had been tried for offences carrying the death penalty and proclaimed it to be a barbaric punishment, was released from prison, and negotiations for constitutional change started. Abolition of the death penalty became a litmus test for the creation of a social order, and a tribunal was established to review all death sentences imposed before July 1990. The last execution was carried out in 1991, and the Minister of Justice proclaimed a formal moratorium on executions in 1992 pending the introduction of a bill of rights. The new Constitutional Court made a landmark judgement in its first case, *the State v. T. Makwanyane and M. Mchunu*,[3] where it concluded that the death penalty was a form of cruel, inhuman or degrading punishment, prohibited by the interim Constitution. Despite opinion polls showing a majority in favour of retaining capital punishment, the African National Congress supported abolition. South Africa's Constitution was adopted in May 1996, and it retained the wording of the 1993 interim Constitution guaranteeing the right to life as a fundamental right and abolishing the death penalty. In 1997, the parliament formally abolished the death penalty for all crimes by passing the Criminal Law Amendment Act, which removed all references

---

3   *In the Matter of the State v. T. Makwanyane and M. Mchunu*, case no. CCT3/94, Constitutional Court of the Republic of South Africa, 1995. Available from www.saflii.org/za/cases/ZACC/1995/3.pdf.

to the death penalty from the statute book, and abolition came into force in 1998. In November 2006, the Constitutional Court ruled that the Government had fully complied with its 1995 judgement on the unconstitutionality of the death penalty.

In Mongolia, President Tsakhiagiin Elbegdorj has been leading the move towards abolition of capital punishment, including acceding to the Second Optional Protocol to the International Convention on Civil and Political Rights, which is the only treaty with global scope to abolish the death penalty. President Elbegdorj initially announced a moratorium on the death penalty in January 2010, emphasising the need to follow the worldwide trend towards abolition. In a landmark speech to the State Great Khural (parliament), President Elbegdorj listed eight reasons for rejecting the death penalty, including the irreparable nature of any error in imposing it, its historical use in political purges, the international community's calls for abolition and its lack of a deterrent effect. He said, "There could be a multitude of reasons and varying circumstances and settings for committing a crime that carries a death penalty. Yet the guiding principle for the Head of State on whether to approve a death penalty must be single. That single principle is to pardon the offender. As the Head of State of Mongolia, I will remain faithful to this principle because it guarantees and safeguards the value of human life."[4] In January 2012, the Mongolian parliament approved a bill to end the death penalty by acceding to the Second Optional Protocol, and later that year, Mongolia acceded to the protocol. Although death-penalty provisions remain in the law until repealed by parliament, accession marked Mongolia's international commitment to abolish the death penalty.

In the United States of America, as of this writing the only country in the Americas carrying out executions in 2013-2014, a number of governors and state legislatures are moving to repeal capital punishment, although at the federal level the death penalty remains in force. Not only has the number of total executions in the United States decreased, but several states have either abolished the death penalty or established an official moratorium. Recent states to abolish

---

4   Tsakhiagiin Elbegdorj, "The path of democratic Mongolia must be clean and bloodless", speech by the president at the State Great Khural, 14 January 2010, available from www.president.mn/eng/newsCenter/viewEvent.php?cid=&newsId=122&newsEvent=President%20on%20Climate%20Change.

the death penalty include Illinois (2011), Connecticut (2012) and Maryland (2013); as of this writing, the total number of abolitionist states was 18. Essential for these developments has been the work of individual state governors, including Patrick Quinn of Illinois, Dannel Malloy of Connecticut and Martin O'Malley of Maryland, who have campaigned for abolition or commuted death sentences to life imprisonment. In November 2011, Governor John Kitzhaber of Oregon imposed a moratorium on executions in the state and said that a re-evaluation of capital punishment was long overdue.[5] In Washington, Governor Jay Inslee announced a moratorium on the death penalty on 11 February 2014 for as long as he is in office.[6] In Connecticut, a bill abolishing the death penalty was passed by the state legislature in April 2012. Governor Malloy, who signed the bill into law, said:

> *I spent years as a prosecutor. . . . I learned first-hand that our system of justice is . . . subject to the fallibility of those who participate in it. I saw people who were poorly served by their counsel. I saw people wrongly accused or mistakenly identified. I saw discrimination. I came to believe that doing away with the death penalty was the only way to ensure it would not be unfairly imposed.[7]*

Governor Malloy highlighted the important role played by victims' families who lobbied the state legislature against the death penalty. When the death penalty was abolished in Connecticut, 48 per cent of the voters of the state were reported to be in favour of the death penalty, with 43 per cent against.[8]

In Rwanda, the death penalty was abolished in the aftermath of the 1994 genocide, in which an estimated 800,000 Rwandans were murdered. The involvement of the international community

---

5   Death Penalty Information Center, "Gov. John Kitzhaber of Oregon declares a moratorium on all executions" (Washington, DC, 26 November 2011).

6   Amnesty International, "Momentum against death penalty continues as Washington state governor announces moratorium on execution" (AI Index No. AMR/51/011/2014, 12 February 2014).

7   International Commission against the Death Penalty, "How states abolish the death penalty" (Geneva, 2013), p. 31.

8   Ibid., p. 31.

in establishing accountability triggered Rwanda's move towards abolition of capital punishment. Prior to the genocide, capital punishment existed in Rwanda for a wide range of criminal offences, and the State Security Court had jurisdiction over cases of a political nature, including offences punishable by death. Executions were occasionally carried out. In 1987, President Juvenal Habyarimana commuted all existing death sentences to life imprisonment, a move that benefitted 537 prisoners. Some of those charged with involvement in the 1994 genocide were tried in Rwandan domestic courts, and in 1998, 22 people convicted of leading the genocide were executed.

Meanwhile, when the United Nations Security Council had established the International Criminal Tribunal for Rwanda (ICTR) in November 1994, the death penalty was excluded as punishment in spite of strong opposition from Rwanda. This decision presented a problem for the government: A fundamental injustice would occur if suspects tried in domestic courts were sentenced to death while thousands of genocide suspects living abroad, some held by the ICTR, including alleged ringleaders, received life imprisonment at most. Indeed, governments detaining suspects who had fled abroad as well as the ICTR refused to extradite them to Rwanda, because of the death penalty as well as concerns about the lack of fair trial guarantees, which had been a long-standing concern in cases related to the death penalty. These concerns first prompted the enactment, in 2007, of a special transfer law prohibiting execution of suspects due to be transferred from the ICTR to local Rwandan courts. In October 2006, the political bureau of the ruling party strongly recommended abolition, and in January 2007, the cabinet approved plans to abolish capital punishment. The Chamber of Deputies and the Senate passed abolition bills, and the Law Relating to the Abolition of the Death Penalty entered into force in July 2007 when it was ratified by President Paul Kagame. It abolished the death penalty for all crimes and removed it from the Penal Code. President Kagame observed that his country's history of genocide was a primary factor in the abolition of the death penalty. All death sentences (about 600) were commuted to life imprisonment.

ICDP COMMISSIONERS' CONTRIBUTIONS

ICDP commissioners[9] all have a strong record of promoting human rights and are committed to providing political leadership to the cause of abolishing the death penalty worldwide. Their experience and knowledge enables them to address politically sensitive issues and engage with senior officials from countries where the death penalty is still retained. This section highlights the leading role some of the commissioners have played in the cause of abolishing the death penalty in their home countries.

Robert Badinter (Minister of Justice, 1981-1986, France) was well known for challenging the death penalty in the courts before becoming Minister of Justice. As a lawyer, he argued successfully, six times between 1976 and 1980, against the death penalty as cruel and inhuman punishment that risked innocent people being executed. French President François Mitterrand, who had declared his opposition to the death penalty a few weeks before the 1981 elections, appointed Mr. Badinter to be Minister of Justice in his new Socialist government. President Mitterrand's call for abolition during the election campaign was controversial, as public opinion largely favoured capital punishment. Mr. Badinter, as Minister of Justice, introduced a death penalty abolition bill in the National Assembly in September 1981 under the quick vote procedure. In October 1981, after the bill passed the National Assembly (363 to 117) and the Senate (160 to 26), the death penalty was abolished for all civil and military offences in France. Abolition followed a long public debate, presidential pardons, a cross-party study group, legal action in the courts and decisive action by President Mitterrand and Minister of Justice Badinter. In 2007, abolition of the death penalty was incorporated in the French Constitution by President Jacques Chirac by means of a constitutional amendment passed in parliament. Article 66-1 of the French Constitution provides that "no one shall be sentenced to the death penalty."[10]

Gloria Macapagal-Arroyo (President, 2001-2010, the Philippines) commuted all death sentences to life imprisonment during her

---

9   Navi Pillay, former High Commissioner for Human Rights, has recently been appointed as ICDP commissioner.
10   Ibid., pp. 13-15; International Commission against the Death Penalty, *Annual Review 2010-2012* (Geneva, 2013), p. 21.

presidency and signed a law abolishing the death penalty in 2006. Philippines presidents played a very important role in the abolition of capital punishment. The Philippines was the first country in Asia to abolish the death penalty for all crimes, in 1987 under President Corazón Aquino. The death penalty was reintroduced in 1993, and executions were resumed in 1999; the last execution was carried out in 2000. In early 2000, the Philippines had one of the highest rates of death sentences in the world. Shortly after assuming the presidency in 2001, Ms. Macapagal-Arroyo announced a death penalty moratorium. This decision followed a campaign against reimposition of capital punishment by civil society organisations including the Catholic Bishops' Conference and the Philippines Commission on Human Rights. On 15 April 2006, on the occasion of Easter, President Macapagal-Arroyo announced the commutation of all death sentences to life imprisonment, affecting over 1,200 people. She wrote a letter to then Senate President Franklin M. Drilon on the urgent need for "abolishing the death penalty as its imposition was shown to have not served its principal purpose of effectively deterring the commission of heinous crimes,"[11] adding that abolition would remedy the findings that the death penalty was anti-poor as it was often those who could not afford legal representation who were sentenced to death. The Philippines Congress took swift action and in June 2006, the Senate (16 to 0, with one abstention) and the House of Representatives (119 to 20) passed bills abolishing the death penalty. President Arroyo issued a statement saying, "We celebrate the victory of life as I thank Congress for its immediate action in abolishing the death penalty law."[12] The law entered into effect on 24 June 2006, with President Macapagal-Arroyo signing the Act Prohibiting the Imposition of the Death Penalty in the Philippines.[13]

Ibrahim Najjar (Minister of Justice, 2008–2011, Lebanon), an eminent lawyer, scholar and law professor, is seen as one of the leaders of the death penalty abolitionist movement in Lebanon. As Minister of Justice, he promoted laws in many fields, including prevention of arbitrary detention and protection of human rights, and

---

11 International Commission against the Death Penalty, "How states abolish the death penalty", p. 21.
12 Ibid., p. 21.
13 Ibid., pp. 20-22; International Commission against the Death Penalty, *Annual Review 2010-2012*, p. 21.

worked to repeal capital punishment in Lebanon's Penal Code. His tenure as Minister of Justice is considered one of the most productive periods for the judiciary and the promotion of draft laws. After recognising that abolition of the death penalty in Lebanon was a contentious issue, he continued working towards the achievement of a "more humane and more efficient justice system."[14] In 2008, he introduced a draft law to abolish the death penalty in Lebanon. Had it been accepted, capital punishment would have been replaced by life imprisonment.[15] In 2010 he was awarded the National Medal for Human Rights in recognition of his draft law to abolish the death penalty in Lebanon. Mr. Najjar continues to advocate the abolition of capital punishment in Lebanon. In June 2014, he was part of a delegation of ICDP commissioners which I led. We held discussions related to the death penalty with Prime Minister Tammam Salam, members of parliament, lawyers, diplomats and important members of civil society. During a speech in Lebanon as an ICDP delegate in June 2014, he said, "In Lebanon, we are witnessing a tendency to steer away from the death penalty when we take note [that] the Parliament has introduced no new legal sanctions constituting expansion of the death penalty in the recent past. The dependence on death penalty has ended. For me, the death penalty is premeditated murder; it is not objective. Its abolition has to be achieved through constant consensus and placed within the context of Lebanese and regional peace."[16]

Lebanon remains a death-penalty-retentionist country; the last executions, of three men, were carried out in January 2004. (The last public executions were carried out in May 1998 and sparked uproar because the gallows did not work properly.) In July 2001, the Lebanese parliament voted unanimously leave the application of the death penalty to the discretion of judges. The Lebanese Constitution requires the signature of the president, the prime minister and the minister of justice to carry out an execution. In September 2011, the Lebanese parliament approved a bill amending law No. 463/2002 on the implementation of sentences, creating a formal status for those

---

14   International Commission against the Death Penalty, *Annual Review 2010-2012*, p. 23.

15   Ibid., p. 21.

16   International Commission against the Death Penalty, "President of ICDP Mr Federico Mayor, Commissioners Ms Hanne Sophie Greve and Mr Ibrahim Najjar leads ICDP mission to Lebanon" (Geneva, 16 June 2014), available from www.icomdp.org/cms/wp-content/uploads/2014/06/18-ICDP-Press-Statement-Lebanon-16-June-2014.pdf.

"sentenced to death without being executed." Although this amendment did not abolish the death penalty, it has enhanced the unofficial position of the Lebanese authorities in favour of a de facto moratorium on executions. As of June 2014, there were at least 57 prisoners sentenced to death in Lebanon.

Bill Richardson (Governor, 2002–2010, New Mexico, USA) signed a death penalty abolition bill into law in March 2009, making the state of New Mexico the 15th US state to abolish capital punishment. He was then in his second term as Governor of New Mexico, re-elected in 2006 with the support of 69 per cent of voters, representing the largest margin of victory for any governor in state history. Since the resumption of executions in the United States in 1977, New Mexico had carried out one execution, in 2001. A statewide poll in 2008 showed that 64 per cent of New Mexicans supported replacing the death penalty with life imprisonment without parole and restitution to victims' families. In New Mexico's case, factors that helped abolition included lobbying against the death penalty by prominent voices within the Catholic Church and families of murder victims, legislators citing the high cost of executions, and a 2008 study by the *New Mexico Law Review* on the application of capital punishment between July 1979 and December 2007 that found that the imposition of the death penalty was influenced by where or when the crime was committed and the race or ethnicity of the victim and the defendant. The death penalty abolition bill was passed with cross-party support by the State Senate (24 to 18) and House of Representatives (40 to 28) in March 2009. Governor Richardson then sought the views of citizens and was urged by former US President Jimmy Carter to support the bill.

Governor Richardson justified his decision to sign the death penalty abolition bill, which he called the most difficult of his life, by referring to inmates who had been exonerated after being sentenced to death: "The sad truth is that the wrong person can still be convicted in this day and age, and in cases where that conviction carries with it the ultimate sanction, we must have ultimate confidence, I would say certitude, that the system is without flaw or prejudice. Unfortunately, this is demonstrably not the case."[17] He also commented: "In a society which values individual life and liberty above all else, where justice and not vengeance is the singular guiding principle of our system of criminal law, the potential for wrongful conviction and, God forbid, execution of an innocent person stands as anathema to our very sensibilities as human beings."[18] Another factor had been the worldwide trend towards abolition of the death penalty: "From an international human rights perspective, there is no reason the United States should be behind the rest of the world in this issue."[19]

CONCLUSION

Political leadership is a key factor in the abolition of the death penalty, which has gained momentum in recent years, with the United Nations now estimating that over 160 countries have abolished capital punishment or do not execute. In Haiti, political leaders have helped lay the groundwork for change in the penal code, while in Senegal, abolition came about due to a change in the President's viewpoint, backed up by the Justice Minister's view that there was no evidence of a deterrent effect. The role of the President was key in Mongolia, which acceded to the Second Optional Protocol to the International Convention on Civil and Political Rights, thereby voluntarily making an international commitment to abolish capital punishment prior to removing it from national law. In Mexico, abolition was a consequence of constitutional amendment, while in South Africa, the Constitutional Court played a key role, during the era ending apartheid, upholding the abolitionist ideals of leaders like Nelson Mandela. Abolition in Rwanda came in the aftermath of the 1994 genocide, with an international tribunal leading the way in ensuring the end of capital punishment. In the United States, governors of 18 states have led the move to abolish capital punishment.

While States have adopted different pathways to end the cruel, inhuman and degrading practice of the death penalty, it is evident that

---

17 Death Penalty Information Centre, "Governor Bill Richardson signs repeal of the death penalty" (Washington, DC, 19 March 2009).

18 "Bill Richardson", *International Commission against the Death Penalty*, available from www.icomdp.org/bill-richardson.

19 International Commission against the Death Penalty, "How states abolish the death penalty", p. 32.

political leadership has played a crucial part in ensuring and deepening the abolitionist trend. The four ICDP commissioners highlighted in this article have played a leading role in the abolition of the death penalty in their countries. The ICDP itself is a manifestation of the need for this political leadership to expand efforts to abolish capital punishment from the national to the international arena. ICDP, I believe, is able to bring experienced, eminent, respected voices to the cause of abolition, in a way that complements the work of other institutions. Rejecting capital punishment is about choosing what kind of society we want to live in, and which values—including human rights and dignity, democracy and the rule of law—we want to uphold.

VOX POPULI, VOX DEI?
A CLOSER LOOK AT THE
"PUBLIC OPINION" ARGUMENT
FOR RETENTION

Mai Sato[1]

For countries and organisations that oppose the death penalty, any state execution is a violation of human rights or risks a miscarriage of justice that is both severe and uncorrectable. Abolitionist states and organisations have urged retentionists—through international treaties, soft-power diplomacy and other campaigns—to change their point of view. An eminent legal scholar predicted nearly 20 years ago that abolition may become a customary norm and reach the status of "*jus cogens* [a fundamental principle of international law from which no derogation is permitted]. . . in the not too distant future."[2] Today, while abolitionist states have become the clear majority, it is also true that retentionist states have continued to carry out the death penalty.

Japan was the first country in the world known to have abolished the death penalty; no executions were carried out from 810 to 1156.[3] Today, however, Japan retains the death penalty.[4] While its use is far from aggressive, with about five executions per year during the last 20 years, prisoners on death row have been hanged every year (except for 2011). The United Nations Human Rights Committee (hereafter the Committee) has repeatedly raised concerns over Japan's failure to fulfil its obligations under the International Covenant on Civil and

---

1   Mai Sato is Research Officer at the Centre for Criminology, University of Oxford. This chapter summarises the main arguments in her book The Death Penalty in Japan: Will the Public Tolerate Abolition? (Berlin, Springer, 2014).
2   W. A. Schabas, The Abolition of the Death Penalty in International Law (Cambridge, Cambridge University Press, 1997), p. 20.
3   D. T. Johnson and F. Zimring, The Next Frontier: National Development, Political Change, and the Death Penalty in Asia (Oxford and New York, Oxford University Press, 2009); K. Kikuta, Q&A: Shikei Mondai no Kiso Chishiki / Q&A: Basic Knowledge of the Issues Surrounding the Death Penalty (Tokyo, Akashi Shoten, 2004).
4   In Japan, 18 crimes are eligible for the death penalty. In practice, however, its use is restricted to a limited subset of these crimes, with almost all prisoners sentenced to death for one of three crimes: murder, robbery resulting in death, or rape on occasion of robbery resulting in death. In relation to murder (as with all other offences on the list), the death penalty is discretionary rather than mandatory and is normally imposed only when a defendant is convicted of multiple killings.

Political Rights,[5] and the Council of Europe has made numerous resolutions critical of Japan, even threatening to take away its observer status.[6] However, Japan has retained its observer status and, despite condemnation by the Committee, has openly and without much (if any) political damage continued to carry out executions.

This illustrates an important limitation of international human rights law: The implementation of human rights norms is possible only if states choose to be bound by them. Human rights is a socially constructed concept that needs to be embraced and accepted to be effective, rather than a set of self-evident principles that exists independently—not a "truth" that people will one day naturally "come round to" but a concept that requires negotiation and persuasion to become operational. This perspective is often neglected or forgotten when abolitionist scholars and international organisations engage with retentionist states.

Public opinion and government legitimacy

The clearest example of this in the Japanese context relates to public opinion, which the Japanese government has raised as the main obstacle to abolition for over 30 years. However, the Committee has not fully engaged with this argument, either to respond to it or to refute it.[7] For example, in responding to Japan's state party report, which consistently makes the public opinion argument, the Committee

---

5   UN Human Rights Committee, "Concluding observations of the Human Rights Committee: Japan", 19 November 1998 (CCPR/C/79Add.102); UN Human Rights Committee, "Concluding observations of the Human Rights Committee: Japan", 18 December 2008 (CCPR/C/JPN/CO/5); UN Human Rights Committee, "Concluding observations of the Human Rights Committee: Japan", 20 August 2014 (CCPR/C/JPN/CO/6) Documents available from: http://tbinternet.ohchr.org/_layouts/treatybodyexternal/TBSearch.aspx-?Lang=en&TreatyID=8&DocTypeID=5. Japan ratified the Covenant in 1979 but has not yet signed or ratified the Second Optional Protocol to the Covenant.

6   Council of Europe, "Resolution 1253 (2001): Abolition of the death penalty in Council of Europe in observer status" (Strasburg, Council of Europe, 2001); Council of Europe, "Resolution 1349 (2003): Abolition of the death penalty in Council of Europe in observer status" (Strasburg, Council of Europe, 2003); Council of Europe, "Doc. 10911: Position of the Parliamentary Assembly as regards the Council of Europe member and observer states which have not abolished the death penalty (Report of the Committee on Legal Affairs and Human Rights of the Parliamentary Assembly of the Council of Europe)" (Strasburg, Council of Europe, 2006). Japan was granted Council of Europe observer status in 1996. Under Statutory Resolution (93) 26, Japan must accept the principles of democracy, the rule of law and the enjoyment of all persons within its jurisdiction of human rights and fundamental freedoms.

7   For a more detailed discussion of the dialogue between the Japanese government and international organisations, see M. Sato, "Challenging the Japanese government's approach to the death penalty", in *Confronting Capital Punishment in Asia: Human Rights, Politics, Public Opinion and Practices*, Roger Hood and Surya Deva, eds. (Oxford, Oxford University Press, 2013) pp. 205-217.

in 2008 wrote, "regardless of opinion polls, the state party should favourably consider abolishing the death penalty"; its 2014 response did not address the issue at all.[8]

The following statement is what the Japanese government wrote in its most recent state party report:

> *Presently, the death penalty is believed to be unavoidable by a large number of Japanese people in cases of extremely malicious or atrocious crimes (affirmed by 85.6 percent in the latest opinion survey conducted from November to December 2009 ... and there is no end to atrocious crimes in Japan.*[9]

The Japanese government's argument is twofold. First it makes a theoretical claim that the decision to retain or abolish should depend on public opinion, based on the idea of popular sovereignty and the importance of maintaining the legitimacy of criminal justice agencies and criminal law. Second, it presents its own survey evidence to support its theoretical position.

While deferring to public opinion on human rights issues is often criticised as unprincipled, the concept of popular sovereignty is in fact enshrined in instruments such Article 1 and 2 of the United Nations Charter and Article 25 of the International Covenant on Civil and Political Rights. It is based on the idea that the legitimacy of the state is formed by the will or consent of its people. The interdependence of law and public opinion, and the need for legal systems to command popular support, have long been recognised.[10] Public perception of the legitimacy of government policies and laws is a key determinant

---

8   UN Human Rights Committee, "Concluding observations of the Human Rights Committee: Japan", 18 December 2008 (CCPR/C/JPN/CO/5), paragraph 6; UN Human Rights Committee, "Concluding observations of the Human Rights Committee: Japan", 20 August 2014 (CCPR/C/JPN/CO/6). Documents available from: http://tbinternet.ohchr.org/_layouts/treatybodyexternal/TBSearch.aspx?Lang=en&TreatyID=8&DocTypeID=5

9   UN Human Rights Committee, "State party report to the Human Rights Committee: Japan", 9 October 2012 (CCPR/C/JPN/6), paragraph 104. Document vailable from: http://tbinternet.ohchr.org/_layouts/treatybodyexternal/TBSearch.aspx?Lang=en&TreatyID=8&DocTypeID=45&DocTypeID=29

10 P. Robinson, "Empirical desert", in Criminal Law Conversations, P. Robinson, S. Garvey and K. Ferzan, eds. (Oxford, Oxford University Press, 2009); P. Robinson and J. Darley, Justice, Liability, and Blame. Community Views and the Criminal Law (Boulder, Colorado: Westview Press, 1995).

of public acceptance of and compliance with them. Criminologists have also argued for the importance of maintaining legitimacy and warned against disregarding public opinion completely.[11] "It is only when the perspectives of everyday members are enshrined in institutions and in the actions of authorities that widespread legitimacy will exist."[12]

Legitimacy based on public perceptions is often called subjective or empirical legitimacy.[13] It can be contrasted with objective legitimacy, which occurs when an institution can be shown to meet criteria for legitimacy, however these criteria are derived. Objective legitimacy involves normative judgments about the criteria to be applied and assessments as to whether these criteria have been met. It is within this top-down perspective that the human rights approach fits. Subjective/empirical legitimacy occurs when citizens perceive an institution as legitimate, regardless of the objective standards that it may (or may not) meet. Clearly it is possible for political and justice institutions to achieve objective legitimacy without subjective legitimacy or vice versa.

The relevance of public opinion to penal policy is not confined to the death penalty debate. For instance, penal populism can result in over-responsiveness to public opinion in penal policy, manifesting itself in counterproductive laws such as "three strikes" provisions for mandatory imprisonment.[14] More positive examples of responsiveness to public opinion include victim impact statements and the use of jury trials.

What happens if subjective legitimacy is eroded? What are the consequences of going against public opinion? One example is Mexico's attempt to combat drug trafficking, which has led to clear damage to the rule of law.[15] A combination of ineffectiveness in policing and extralegal

---

11 D. Garland, "A note on penal populism", in Globalised Penal Populism and Its Countermeasures, Japanese Association of Sociological Criminology, ed. (Tokyo, Gendaijinbunsha, 2009); J. Roberts and M. Hough, Understanding Public Attitudes to Criminal Justice (Maidenhead: Open University Press, 2005).

12 T. Tyler, Why People Obey the Law (Princeton, New Jersey: Princeton University Press, 2006).

13 M. Zelditch, "Theories of legitimacy", in The Psychology of Legitimacy: Emerging Perspectives on Ideology, Justice, and Intergroup Relations, J. T. Jost and B. Major, eds. (Cambridge: Cambridge University Press, 2001).

14 F. E. Zimring, G. Hawkins, and S. Kamin, Punishment and Democracy: Three Strikes and You're Out in California (Oxford: Oxford University Press, 2001).

15 T. R. Tyler, ed., Legitimacy and Criminal Justice (New York, Russell Sage, 2007).

practices led to loss of public trust in the criminal justice system, which in turn led to the establishment by activists of a new grass-roots system operating outside the formal legal structure. Unpaid volunteers have acted as police, court and penal system, often using torture and vigilantism. Governments are naturally concerned that their penal policies, including abolition of the death penalty, do not erode public perceptions of the legitimacy of the criminal justice system—which could result in noncompliance with the law, lack of cooperation with the criminal justice system, and vigilantism. One country where the death penalty policy was at least claimed to be central to popular trust in the criminal justice system was the Philippines. The government explained to the Committee in 2002 that the abolition of the death penalty had "undermined the people's faith in the Government and the latter's ability to maintain peace and order in the country."[16]

> "WHETHER OR NOT THERE IS A DETERRENT EFFECT IS A MATTER OF EVIDENCE AND NOT OPINION."
>
> —Mai Sato

As noted earlier, the public-opinion-based argument for retention of the death penalty has two elements. It must demonstrate that retention is central to popular trust in the criminal justice system and that abolition would result in the erosion of political and judicial legitimacy. This would establish a *theoretical* basis for the argument. However, my view is that the biggest challenge to this approach is in proving *empirically* that legitimacy depends on retention. For example, the Japanese government's argument for retaining the death penalty is based on the assumption that the survey it conducts has accurately captured public opinion—a claim that is challenged below.

A closer look at the Japanese survey results

Some retentionist states may claim that there is strong public support for retention without offering evidence or based on a survey conducted elsewhere on an ad hoc basis. The Japanese government

---

16   UN Human Rights Committee, "State party report to the Human Rights Committee: Phillippines", 18 September 2012 (CCPR/C/PHL/2002/2), paragraph 494. Document vailable from: http://tbinternet.ohchr.org/_layouts/treatybodyexternal/TBSearch.aspx?Lang=en&TreatyID=8&DocTypeID=45&DocTypeID=29

takes the argument more seriously by carrying out its own survey (hereafter the survey), which is contracted to an independent market research company and has been carried out approximately every five years since 1956. Each survey has interviewed nationally representative samples of Japanese men and women aged 20 and over, using two-stage stratified random sampling. This needs to be acknowledged as a systematic attempt to measure public opinion. But does the result demonstrate that retention of the death penalty is critical to maintaining social order and legitimacy?

The most recent survey was conducted at the end of 2014; reportedly, 80 per cent of respondents were in favour of retention. The result has been cited by the Ministry of Justice as proof that abolition is not yet possible.[17] Arguably, however, the survey results do not prove that abolition of the death penalty would harm the criminal justice system's legitimacy.

For the last five sweeps of the survey, the government has used the same measure of support for retention. Respondents are invited to choose from two statements the one that reflects their viewpoint. The retentionist position is phrased in broad terms: "The death penalty is unavoidable in some cases." By contrast, the abolitionist option states, "The death penalty should be abolished under all circumstances." The 80 per cent response reported as supporting the death penalty refers to respondents who considered that the death penalty is unavoidable in *some* cases rather than enthusiastically embracing retention.[18]

The retention option also includes an option to support future abolition. Of the 80 per cent of respondents who considered the death penalty to be unavoidable in some cases, 41 per cent (a third of the total sample) supported future abolition. When respondents who support future abolition are not included, under half (46 per cent) of the total sample can be considered to whole-heartedly support retention.

In addition to the question concerning future abolition, one new question was added to the 2014 survey. It concerned the introduction of life imprisonment without parole as an alternative to the

---

17   Minutes of the press conference available from the MoJ website: http://www.moj.go.jp/ hisho/kouhou/hisho08_00616.html).

18   Even with this wording, the percentage of people who chose this option dropped by 6 per cent from the 2009 survey.

death penalty. This question further qualifies public commitment to retention. Of the respondents, 38 per cent said that the death penalty should be abolished if life imprisonment without parole was introduced, 52 per cent said that it should be kept, and 11 per cent said they didn't know.[19]

Based on the 2014 survey results, it is possible to argue that respondents who (1) consider the death penalty to be unavoidable in some cases, (2) do not accept the possibility of future abolition, and (3) do not agree with replacing the death penalty with life imprisonment without parole amount to only 34 per cent of all respondents. In other words, behind the 80 per cent support reported in headlines, the majority of the public do in fact accept the possibility of future abolition, especially if alternative punishments are available. If hardcore retentionists make up only 34 per cent of the public, it does not seem persuasive to argue that abolition would erode trust in the criminal justice system.

Another vulnerability of this argument is the question: What figure should be the threshold when judging how essential retaining the death penalty is to maintaining legitimacy? The Japanese government has not attempted to answer this question. It is obviously not an easy question to answer, but it is essential to any public-opinion-based argument for keeping the death penalty.

One further point undermines the presumed importance of retention for the Japanese public. Those who are committed to retaining the death penalty tend to hold inaccurate beliefs about its effect. The survey asks respondents about their perception of the deterrent effect of the death penalty. In the 2014 survey, 58 per cent of respondents thought crime would increase if the death penalty were abolished, 14 per cent thought it would not increase, and 28 per cent chose "don't know/cannot say"—which is the correct answer if one accepts the increasing academic consensus that it is virtually impossible to prove or disapprove a deterrent effect.[20]

---

19   The percentages do not add up to 100 due to the rounding up of figures.
20   See National Research Council, *Deterrence and the Death Penalty*, Daniel S. Nagin and John V. Pepper, eds. (Washington, DC, National Academies Press, 2012).

In addition, whether or not there is a deterrent effect is a matter of evidence and not opinion. Hence, it is puzzling as to why the survey has consistently included this question for over 50 years. Nothing has been done to address public misconceptions about deterrence, nor has any analysis taken into account those respondents who express support for the death penalty based on inaccurate beliefs.

Linked to the issue of inaccurate public beliefs, secrecy is a salient feature of the Japanese death penalty system. In December 2007 the Japanese government, for the first time, announced the names of prisoners and the crimes they committed after each execution. Before this, the number of executions was published in newspapers in just one sentence such as, "Today, two people were executed." It is still the case that prisoners about to be executed are notified only a few hours before the execution, which gives no time for them to get in touch with their lawyer or their family.[21] In most cases, the families of prisoners are informed only after the execution has taken place. Furthermore, there is still no official information regarding how prisoners are selected for execution, the treatment of prisoners on death row, or the cost of executions. This has led scholars to state that "the secrecy that surrounds capital punishment in Japan is taken to extremes not seen in other nations"[22] and that the public only has a very abstract idea of the punishment.[23] Recently, a series of social experiments showed that the vast majority of the public did not possess basic knowledge about the death penalty, including whether an execution had taken place in the current year, and that many people changed their views when they received additional information.[24] The government has so far failed to reconcile its secrecy on the use of the death penalty with its delegation of power to the (poorly informed) public to decide whether to retain it.

Examination of the 2014 survey demonstrated that the wording of a question and the knowledge of a respondent can dramatically affect survey results. Does this render surveys unreliable? Furthermore, critics who question the relevance of public opinion to death-penalty policy

---

21   K. Kikuta, *Q&A*, pp. 73-78.

22   D. T. Johnson, "When the state kills in secret: capital punishment in Japan", *Punishment and Society*, vol. 8, no. 3 (2006), pp. 251-285, at p. 251.

23   S. Dando, "Toward the abolition of the death penalty", *Indiana Law Journal*, vol. 72 (1996), pp. 7-19, at p. 10.

24   M. Sato, *The Death Penalty in Japan*.

argue that almost all countries that abolished the death penalty did so through judicial or political leadership, despite public support for the death penalty.[25] In my view, these criticisms do not disprove the value of survey evidence as a social barometer to inform policy decisions. If, contrary to expectations based on survey results, countries have abolished the death penalty without eroding the legitimacy of the criminal justice system, this should cause us to question the reliability of those survey results—and more importantly, their interpretation—not to negate a role for public opinion in the death penalty debate.

Concluding remarks

The Japanese government's justification for retaining the death penalty is that abolition would erode the legitimacy of and public trust in the criminal justice system, leading to victims' families taking justice into their own hands. This justification is based on the results of a regularly administered public opinion survey, which is said to show strong public support for the death penalty. However, a close analysis of the results of the 2014 survey fails to validate this claim. Just over a third of respondents were committed to retaining the death penalty at all costs, while the rest accepted the possibility of future abolition, with some of them seeing this as contingent on the introduction of life imprisonment without parole as an alternative sentence. These findings hardly describe a society that expects the strict application of the death penalty and whose trust in justice depends on the government's commitment to retaining it. My reading of the 2014 survey is that the Japanese public is ready to embrace abolition. Japan, after all, is a signatory to the International Covenant on Civil and Political Rights, which calls on states not to delay or prevent abolition, so this should be welcome news for the Japanese government!

---

25 P. Hodgkinson, "Replacing capital punishment: an issue of effective penal policy", in *The International Leadership Conference on Human Rights and the Death Penalty, Conference Brochure 1* (European Commission, American Bar Associations, and Japan Federation of Bar Associations, unpublished, 2005); R. Hood and C. Hoyle, *The Death Penalty: A Worldwide Perspective* (Oxford, Oxford University Press, 2015); D. T. Johnson and F. Zimring, *The Next Frontier: National Development, Political Change, and the Death Penalty in Asia* (Oxford and New York, Oxford University Press, 2009). Hodgkinson (p. 46) argued that "universally public opinion supports the death penalty and this is important in that politicians many of whom are mesmerised by such polls are reluctant to question them or to encourage a more authoritative evaluation. . . . Few countries would have abolished the death penalty if they had waited for public approval."

LEADERSHIP THROUGH DIALOGUE

Didier Burkhalter[1]

Each country has its own way of dealing with the death penalty, and Switzerland is no exception. In the Swiss case, use of the death penalty had been steadily declining when legal experts working on the unification of the Swiss penal code in the 1930s decided that it was time to end the problematic punishment. Thus, abolition of the death penalty for ordinary crimes entered into force in 1942 and for military crimes in 1992. Since 2000, the Swiss Constitution has forbidden the use of the death penalty. The Swiss experience demonstrates the length of time an abolition process can take, from initial questioning to full *de jure* abolition. This is a process that needs to be driven by leadership.

Switzerland's ambition is to act as a catalyst in the universal abolitionist movement. One cannot create political will in countries where there is none, nor can one impose abolition where there hasn't been a mature and serious debate on the death penalty. But we can kindle the flame already burning in those countries that have yet to complete their abolition process. As foreign minister, I have set universal death penalty abolition as a Swiss foreign policy priority and as a goal, shared with many colleagues around the world, to be reached by 2025.

Switzerland's strategy is straightforward. Bilaterally, we foster and support discussions between key actors who are open to sharing their views on the death penalty. We nourish those discussions with facts, expert analyses and technical support. Where there is growing agreement that steps can be taken towards abolition, we remain ready to provide pragmatic assistance when appropriate. Multilaterally, we also play a proactive role in shaping international norms and standards towards a more restrictive use of the death penalty.

There is increasing awareness that the death penalty cannot be carried out without violating international human rights law. Executions

---

1   Didier Burkhalter is a member of the Federal Council and the minister of foreign affairs of Switzerland.

constitute inhumane and degrading treatment and fundamentally contradict Article 10 of the International Covenant on Civil and Political Rights, which states that the essential aim of any penitentiary system shall be the reformation and social rehabilitation of prisoners. The death penalty also takes a heavy toll on prisoners' families, particularly their children, violating the fundamental right of each child to have a family. These are but a few of the principles that Switzerland defends in international forums, foremost the United Nations Human Rights Council and General Assembly.

Through the strength of its convictions and its openness to sharing ideas and experiences, Switzerland is committed to remaining active in efforts to abolish the death penalty.

THE MANY FACETS OF THE DEATH PENALTY DEBATE

The global trend towards abolition of the death penalty is undeniable. In December 2014, Madagascar adopted a bill to abolish the death penalty. In February 2015, Fiji completed its full de jure abolition process. In March, Côte d'Ivoire and Suriname both scrapped the death penalty. Whilst a few countries have resumed executions, there is a growing international consensus that the death penalty is neither a useful nor a viable sentence.

In the handful of countries where there seems to be little or no hope of abolition in the near future, what we confront is not a hard bedrock of unshakable opposition, but rather a sturdy door. Trying to break down the door will only alienate those on the other side. But by respectfully ringing the doorbell and showing patience, one can engage in productive conversations with those who disagree. However strong the differences, it is the experience of Switzerland that when it comes to the death penalty, there is always room for discussion. Sometimes the exchanges can be technical, on topics such as criminal justice reform and alternative sentencing. Other times they are ideological, philosophical, or even theological, for instance on the purpose of criminal justice. Overall, though, abolition of the death penalty is a human rights issue that transcends cultural barriers and speaks to our common humanity. Compassion is common to every civilization, religion and region. Rehabilitation as the central goal of the criminal justice system is an accepted norm of international law, enshrined in the International Covenant on Civil and Political Rights. Countries from every region of the world have set an example in ending the use of capital punishment, including Benin, Cambodia, Canada, Cap Verde, Costa Rica, Latvia, Mexico, Mongolia and Timor-Leste.

CHALLENGING THE MYTH OF DETERRENCE

Though a conversation on abolition is always possible, it isn't always easy. There are often technical issues that need to be resolved, such as penal code reform. In countries willing to revisit the death penalty issue, revising sentencing practices and finding alternatives to capital punishment can be a lengthy but necessary process. And there is always a need for local experts to lead the work on legal reform, at times also to exchange experiences with international experts from countries with similar justice systems, before abolishing the death penalty.

The persisting myth of deterrence is a challenge almost everywhere. It is tempting to assume that the threat of execution must discourage heinous crimes. However, compelling research has shown that the death penalty does not deter violent crime any more than harsh alternative sanctions such as life imprisonment. Other factors, such as having an efficient police force, are the ones that actually matter in effectively fighting crime.

Executing drug mules would not stop the flow of illicit drugs. Trafficking will continue as long as there are consumers, as well as people desperate enough to risk entering the drug trafficking business for rapid but often small economic gain. Executing the mentally ill would not make the community safer, but putting in place programs to address mental illness will. Both of these scenarios would not only violate international law, they would also be unethical, inhumane and ultimately pointless.

Yet one of the most common arguments in defence of the death penalty is linked to the same illusion of deterrence. Executing individuals who are incarcerated, and thus have already ceased to be a threat to society, is not being tough on crime. Emphasizing the deterrence rationale is fear mongering, and it is dishonest towards citizens who have legitimate concerns about their safety. We need to move away from reliance on this cruel punishment and to focus instead on effective and efficient crime prevention.

For Switzerland, leadership is expressed in action rather than grand discourse. My country is opposed to the death penalty everywhere and under all circumstances, but it is unrealistic to expect that retentionist countries will accept this stance immediately. Long-term engagement, incremental action, attentiveness and fact-based discussion are the means by which to move forward. With the right amount of research, and dissemination to the right actors, it is possible to revive dialogue everywhere, even where it seems to be dying out.

THE INTERNATIONAL MOVEMENT FOR ABOLITION

Finding the right interlocutor and the proper approach can be daunting challenges, as every abolition process is different, with its own context and opportunities. In some countries, abolition requires the political courage of a few committed leaders. This was famously the case in France, where Robert Badinter, then minister of justice, spearheaded abolition through incisive and eloquent prose. In most countries, however, there is no single event or single politician that changes the political landscape. Instead it is often a lengthy process, edged forward by the tenacity of committed parliamentarians and political leaders. These commendable women and men deserve the support of the international community.

In other countries, the judiciary can be the best entry point for addressing capital punishment. Though the death penalty is technically permitted under international law, legally putting someone to death is impossible. International law restricts the use of the death penalty to only the most serious crimes, while mandatory death sentencing is illegal. In the rarest-of-the-rare cases where the death penalty could be applicable, there has to be due process. Every prisoner has the right to appeal up to the highest judicial body of his or her country, as well as to request clemency. Appeal and clemency procedures invariably take years, during which the condemned is subjected to the intense psychological hardship of impending death. Any individual would be severely psychologically affected by such a process, which amounts to cruel and degrading treatment. In addition, in every country that still practices the death penalty, it is disproportionately imposed on the marginalized, the weak, the poor and the vulnerable. Though capital punishment may at first seem consistent with international law, there is a strong empirical argument to be made that its use inevitably violates human rights—a case Switzerland is making with a broad coalition of like-minded countries in international forums.

Public opinion is important, but can be a double-edged sword in the push for universal abolition, as few people are genuinely committed to learning about the death penalty's true consequences. To make matters worse, some politicians misuse perceived majority support for the death penalty as the primary justification for not opposing it. In the numerous countries where abolition took place in spite of majority opposition, opinions evolved gradually to favour abolition. Indeed, opinions can change quickly when people are presented with facts. This has for instance been the case in California, the most populous state in the United States, where there has been a gradual shift in public attitudes towards the death penalty. Support for capital punishment dropped from 63% in 2000 to 52% in 2012, when the state voted on abolition. Criminologists in particular have been instrumental in demonstrating that public support for capital punishment, even in the most hard-line countries, is limited at best.

> "DEATH PENALTY CANNOT BE CARRIED OUT WITHOUT VIOLATING INTERNATIONAL HUMAN RIGHTS LAW."
> —Didier Burkhalter

Transparent reporting and public action can be a substantial force for abolition. Victims' families in countries including the United States and Japan have been vocal in saying that the death penalty does not offer closure for the loss of a loved one; rather, it perpetuates violence and hatred. Hundreds of innocent people have now been exonerated from death row because of wrongful convictions and, knowing better than anyone the pain of that experience, several have been touring the world to tell their story or have it recorded by the media. Hearing about the injustice of wrongful convictions and executions is uncomfortable, but it is important to realize the implications of what can otherwise be too easily forgotten: No criminal justice system is without error. Prosecutors and judges are human, and despite the best efforts and safeguards, they make mistakes like anyone else.

SMART LEADERSHIP

The death penalty debate is complex, multifaceted, politically sensitive and often misunderstood. Doing research, disseminating information and holding conferences, seminars and workshops – all of these are important, but they are not sufficient to achieve abolition. Leadership is always necessary to instigate major change.

The abolitionist movement needs to adapt to remaining challenges and move forward by committing to a new, smart form of leadership, in which governments, parliamentarians, judges, academics, members of the media, artists and activists all build on each other's complementary strengths. An unwaveringly principled stance needs to be combined with inclusive and respectful engagement. Switzerland has been proactive in consolidating a network of smart leaders, many of whom have years of experience working for universal abolition of the death penalty. To facilitate the emergence of new leaders, especially where nearly everything has yet to be done, is a gratifying task.

Dialogue may not be what immediately comes to mind when talking about leadership. Yet some of the greatest progress towards abolition has been achieved thanks to individuals willing to engage in productive dialogue. Spending time and resources, fostering dialogue, providing facts, listening to arguments and striving to find a way forward is in itself a valuable form of leadership. There is enough work remaining to be done for each of us to have a leadership role to play. There is also potential for complementarity between gentle support and full-throated advocacy, as long as actors in both these roles take the time to study and strategize together. This collaborative planning is the essence of smart leadership.

I am personally convinced that there are no good arguments in favour of the death penalty. Quite the contrary: the death penalty creates more problems than it purports to solve. I believe that under no circumstances is it just for a human being to take the life of another human being. We are all flawed, we make mistakes, and our imperfection needs to be acknowledged in the way in which we construct our criminal justice systems. The death penalty does not make the world safer, and it most certainly does not make it better.

Switzerland will continue to lead through dialogue in the years to come. We are counting on the support of many partner countries interested in open and comprehensive engagement. I believe additional partners will join us soon, and working together with the few countries still using the death penalty, we can achieve universal abolition by 2025.

MONGOLIA HONOURS HUMAN LIFE AND DIGNITY

Tsakhiagiin Elbegdorj[1]

I am glad to be part of the movement away from the death penalty, and I am confident that this book will be an indispensable reference to national leaders working to advance a moratorium on the imposition of the death penalty and its eventual abolition.

In 2010 Mongolia announced a moratorium on executions as a first step towards abolition of the death penalty. Our decision received acclamation internationally and set the standard for other countries in the "worst executioner" region. It was a dramatic decision. No known human society has been fully able to prevent humans from killing one another. Every community demands from its state severe punishment of criminals. Yet states have the ability to stop taking citizens' lives. None of the abolitionist countries repealed the death penalty under pressure from public opinion. But the number of countries that have abolished this punishment grows year by year.

> "WE CANNOT REPAIR ONE DEATH WITH ANOTHER."
> —Tsakhiagiin Elbegdorj

Mongolia is a dignified country, and our citizens are dignified people. As president, I encouraged my people to end the death penalty, which degrades our dignity. I said I wanted to be a president who can tell his citizens: "I will not deprive you of your life under any circumstances, knowingly, on behalf of the state." Our people say that a human life is more precious than all the wealth that the Earth can carry. The road that a democratic Mongolia takes should be clean and bloodless.

Mongolians have suffered enough from the death sentence. Between October 1937 and April 1939, in 51 sessions of the Special Full-Power Committee, which then functioned in place of the courts, 20,474 Mongolian citizens were sentenced to death. In just one session, a mass death sentence for 1,228 people was issued, including eight women.

---

1 Tsakhiagiin Elbegdorj is president of Mongolia. This article draws on the statement he made at the Leadership and Moving Away from the Death Penalty event at the United Nations in New York on 25 September 2014.

Mongolia was one of the few countries to re-introduce the death penalty. In 1953, the Presidium of the People's Great Khural adopted Decree 93, which resolved to abandon capital punishment, but 10 months later it retreated from this decision. Most of those sentenced to death were people in their 20s to 40s. And most of them had committed a crime for the first time.

I would like to mention the main arguments that led me to oppose the death penalty:

- Removing the death penalty does not mean removing punishment. Criminals fear justice, and justice must be imminent and unavoidable. But we cannot repair one death with another.

- The state has no right to risk making a judicial or procedural mistake when deciding a question of life and death. Such mistakes are unacceptable. Mistakes and miscarriages of justice in applying the death penalty can only be prevented by closing the door to it altogether. Only then will we be able to genuinely honour human life and human rights and create conditions to safeguard them.

On 13 March 2012, the Mongolian Parliament ratified the Second Optional Protocol to the International Covenant on Civil and Political Rights, indicating that the country is poised to completely abolish the death penalty.

Mongolia is taking steps to abolish the death penalty both in law and practice. The criminal code is being amended to comply with the Second Optional Protocol. Comments from Amnesty International and specialized United Nations agencies were solicited in the course of the drafting. The draft Law on Crimes proposed life imprisonment as the harshest criminal sentence.

Mongolia is committed to contributing to international cooperation to abolish the death penalty. Mongolia shares the concern over the continued use of the death penalty in a number of countries. Consistent with our opposition to capital punishment, Mongolia calls upon all states that have not yet done so to join the vast majority of countries that do not execute in the name of the law. It is important to underline the role and critical importance of international and regional organizations, particularly the United Nations, in the effort to abolish the death penalty.

TOWARDS UNIVERSAL ABOLITION OF THE DEATH PENALTY

Laurent Fabius[1]

France's commitment to universal abolition of the death penalty is a fight for the progress of mankind.

It is a fight that we share with the whole abolitionist movement. It is by joining our efforts that all of us, governments, regional and international organizations, parliamentarians, militants, researchers, advocates, and citizens, will get there.

The articles that appear in the publication that you are holding reflect the mobilization of all sectors of society and regions of the world towards abolition. France is especially pleased to contribute to spreading this publication in francophone and Arabic-speaking regions, and I hereby thank the High Commissioner for Human Rights for his active engagement in this cause.

The testimonies of individuals who have been wrongly convicted, the studies of the researchers, the articles written by NGO representatives remind us that the death penalty is ineffective, it is unjust and it is inhumane.

The evidence is in that it is not an effective punishment against criminal behavior: it doesn't deter crime.

The unjust nature of the death penalty is confirmed by the inequality it perpetuates: the punishment varies depending on social status or ethnic affiliation. How can one accept that those factors determine life and death?

Because mistakes are unavoidable and irreversible, the death penalty is fundamentally a human rights violation. It is not justice. It is the failure and the negation of justice.

---

1 Laurent Fabius is the Minister of Foreign Affairs and International Development of France.

The majority of States already share the conviction that the death penalty is the opposite of justice.

During the last few decades, the death penalty has lost ground. Two thirds of the world have already abolished it or have adopted a moratorium, as compared to only 16 in 1977. Each time an execution is stayed, each time a death sentence is commuted or a new moratorium is adopted, it is a victory.

But we should stay engaged, as the fight for universal abolition has not ended yet.

First of all, because a moratorium remains reversible, and a number of States have broken what until now they had respected, at times for long periods.

Also, because every year worldwide thousands of women and men are still sentenced to death: in 2014, the number of death sentences increased by 28% compared to the previous year, according to the latest report by Amnesty International.

Finally, because every year more than a dozen of countries continue to execute hundreds or even thousands of people on death row.

In view of these long-term advances but also taking into account short-term backtracking, it is essential to ensure a strong mobilization towards universal abolition, for all crimes.

This is the reason why I chose to prioritize this fight in the context of the French diplomacy, by launching a world campaign towards universal abolition of the death penalty. This campaign mobilizes our entire network at different levels.

What do we do concretely?

Our embassies and cultural centers are active on the ground to alert, mobilize, advocate. By organizing conferences, partnerships with NGOs, media awareness campaigns, creation or strengthening of abolitionist networks around the world, our diplomats are consistently engaged in the abolitionist fight.

"PUBLIC OPINION CANNOT BE USED AS A PRETEXT TO MAINTAIN CAPITAL PUNISHMENT."

—Laurent Fabius

We engage with all key stakeholders: parliamentarians, as abolition is the result of legislative revision; attorneys, who are on the frontline defending people on death row and who contribute to evolving the thinking on the death penalty; journalists, who can inform about the reality surrounding the death penalty, especially in those countries where executions are carried out in secret; but also the youth, because they are tomorrow's citizens and decision-makers.

We are also engaged, together with our EU partners, at the multilateral level. In the context of the UN, we use our influence to strengthen the abolitionist movement.

In the General Assembly, France is fully engaged in the fight for the adoption of the resolution on a universal moratorium, as a first step towards complete abolition. In the Human Rights Council, France has made the fight against the death penalty a priority, including by acknowledging the human rights violations stemming from it.

The international community has a special responsibility, as capital punishment is a threat to the universal principles it supports.

However, we should not forget the role that each individual can play, our personal responsibility on the path towards abolition.

All the countries that have succeeded in the fight against capital punishment have been able to do so because of the strong political will and determination of a few individuals.

This is exactly what happened in France. Our path towards abolition was particularly long: the first attempts to abolish capital punishment date back to the beginning of the French Revolution. This issue divided France, one of the last countries in Western Europe to abolish it, in 1981. At the time, public opinion was mostly in favor of the death penalty.

However, public opinion cannot be used as a pretext to maintain capital punishment. In order to abolish it, one needs to be ahead of society, show it the way. To this end, one needs courage, determination and perseverance.

The abolitionist cause requires speaking out against fake certitudes, fighting bias. Public opinion, urgent priorities or the need to fight threats such as terrorism or drug trafficking are often invoked to justify the death penalty. These arguments cannot justify maintaining such a cruel, degrading and inhumane punishment. Those who support the death penalty often see it as a trade off against the need for security. One can support the need for security – we all do – while at the same time opposing the death penalty.

In view of the obligation to protect life, each political or judicial actor should appeal to his/her courage.

The French experience confirms that courage will pay off. Today, the majority of the French population supports the choice made by our leaders thirty years ago, despite the then public opinion. Abolition has been reflected in our constitution in 2007. It is now part of our heritage.

The decision to abolish capital punishment is not a matter of political expediency. It is not a matter of culture, despite what some claim. It is a matter of principle.

We must pursue our efforts to advocate that it is both just and possible to abolish capital punishment, regardless of the circumstances.

The path towards abolition is long and winded. But in view of our shared ideals of justice and human dignity, each person on death row is one too many.

To those who still resort to the death penalty or remain hesitant we say, using the words of Victor Hugo, "*you may not abolish capital punishment today, but make no mistake about it, you will abolish it tomorrow or your successors will*".

Let's not waste time or lives. Abolishing the death penalty is allowing justice and mankind to evolve. All those who commit to this path, will find France standing by their side.

CHALLENGES RELATED TO ABOLITION OF THE DEATH PENALTY IN ARAB AND ISLAMIC COUNTRIES: TUNISIA'S MODEL

Mohamed Moncef Marzouki[1]

A few days after my election as president of the Republic of Tunisia on 12 December 2011, I discovered to my astonishment that there were 220 prisoners on death row. Many in this group had been sentenced to death a long time ago, but they had neither been executed nor had their sentence commuted to life imprisonment. Before he was ousted by the revolution, the dictator had adopted the policy of neither applying the sentences (as they would further tarnish his dark record of human rights violations) nor commuting them (as he did not want to turn public opinion, which supported the death penalty, against him).

I signed a decree to replace the death penalty with life imprisonment, a decision that in my opinion has changed the lives of many people who had to bear the weight of psychological torture for years. I was soon faced with the consequences of this act. Each time the amnesty committee brought me an amnesty decree, I signed it as a matter of principle, without even looking at the case. On one occasion the Minister of Justice insisted that I hear the details of the case, perhaps with the hope that I would not readily approve the amnesty. So I went through the details of a horrendous crime. To everyone's astonishment I signed the amnesty in the midst of what felt like silent yet heavy disapproval. I knew that that move would further complicate matters for me, including at the political level.

It was customary to reduce overcrowding in prisons by releasing young or sick detainees, or those convicted of minor crimes, on national holidays. But on each occasion the opposition accused me of releasing dangerous criminals. These attacks were widely supported by the media, which used to report on every crime that occurred as a crime committed by someone who was pardoned by the president.

---

1   Mohamed Moncef Marzouki is the former president of the Republic of Tunisia.

In other words, I was digging my own political grave by systematically pardoning people who were sentenced to death and pardoning other detainees on national holidays.

What complicated things further for me was the constitutional struggle, as I strived for the inclusion of an article on the abolition of the death penalty. I had been working for abolition since the early 1990s, as soon as I became chairman of the Tunisian League for Human Rights. I remember that the fight started when a well-known newspaper made a call in a large headline to execute 12 times a criminal who had raped and killed 12 children. That day even the members of the executive board of the League preferred not to take an active stance against the death penalty, as society was deeply shocked by this atrocious crime. But I insisted that it was, on the contrary, an opportunity for us to assume our intellectual responsibility and confront the (understandably tense) public with our ideas.

In articles and heated public debates, I reiterated the usual arguments against capital punishment, and these were the same arguments that I used in my speech to Tunisia's National Constituent Assembly to call for abolition:

- The death sentence neither cancels nor compensates for the atrocity of the crime, but rather adds another layer of atrocity.

- There is no proven link between the application of this sentence and a decline in crime rates; sometimes the opposite happens.

- Most convicts receiving the sentence come from the poorest sections of society as well as minorities and the political opposition.

- Judicial errors are more common that we think, and they cannot be redressed after an execution is carried out.

These logical arguments, which reject the use of a cure that is more painful than the disease itself, failed to convince the 217 members of the Constituent Assembly, and therefore the draft law was not debated.

I was appalled that my closest friends and colleagues in human rights organizations did nothing either.

I am very proud of the constitution ratified by the Constituent Assembly on 27 January 2014, which guarantees many rights and freedoms. But I would have been even more proud had Tunisia become the first Arab country to join the circle of democratic countries and civilized nations that have abolished this barbaric punishment.

> "I WAS DIGGING MY OWN POLITICAL GRAVE
> BY SYSTEMATICALLY PARDONING PEOPLE WHO
> WERE SENTENCED TO DEATH."
> —Mohamed Moncef Marzouki

We need to make sense of this failure in a country that was offered an historic opportunity, having known a democratic revolution, a strong human rights movement, and a fervent opponent of capital punishment as head of state.

There are two causes for this failure, one contextual and one structural.

Contextually, the drafting of the constitution, which started after the October 2011 elections and lasted until January 2013, was marred with terrorist attacks that resulted in many losses in the ranks of the army and the police. At these martyrs' funerals and subsequent meetings with their families at the Carthage Palace, all I could hear were the cries of these families for retaliation against those who killed their sons, sometimes expressed with extremely violent imagery. In such circumstances it is very difficult to advocate for abolition.

The structural cause was even more difficult to overcome: the dominant religious culture that considers capital punishment part of Islamic sharia law, and therefore not open to debate. For many years in the human rights struggle, I consistently made reference to verses of the Koran that encourage pardon, forgiveness and mercy, all of which are core values of our noble Islamic religion.

But every reference I made was countered by a reference to other parts of the Koran that explicitly call for retaliation. Such a position leads nowhere, because it gives us only two choices: Advocate for abolition outside the Islamic framework, or accept the death penalty and give up our hope of seeing Tunisia in the circle of civilized countries.

But because I am a faithful Muslim and cannot extract myself from the value system within which I grew up, I found an answer in the following verse: "Whoever kills a soul unless for a soul or for corruption in the land, it is as if he had killed all mankind, and whoever saves it, it is as if he saved all mankind." In my opinion, this verse warns against killing an innocent person mistakenly or unfairly—which is common under capital punishment—because the act of killing all mankind, even symbolically, is an extraordinary responsibility no one is able to bear.

This is why I argue that we have to give up a right which the Koran considers lawful but which, when interpreted and applied by humans, has led to killing all mankind on countless occasions. The Koran does not accept this.

The intellectual debate on this issue will certainly continue for years, and it will be difficult to convince society even after terrorism has been defeated. But our mission as human rights defenders is to continue advocating, because the matter is not just about people whom we need to save from a barbaric and ineffective punishment, but also about helping society advance towards a higher degree of civilization.

THE ROLE OF LEADERSHIP

Matteo Renzi[1]

As a country that has traditionally supported multilateralism and is inclined towards dialogue and mediation, for both historical and geographical reasons, Italy has always attached great importance to the promotion of human rights in international relations. In particular, Italy has been actively engaged in the campaign for a moratorium on the death penalty, which was one of the priorities of the Italian rotating Presidency of the Council of the European Union for the second semester of 2014.[2] I am therefore very grateful for the opportunity to contribute to this publication and elaborate on the role of leadership in advancing this campaign.

The United Nations plays a unique role in calling on the entire international community to work in a more coordinated and effective manner to ensure the respect of human rights and fundamental freedoms. I would like to thank in particular Secretary-General Ban Ki-moon for his tireless work in advocating for a moratorium of the use of the death penalty worldwide. His strong leadership, deep personal commitment and inspiring words are instrumental to the success of the campaign. I would also like to thank the Assistant Secretary-General for Human Rights Šimonović and the Office of the High Commissioner for Human Rights for their excellent work in assisting and coordinating activities in this field.

Since my appointment as prime minister of Italy, I have grown even further in my firm belief in the importance of promoting and protecting human rights and fundamental freedoms. Promoting respect for human rights for all without distinction is not only a matter of ethics, but a necessary condition to maintain international peace and security and foster economic and social development.

---

1   Matteo Renzi is president of the Council of Ministers of the Republic of Italy.
2   The Italian Presidency had the following priorities in the field of human rights: to further the campaign for a moratorium on executions, to ensure freedom of religion and belief and the protection of religious minorities, and to promote women's rights (in particular, by combating gender-based violence, female genital mutilation and early and forced marriages).

Every country has a responsibility to respect human rights for the good of their own people and for the rest of humankind. We should exercise our individual and shared responsibility not just in the interest of people living today, but for all future generations.

As prime minister of Italy, I take pride in the fact that my country is highly regarded for its engagement in the campaign for a moratorium on the death penalty. This endeavour is deeply rooted in the Italian identity; historical, cultural and religious factors have all played a fundamental role. But let me be clear: This is also a success story about good leadership.

More than two centuries ago, in 1786, the Grand Duke of Tuscany, Leopold I, abolished capital punishment in his territories. This decision was inspired by the philosophical and juridical reflection of another great Italian, Cesare Beccaria, who 20 years before had published a book titled *On Crimes and Punishments*, in which he condemned the use of torture and capital punishment and underlined the lack of scientific evidence on the deterrent value of the death penalty. Beccaria was able to show that the death penalty is useless and unnecessary, affirming at the same time that its abolition would represent a significant contribution to human progress.

In the 18th century Italy was not the unified state it is today, but in many aspects it was already a nation, with a common heritage, language, history and values. The arguments provided by Cesare Beccaria and the example set by Grand Duke Leopold have remained vivid in the hearts and minds of Italians until today. Great leadership inspired by ideas and a clear vision of the future can make change happen. In 1889, the now unified Kingdom of Italy abolished the death penalty, except in the military code. Under fascism, the death penalty was reintroduced, but as soon as democracy was re-established after the Second World War, the death penalty during peacetime was completely abolished. Further steps were later taken to completely abolish the use of capital punishment under all circumstances, and today Italian legislation is fully compliant with the standards set by the United Nations and the Council of Europe. But even in a country where the campaign for abolition of the death penalty has deep roots in history and enjoys a wide consensus among the population, it has taken time and effort to introduce the necessary legislative reforms to fully enact it.

Italian opposition to the death penalty is grounded in history, but it looks to the future as well. Building on the progress achieved at home, it was natural for Italy to set out on a worldwide campaign for a moratorium on the death penalty and to put it at the forefront of its foreign policy priorities. Italy first tabled a draft resolution on a moratorium at the United Nations General Assembly in 1994. While the resolution failed (by only a handful of votes), this outcome confirmed the importance and the urgency of the campaign. There was wide support for our initiative, but it became clear that enhanced efforts were needed to win the hearts and minds of all members of the international community. Indeed, Italy continued to work on building a broad international coalition in favour of the moratorium, in close cooperation with its European partners and with the strong support of civil society organisations. I personally remember the initiatives and debates on this topic within Italian civil society, including the youth movement. It was thanks to these tremendous collective efforts that the first resolution on a moratorium on the use of the death penalty was adopted in 2007. This was indeed a historical moment for the entire international community!

Four more resolutions were approved in 2008, 2010, 2012 and 2014. Each resolution has been a landmark for the campaign on the moratorium as it has focused attention on different aspects of this issue. For instance, the 2012 resolution called for the first time on states to progressively restrict executions involving children and pregnant women. It also more clearly identified the information states should make available on their use of the death penalty—the number of people sentenced to death, the number of people on death row and the number of executions carried out.

The most recent resolution was tabled for approval at the 69th Session of the United Nations General Assembly in December 2014. Italy worked with enhanced efforts alongside the cross-regional group of co-sponsors to obtain the widest possible support for the new resolution. I am honoured to have contributed to the outreach to other countries by participating in the supporting event Moving Away from the Death Penalty: National Leadership, organized by Italy and the United Nations—along with Benin, Mongolia and Tunisia—during the 69th General Assembly session in September 2014.

When we first started the campaign for a moratorium on the death penalty, many looked with scepticism at our efforts and our chances of success. Some argued that a resolution should not cover a topic that is still considered by many states to be a matter of domestic jurisdiction; for others, the non-binding nature of the resolutions meant they were unlikely to bring about significant change. However, we believed, and we still do, that every battle for the promotion of human rights is worth fighting. And it pays off. The increasing number of countries that over the years have voted in favour of the moratorium (or abstained) shows a clear international trend in favour of limiting the scope and consequences of the death penalty. In a true testimony to the importance and universality of this campaign, the United Nations General Assembly resolutions have received the support of ever more countries from all regions of the world, at different stages of economic development, with populations belonging to different religions.

> "POLITICAL LEADERS ARE CALLED TO PLAY A
> GUIDING ROLE AND MAKE THE CASE FOR THE
> ABOLITION OF THE DEATH PENALTY."
> —Matteo Renzi

By emphasising the need to establish a moratorium on executions with a view to abolishing the death penalty, the resolutions have been supported by countries that have legally abolished the death penalty (perhaps a long time ago), as well as by countries that have introduced a de facto moratorium or intend to do so, while the death penalty remains part of their legal framework. Many countries have not been able to abolish the death penalty but have taken steps in this direction. The campaign for the moratorium has kept the momentum going and focused the attention of the international community on this important topic.

One of the lessons we have learned in this experience is that no single strategy can be considered more successful than others to advance the movement in favour of the moratorium. However, undoubtedly, strong leadership is always necessary.

Political leaders have a special responsibility in this regard. First and foremost, they can build consensus in favour of a moratorium within the wider political community of their country. I am honoured that all Italian political actors and institutions have shown full and unwavering support for the campaign. This level of support is particularly important in countries where capital punishment still exists. In these circumstances, political leaders are called to engage constructively with parliaments to facilitate the legal reforms required, so that changes to establish a de jure moratorium or abolition can be enacted according to a sustainable reform path and within an appropriate time frame.

Political leaders also play an important role in mobilising public opinion in favour of the abolition of the death penalty, for instance through awareness campaigns, public debates and specific educational programs in schools. I am deeply touched by the experiences of those political leaders that have directly witnessed the effects of the use of the death penalty and are actively engaged in the campaign for the moratorium.

Such strong leadership is even more necessary when countries confront significant threats to their security, including organized crime and terrorism. Although there is increasing evidence that the death penalty is not an effective deterrent to crime, statistics are not always enough to sway public opinion. The sense of insecurity caused by extremism and widespread violence may lead people to believe that the death penalty could restore security. It is exactly in such cases, however, that political leaders are called to play a guiding role and make the case for the abolition of the death penalty, even if it may seem difficult to justify. Political responsibility to stop crime and violence does not need to lead to compromises in terms of human rights. On the contrary, it makes the promotion and protection of human rights and fundamental freedoms even more necessary. For instance, enhanced efforts could be made to ensure that terrorists and those responsible for violations of international humanitarian or human rights law are held to account through existing international criminal justice mechanisms.

The success of the campaign for a moratorium does not depend only on the contribution of political leadership. All international and national institutions and all sectors of civil society should play a leading role. It is crucial, for example, to enhance cooperation between political institutions and nongovernmental organizations that possess specific expertise on the subject. In this regard, I would like to recall

Italy's experience as a useful example of positive synergy between national governments and civil society organisations. The Italian Ministry of Foreign Affairs and International Cooperation has established a special partnership with Comunità di Sant'Egidio, Hands off Cain and the Italian branch of Amnesty International. These organisations have been engaged for a long time in awareness-raising projects. Their global outreach has significantly contributed to the success of the campaign for a moratorium on the death penalty. Their efforts have effectively complemented activities undertaken at the institutional level.

In many countries, religious leaders can also play a role in the campaign for the moratorium, in particular where religion and politics are closely intertwined, or for instance the judicial power is held by a religious authority. In some cases such a positive interaction could be more complex, but constructive dialogue is always the best tool for promoting human rights, even in the most difficult contexts.

Other examples of successful outreach include initiatives carried out together with the academic or judiciary community of countries where capital punishment is still practised. Although in such countries the abolition of the death penalty may not be possible in the short term, dialogue between human rights experts and legal practitioners could produce significant results and pave the way for future changes. In this regard, the support of the United Nations, mainly through the activities of the Office of the High Commissioner for Human Rights, can provide invaluable help.

In conclusion, the conditions of individual countries may differ, but the campaign for a moratorium on the use of the death penalty with a view to its eventual full abolition will only be successful if it can count on strong leadership at all levels. Successful political leaders are able to overcome setbacks and difficulties by reaching out to all interested parties at the institutional level and within civil society. This continuous dialogue is instrumental to building the consensus we need to steadily progress towards a world where justice does not require the loss of a human life.

A FIGHT FOR THE PROGRESS OF HUMANITY

Boni Yayi[1]

The death penalty has turned out to be ineffective in the fight against crime. It never helped curb the crime rate in the countries that make use of it; in fact, as criminals know what fate is in store for them, they become more aggressive.

The death penalty does not provide satisfaction to the families of the victims, as an execution cannot soothe their pain. Also, the numerous judicial errors that have been discovered, leading to stays of execution, should force a reflection in society about the need to abandon this form of punishment.

The Republic of Benin has fully adhered to the Second Optional Protocol of the International Covenant on Civil and Political Rights, aiming at abolishing the death penalty, since 2013.

Even before 2013, death sentences imposed by the courts of Benin were not carried out. The last execution took place in 1987; after that, Benin observed a de facto moratorium. Since Benin became party to the Second Optional Protocol, no court in Benin can sentence people to death. The government informed all courts of Benin accordingly, specifying the new international norm to which Benin had become a party. Benin's new draft penal code has annulled all provisions relating to the death penalty, based on the principle of the superiority of ratified international law over domestic legislation.

It is important to recognize that the practice followed in Benin is the result of a process of sensitisation which gained the trust of the people of Benin, who traditionally value human life and believe that the death penalty is not justice but rather a failure of justice. These outreach campaigns have been very successful.

---

1   Boni Yayi is the president (chief of state and head of government) of the Republic of Benin.

> **"THE DEATH PENALTY HAS TURNED OUT TO BE INEFFECTIVE IN THE FIGHT AGAINST CRIME."**
> —Boni Yayi

The main challenge the government faces is the need to mobilize the necessary means and financial resources to refurbish or build modern infrastructure including high-security prisons, in line with international standards, to carry out life sentences. The goal is to ensure that perpetrators of armed robberies resulting in casualties are not released to resume their criminal activities at the expense of society.

We consider that the international community should pursue and strengthen its outreach efforts to convince an increasing number of states to adopt a moratorium with a view to abolishing the death penalty. The abolition of the death penalty is a fight for the progress of humanity, and Benin wishes to thank civil society organisations for their remarkable work towards an evolution of minds and mentalities to that end.

At the United Nations, this progress is already visible and needs to be strengthened. It is heartening to see that several states that used to abstain or vote against the resolution on the moratorium are changing their vote, and we have to pursue our efforts to support them further.

"Rejecting capital punishment is about choosing what kind of society we want to live in, and which values—including human rights and dignity, democracy and the rule of law—we want to uphold.

— *Federico Mayor*

CHAPTER 6
TRENDS AND PERSPECTIVES

This chapter deals with empirically measurable trends regarding the death penalty and the role of political leadership in shaping those trends. Although there is a clear long-term trend away from the death penalty, data about increases in passed death sentences in 2014 are deeply concerning. Political leadership is urgently needed to keep us on the abolitionist track.

<u>Salil Shetty</u>, Secretary General of Amnesty International, offers a cautiously optimistic analysis of global trends in the death penalty from 2014. Amnesty International has been monitoring trends in the use of the death penalty for more than three decades. There is no doubt that the world has moved away from the death penalty during this time. In 1945 only eight countries had abolished the death penalty; today, 100 countries have fully abolished it. However, each year there is both good and bad news. According to Amnesty International, in 2014, the number of passed death sentences rose by 28 per cent compared to the previous year.

In 2014, an alarming number of countries used the death penalty to respond to real or perceived threats to state security and public safety posed by terrorism, crime (especially drug trafficking) or internal instability. As in the past, unfair trials, "confessions" extracted through torture or other ill-treatment, the use of the death penalty against juvenile offenders and people with mental or intellectual disabilities, and for crimes other than "intentional killing" continued to be concerning features of the use of the death penalty.

GLOBAL DEATH PENALTY TRENDS IN 2014

Salil Shetty[1]

Amnesty International has been campaigning for abolition of the death penalty since 1977. As part of this work, the organization monitors the use of capital punishment globally and publishes annual figures on the number of countries known to have carried out judicial executions, as well as the number of people known to have been sentenced to death or executed. This annual report also looks at how capital punishment is applied and at trends in its use, as far as these can be determined.

One of the greatest challenges we face each year is the lack of official information on the application of the death penalty in most countries that retain it. Using a variety of non-governmental sources, we are able to establish what we term credible minimum figures—meaning that we can say that at least this number of people were executed or sentenced to death. The true figures are often higher.

THE 2014 FIGURES

Amnesty International recorded executions in 22 countries in 2014, the same number of countries as in 2013.[2] Although the number remained constant, there were some changes in the countries carrying out executions. Seven countries that executed in 2013 did not do so in 2014 (Bangladesh, Botswana, Indonesia, India, Kuwait, Nigeria and South Sudan), while seven others resumed executions (Belarus, Egypt, Equatorial Guinea, Jordan, Pakistan, Singapore and the United Arab Emirates).

At least 607 people were executed, and at least 2,466 people were sentenced to death. These figures represent a decrease in the number of executions compared to in 2013 (at least 778) but a sharp increase in

---

1 Salil Shetty is secretary-general of Amnesty International.
2 All data in this article are drawn from Amnesty International, *Death Sentences and Executions in 2014* (London, Amnesty International, 2015), available from www.amnestyusa.org/research/reports/death-sentences-and-executions-2014.

the number of death sentences (at least 1,925). Whilst the challenges of data collection referred to above mean that year-on-year comparisons should be treated with caution, some specific developments during 2014—such as mass death sentences imposed in Egypt—shed light on the increase in this figure.

At least 509 death sentences were imposed in Egypt in 2014. These included the mass death sentences handed down by Egyptian courts after mass trials that were grossly unfair. For example, the Minya criminal court imposed death sentences on 37 people in April 2014 and 183 people in June 2014.[3] In December 2014, the Giza criminal court recommended death sentences against 188 people for involvement in the killing of 11 police officers in Giza in August 2013.

> "WHEN IT COMES TO THE DEATH PENALTY, HUMANITY'S GOAL IS CLEAR"
>
> —Salil Shetty,
> Amnesty International

Amnesty International's annual figures do not include the thousands of people sentenced to death and executed in China. In 2009, Amnesty International stopped publishing estimates for China, where data on capital punishment are considered a state secret. Instead, we challenge the Chinese authorities to prove their claims that they are reducing the application of the death penalty by publishing the figures themselves.

In 2014, as in 2013, it was also impossible to confirm if judicial executions took place in Syria. In addition, no information could be confirmed on North Korea.

The following methods of executions were used: beheading (Saudi Arabia), hanging (Afghanistan, Bangladesh, Egypt, Iran, Iraq, Japan, Jordan, Malaysia, Pakistan, Palestine, Singapore, Sudan), lethal injection (China, United States, Viet Nam) and shooting (Belarus, China, Equatorial Guinea, North Korea, Palestine, Saudi Arabia, Somalia, Taiwan, United Arab Emirates, Yemen). As in previous years, there

---

3   The death sentences followed referrals from the court to the grand mufti, Egypt's highest religious official. Egyptian criminal courts must refer a case to the grand mufti for review before handing down a death sentence; however, the opinion of the grand mufti is advisory and not binding.

were no reports of judicial executions carried out by stoning. In the United Arab Emirates, one woman was sentenced to death by stoning for committing "adultery" while married. Public executions were carried out in Iran and Saudi Arabia.

Justifications for the use of the death penalty

In 2014 an alarming number of countries used the death penalty to respond to real or perceived threats to state security and public safety posed by terrorism, crime or internal instability. This is not a new phenomenon, but it has become a serious concern for the abolitionist movement as we see more countries and politicians attempt to defend the use, or resumption, of executions as a solution to crime and terrorism. As this publication and others have made clear, there is no evidence that the death penalty has a greater deterrent effect on crime than imprisonment. When governments present the death penalty as a solution to crime or insecurity, they are not only misleading the public but also failing, in many cases, to take the necessary action to prevent and respond to crime through robust and rights-respecting criminal justice systems.[4]

China, Iran, Iraq and Pakistan executed people convicted of terrorism in 2014, while Cameroon and the United Arab Emirates expanded the scope of the death penalty to include terrorism-related crimes.

On 17 December 2014, Pakistan lifted a six-year moratorium on civilian executions for terrorism-related offences. The decision was in response to a horrific attack the day before on a school in Peshawar that left more than 149 people dead, including 132 children. Seven people, all of whom had been convicted under an anti-terrorism law, were executed in less than two weeks. The government also pledged to execute hundreds of people on death row who had been convicted of terrorism-related offences. By 28 April 2015, the country had already executed 100 people.

---

4   See Amnesty International, *Not Making Us Safer: Crime, Public Safety and the Death Penalty* (London, Amnesty International, 2013), available from www.amnesty.org/en/documents/document/?indexnumber=act51%2f002%2f2013&language=en.

Also in December 2014, Indonesia announced its intention to resume executions for drug-related offences to confront what it called a national emergency. On 19 January 2015, six people were executed and the Indonesian authorities announced plans to put more people to death throughout the year. On 28 April, eight people, including Indonesian and foreign nationals, were executed by firing squad. All of them had been convicted of drug trafficking. The executions went ahead despite international calls for clemency.

China made use of the death penalty as a tool in the Strike Hard campaign against terrorism and violent crime in the Xinjiang Uighur Autonomous Region. Three people were sentenced to death in a mass sentencing event that was held in an outdoor sports arena in May 2014. Those sentenced had been convicted of terrorism, separatism and murder. Between June and August, 21 people were executed in the Xinjiang Uighur Autonomous Region in relation to various terrorist attacks.

Jordan resumed executions at the end of 2014 after an eight-year hiatus, executing 11 men for murder. The executions followed the establishment, weeks before, of a special committee of the Cabinet to look into lifting the suspension on executions as a deterrent to murder and in response to public demand.

The ongoing use of the death penalty in contravention of international law

In 2014, as in the past, many of the states that retain the death penalty continued to use it in contravention of international law and standards. Unfair trials, "confessions" extracted through torture or other ill-treatment, and the use of the death penalty against juvenile offenders and people with mental or intellectual disabilities and for crimes other than intentional killing continued to be concerning features of the use of the death penalty.

People with mental or intellectual disabilities were under sentence of death in several countries including Indonesia, Japan, Malaysia, Pakistan, Trinidad and Tobago and the United States.

Several countries continued to hand down death sentences and execute people for crimes that did not involve intentional killing and therefore did not meet the threshold of "most serious crimes" prescribed by Article 6 of the International Covenant on Civil and Political Rights, which is widely understood to mean crimes involving intentional killing. The death penalty was imposed or implemented for drug-related offences in China, Indonesia, Iran, Malaysia, Saudi Arabia, Singapore, Sri Lanka, Thailand, the United Arab Emirates and Viet Nam.

Other capital crimes that did not meet the standard of "most serious crimes" but for which the death penalty was imposed in 2014 included economic crimes such as corruption (China, North Korea and Viet Nam), armed robbery (Democratic Republic of the Congo), committing adultery while married (United Arab Emirates), rape that resulted in death (Afghanistan), rape committed by a repeat rape offender (India), rape (Saudi Arabia, United Arab Emirates), kidnapping (Saudi Arabia), torture (Saudi Arabia), insulting the prophet of Islam (Iran), blasphemy (Pakistan), and witchcraft and sorcery (Saudi Arabia).

Finally, acts described as treason, acts against national security, collaboration with a foreign entity, espionage, participation in an insurrectional movement, terrorism and other crimes against the state, whether or not they led to a loss of life, were punished with death sentences in Lebanon, North Korea, Palestine (in the West Bank and in Gaza), Qatar and Saudi Arabia.

REGIONAL DEVELOPMENTS

Amnesty International recorded at least 46 executions in three countries in sub-Saharan Africa in 2014, compared to 64 in five countries in 2013. The countries known to have executed people were Equatorial Guinea, Somalia and Sudan. Sub-Saharan Africa also saw several positive developments with states taking steps towards abolition, as discussed in the next section.

The number of judicial executions confirmed in the Middle East and North Africa decreased from at least 638 in 2013 to at least 491 in

2014. However, it should be noted that obtaining complete and reliable data on the use of the death penalty in the region is particularly difficult, especially for countries such as Iran, Iraq, Saudi Arabia and Yemen. The internal armed conflict in Syria meant that information on the use of the death penalty in the country could not be confirmed.

In the Americas, the United States remained the only country to carry out judicial executions. However, the number of executions dropped from 39 in 2013 to 35 last year, reflecting a steady decline in executions over the past years.[5] Only seven states executed in 2014 (down from nine in 2013), with four (Texas, Missouri, Florida and Oklahoma) responsible for 89 per cent of all executions. The state of Washington imposed a moratorium on executions in February 2014. The overall number of death sentences decreased from 95 in 2013 to 77 in 2014.

Amnesty International recorded 32 executions in the Asia-Pacific region (excluding China), compared to 37 in 2013. The number of death sentences recorded in 2014 decreased by 335 compared to 2013 (from 1,030 to 695—again, excluding China). Pakistan and Singapore resumed executions in 2014, and Indonesia announced its intention to end a moratorium on civilian executions—acting on this statement of intent in 2015, as noted above.

The Pacific continued to be the world's only virtually death-penalty-free zone, although the governments of both Papua New Guinea and Kiribati took steps to resume executions or introduce the death penalty.

In Europe and Central Asia, Belarus—the only country in the region that executes people —put at least three people to death during the year, ending a 24-month hiatus. The executions were marked by secrecy; family members and lawyers were informed only after the fact.

---

5   Death Penalty Information Center, "Executions in the United States," available from www. deathpenaltyinfo.org/executions-united-states; Amnesty International, "Death penalty," www. amnesty.org/en/what-we-do/death-penalty/.

POSITIVE DEVELOPMENTS IN 2014

There were positive developments recorded in 2014 that are worth celebrating. In December 2014, the National Assembly of Madagascar adopted a bill to abolish the death penalty. Similar bills were pending before legislative bodies in Benin, Chad and Mongolia and were approved by the parliaments of Fiji and Suriname early in 2015. The Parliament of Barbados has started considering draft legislation aimed at abolishing the mandatory death penalty.

States gave more support to international treaties and resolutions favouring abolition of the death penalty. El Salvador, Gabon and Poland became state parties to the Second Optional Protocol to the International Covenant on Civil and Political Rights, aiming at the abolition of the death penalty. In May 2014, Poland also ratified Protocol No. 13 to the (European) Convention for the Protection of Human Rights and Fundamental Freedoms, concerning the abolition of the death penalty in all circumstances.

In December the UN General Assembly adopted its fifth resolution on a moratorium on the use of the death penalty. The number of votes in favour of Resolution 69/186 increased by six, from 111 in 2012 to 117 in 2014, while 38 countries voted against and 34 countries abstained. New votes in favour of the 2014 resolution came from Equatorial Guinea, Eritrea, Fiji, Niger and Suriname. In a further positive sign, Bahrain, Myanmar, Tonga and Uganda moved from opposition to abstention.

Amnesty International recorded 112 exonerations of death row prisoners in nine countries: Bangladesh (4), China (2), Jordan (1), Nigeria (32), Sudan (4), Tanzania (59), United States (7), Viet Nam (2) and Zimbabwe (1). These are minimum figures, and the real figures may be higher. The release of prisoners from death row on the grounds of innocence exposes the fallibility of human justice and has sparked debates on the death penalty in several countries, including countries where support for it has traditionally been strong, such as China, Japan, the United States and Viet Nam.

In 2014, activism by people committed to abolition of the death penalty helped to stop executions in several countries. Chandran s/o

Paskaran was spared execution in Malaysia on 7 February 2014 after an outcry from human rights groups, including Amnesty International.

ThankGod Ebhos was sentenced to death in Nigeria in 1995. On 23 June 2013, he was taken to the gallows with four other men, all of whom were hanged in front of him. At the last minute, the prison authorities realized that ThankGod Ebhos's death sentence required a firing squad and he was returned to his cell. On 24 October 2014, following campaigns against his execution, ThankGod Ebhos was released from death row.

Meriam Yehya Ibrahim was released from prison in Sudan on 23 June 2014. Her death sentence for apostasy, imposed by a Khartoum court on 15 May, was overturned by an appeals court. Meriam Yehya Ibrahim's case attracted widespread international attention, with over one million people responding to Amnesty International's appeal for her release.

Although each year Amnesty International records both negative and positive developments on the death penalty, the long-term global trend is unmistakably positive. In 2014, 22 countries executed; two decades ago, in 1995, that number stood at 41. Today 100 countries have fully abolished the death penalty, and many more have not executed anyone for so long that Amnesty International considers them to be "abolitionist in practice." In total 140 countries, over 70 per cent of the countries in the world, are abolitionist in law or practice.

Amnesty International opposes the death penalty in all cases without exception regardless of the nature or circumstances of the crime; guilt, innocence or other characteristics of the individual; or the method used by the state to carry out the execution. The death penalty violates the right to life and is the ultimate cruel, inhuman and degrading punishment; it should be totally abolished.

AFTERWORD

It is vital that we encourage people to join the movement to end the death penalty, which negates the right to life and raises important human rights concerns.

No judiciary is mistake-free. In practice, the decision to put someone to death is often arbitrary, and the odds are often stacked against the poor, the powerless, and people who belong to racial, religious, ethnic or sexual minorities. An alarming body of evidence also indicates that even well-functioning legal systems have sentenced to death men and women who were subsequently proved innocent. When a miscarriage of justice results in someone being put to death, the state becomes a murderer. Furthermore, there is no evidence that the death penalty deters crime. The real deterrent is not the severity of punishment but its certainty. We need to focus resources and policy on strengthening the justice system—not on the brutal and arbitrary practice of executions.

> "CONSIDER THE FACTS WITH AN OPEN MIND."
> —Zeid Ra'ad Al Hussein

The global trend towards the abolition of the death penalty has accelerated remarkably in recent years, and today most countries either have abolished it or observe a moratorium. Distressingly, among the states that do continue to execute people, several use this penalty for offences that do not meet the threshold of "most serious crimes," after legal proceedings that clearly violate human rights standards for a fair trial.

I urge every reader to consider the facts with an open mind. To me, the arguments are convincing and decisive: On every level—from principle to practice—the death penalty is wrong.

Zeid Ra'ad Al Hussein
United Nations High Commissioner for Human Rights

ACKNOWLEDGEMENTS

Many people contributed to this publication in different ways.

Secretary-General Ban Ki-Moon not only provided the preface for this book, he participated in four of our death-penalty-related events as the keynote speaker. His involvement helped to mobilise a large participation by Member States as well as civil society, including academia, at the events.

Amnesty International and others helped us establish contacts with many panellists whose contributions are included in this book. The Governments of Benin, Chile, Italy, Mongolia, the Philippines and Tunisia co-organised events with us, and the Government of Italy contributed financially to the production of this publication.

The Colosseum is illuminated with the 'Cities of Life' logo to support the campaign against the death penalty, in Rome, Italy, 30 November 2011.
© EPA/Alessandro di Meo

Colleagues from the Office of the High Commissioner for Human Rights in Geneva led by Navi Pillay, the High Commissioner for Human Rights until recently and the new High Commissioner Zeid Ra'ad al-Hussein, have been extremely supportive of the New York-based panels on the death penalty as well as this publication.

Daily challenges would not have allowed me to edit this book without help and support from all New York Office of the High Commissioner staff.

Thank you all!

Ivan Šimonović
Editor